Fearless Freedom Becoming SoulFire

Fearless Freedom
Becoming SoulFire

book one

Soul Fire

ISBN: 1542871050
ISBN 13: 9781542871051
Library of Congress Control Number: 2017901595
CreateSpace Independent Publishing Platform
North Charleston, South Carolina

Dedicated to all the angels in my life, on earth and in heaven,
to my three mothers, my three fathers,
and to my daughter-my teacher and inspiration.

To each and every one of you reading my words:
May you awaken to your free heart and soul fire within.

"Someday, after mastering the winds, the waves, the tides and gravity, we shall harness for God the energies of love, and then, for a second time in the history of the world, man will have discovered fire."

~ Pierre Teilhard de Chardin

Flower of Contents

Namaste,

When I first signed the contract with the publishing company in January 2015, I inquired how long it usually takes someone to get a manuscript to them. "Do people take a year?" I asked jokingly. "That's crazy, not me, " I said. "I will get it to you in a month. It's already written, I just need to organize it."

My initial idea was to gather the blogs I had already written over the last eight years and compile them into a book. As I started arranging them, the thought entered my mind that I should include more of my personal story. I began writing, still with the intention of keeping it as a short story/blog with more emphasis on yoga and meditation.

However, God and the Universe had different plans.

Fate had it three months later in May, just as I finished the introduction on how I healed my life-long abandonment issue and am finally in a beautiful healthy relationship with my true love, he walked out on me.

Completely devastated. I spiraled down to the darkness… again.

In the garbage went my manuscript, and I began over. It turns out that my book was not going to be the nice easy blog compilation after all, but the vulnerable story of my life. This was the last undertaking I wanted to go on. I was trying to move on from my past, not re-live it. Nevertheless, somewhere in my awareness, I knew it was all happening for a reason.

I have come to learn that my life story is my teaching. My experiences of abandonment from birth until now have had a powerful purpose: to show others that it is possible, no matter what circumstances you came into the world with, to rise out of it, find your wings and soar. The abandonment, suffering and pain, *I chose*. I chose it however not to wallow in it, but to experience it, transform it and be a light for others. After all, it is not until we fully know darkness that we can fully know freedom.

After working with different editors, although they were helpful in one regard, I felt like my voice was being diluted and my message disappearing. The joy of writing was gone and feeling disheartened, I almost gave up at one point-then I re-remembered the reason for writing my book in the first place. The whole point of my life is not about fitting into a box, after all, but breaking free, being a trailblazer and forging new energetic pathways. So I decided not to use an editor and keep my book as is: in my voice, uncensored, real and raw. In allowing myself to write my story without worrying about "correct" parameters or trying to conform, I found the fluidity, freedom and truth of my soul's song. I wrote for me, from the trueness of my heart.

When I started this journey I had no idea how powerful and cathartic it would be. The month turned into nearly two years as I journeyed into the center of my sorrow and my deepest pain. I had to walk away from writing numerous times as the past became alive again, along with the feelings I was trying to avoid. Tears are transformation though. The process of writing my life story healed me as I watched my sorrow turn into joy and my life transform. If no one reads my book, that in itself was worth it.

Although I finished writing my life story, a creative portal was open for me and I continued to receive inspired messages and continued to write. The quote I have taped on my laptop from a fortune cookie which I need constant reminder of is: "Four basic premises of writing: clarity, brevity, simplicity and humanity. I divided the manuscript into two books since there was so much. Hence, this is book one. Book two will be released shortly, and I've come to learn there will be a book three.

This book is multi-dimensional. I share my past but from my soul's understanding and awakening now; part of the book is present moment realizations as I am writing, and part of the book is told verbatim in a journal format. I have included poems, parables, prayers, quotes, and excerpts from my favorite authors' books for inspiration as well. I have found that people respond to metaphors as a way of learning; maybe it's because it bypasses the logical left side of the brain and goes into the intuitive right side of the brain and down into the knowing heart.

The wisdom teachings of my soul, which you may recognize, are underlined and woven throughout the book. My story is not about the suffering or staying stuck in the human drama; rather, transcending it and coming home to the freedom, love and peace that we already are. It's not about fighting the darkness anymore, it's about simply choosing the light.

As a little girl I questioned what life was really about, thinking was this all there was to it? You are born, barely get by, work hard, sacrifice your dreams, retire, age, suffer, then die? I questioned all the needless suffering in the world- how one person, for example, could make millions of dollars to play a game with a ball for entertainment while thousands of innocent babies and children died every day from starvation. I didn't understand religion or God. What I was taught didn't make sense to me. I was born a seeker of truth and in my awakening I found it. What I have included in my book is what I have learned from my teachers and other enlightened beings, past and present, along with my own personal realizations. There is only one truth, but different interpretations and expressions of it.

Socrates said, "Learning is remembering." Universal truth and knowledge is not something that someone just now created, it's always been there waiting for us to uncover. Benjamin Franklin didn't invent electricity just as Galileo didn't invent gravity. They simply discovered it. We are at a point in our evolution as a species that we are discovering that what's within us, our consciousness, our light, our soul, is the most powerful resource we have and the only thing left we haven't tried that is going to save the world. Being a devoted student, hungry for healing and understanding on the spiritual path for the last sixteen years has shown me that there is no difference between science, quantum physics, yoga, Universal Law, original religion (before man got a hold of it), spirituality and love. Underlying all of it there is a basic truth- which is what this book is about.

There is a shift happening on the planet. We probably sense it, a stirring, an awakening. People are beginning to question their beliefs, their world view, question many things. There is a desire for less material goods and objects, and for more meaning, fulfillment, kindness, peace in the world and peace in our hearts. We are remembering that we are not separate-even though our bodies might say we are, that the countries and borders of our lands might say we are, but there is another Reality. We are re-remembering we are all brothers and sisters in consciousness, a global family and that all life is interconnected, interrelated, and interdependent, including Gaia, Mother Earth. The divine truth is that we are One-One Spirit, many forms. It's time to wake up and work together. It is time to be our brother's and sister's keeper.

I honor all people wherever they are in their journey as we are all in different phases of our spiritual unfoldment. As you read my book, all I ask of you is to keep an open mind and read with your instinctual awareness and intuitive nature that is always present. Feel the energy between the words and the essence of spirit behind what they are expressing. It can serve as a spark to ignite what you already know deep within. Words are not truth. Truth is eternal. Words are a symbol. As I wrote this book I felt it shifting, changing, and growing as I was evolving along side of it. What may be my truth might just be a seed of awakening for you, like a sunflower drawing darkness from roots to sunlight.

I have infused my healing love into this book, it has been blessed with the most highest of intentions. My hope is that it brings you back to your free heart, wakes you up to the glory, wonderment and truth of who you really are and ignites the fire within your own beautiful soul. You are light, you are love and you are loved.

> May the beauty of all that you are be reflected back upon you and may you emanate it out into the world for all to bask in. ~ SoulFire

> "As each person releases shame and self-loathing and chooses instead to love themselves, they make it easier for every person on Earth to replace self-judgment with self-love. That is, they create a vibration or resonance of love that radiates well beyond their immediate sphere. It is said that the flutter of a butterfly's wings can cause gale-force winds on the other side of the globe. In the same way, our decisions to love ourselves have far-reaching energetic effects. As we shift from the perspective of the personality to that of the soul, we recall a truth we knew long before we were born-that our actions, words, and thoughts impinge upon the entire world. By surmounting the challenges we planned before birth, we create a resonance that heals humanity." ~*Your Soul's Plan* by Robert Schwartz

PETAL 1

Silver Linings

***Broken

As I LAY crumpled on the floor gasping for air after being hit across the face by my fiancee, I sobbed and prayed to God and my angels, "Help me, please help me get up. Help me make it though this night."

It wasn't the hit in the face so much that knocked me down and left me breathless; it was the fear his parting words created as he walked out the door, "It's over," he announced, "beyond repair now." The sting in my face paled to the pain in my heart. Fatherless family again.

This sudden and violent abandonment compounded the burden of guilt and grief I carried with me since my daughter's father took his life eight years prior, when she was two years old. I still hadn't healed from that agonizing event. With this new abandonment, I feared I would break. Yet, from this crisis arose the beginning of my awakening, my way back home.

***Becoming a Mother

I met my daughter's father, Eugene, eleven years earlier at a night club. We danced all night, flowing and moving in harmony to the music. Dancing was one of the joys we had in common, that and music. He kissed me on the forehead at the end of the night and that was it. I was hooked.

We fell in love. I was only 22 years old, he was 21. We had the same birthday. I didn't have a job though I had graduated Magna Cum Laude from Providence College that year. Eugene was escaping from the trying life of Brownsville, Brooklyn, looking to make a fresh start in the suburbs of Long Island. We were an unlikely match, but destiny brought us together.

After about a year, I became pregnant but decided to have an abortion. There was no way I was ready to be a parent. I still had dreams of getting my Masters degree in International Business or traveling around the world with Green Peace. The shame of the abortion, however, took over my soul.

(I have since come to understand that the soul is not harmed from an abortion or miscarriage. The soul will find another vessel to be conceived in and birthed). At the time, however, I was a guilt-stricken mess. It probably had to do with my Catholic upbringing, and it didn't help that every time I turned on the TV, pro life commercials seemed like they were talking directly to me.

One night in the middle of a meltdown, crying out in despair, I promised God that if I got pregnant again, I would have the baby. Two months later, I was pregnant. *Wow, that was fast,* I thought. I was not willing to break a promise to God, so I became a Mommy at twenty three years old. This soul was coming in whether I liked it or not!

Pregnancy was not my friend. The doctor said my baby wasn't growing or getting enough oxygen and nutrients though the umbilical cord, and I wasn't gaining enough weight. Working full time in the city and commuting by the Long Island Railroad 2 1/2 hours each way, left nothing for the baby.

So I was bed ridden for the last four months. Doctors orders: stay in bed and eat! Eat bagels, ice cream, milkshakes, anything, just eat. For some it would have been a dream come true, a convenient excuse to indulge in goodies and sweets, but not me. I'd rather run for five miles than eat a pint of Ben & Jerry's ice cream.

This was not fun for me. I was a type A personality with lots of energy. Exercise, fitness, dancing -anything physical was my passion. My advised bed rest was during Thanksgiving and Christmas holidays on top of it all. The doctor wouldn't even let me go to the supermarket, so Christmas shopping was definitely out. And in 1992, Amazon and online shopping had not yet been born. It was torture to lie in bed every day.

Eugene took very good care of me though. He even made me eat liver once a week, said it would be good for our baby's brain. I had to smother it in onions and ketchup to get it down, but I ate it. In the 36th week, my baby went breech, and the doctor told me I would probably have to get a C section. I wanted to have a natural birth so I decided to watch TV upside down in a modified headstand, hoping she would flip around.

It worked! I earned a front row seat to this gymnastic Olympic event in my body. Feisty and stubborn even in the womb and two weeks past her due date, I had to be induced. In the middle of winter, on our way to the hospital the car doors were frozen shut. Panic, then solution: blow dry the car doors open. Nothing about this pregnancy was easy.

Anyone who has been induced knows how painful it is. The waves of contractions come on fast, strong and hard. I was in Stony Brook Hospital in twelve hours of back labor and all I could hear was a woman bellowing through the vents, "Get it out of me!" Not how you want to begin the birthing process. I learned later the women had quadruplets.

Poor Eugene, he tried so hard to make me comfortable. He even brought a boom box and played Enya in the hospital room to relax me, but those contractions were in my back and they didn't let up for twelve hours. To this day I have a hard time listening to Enya. Eugene, freaking out but trying to remain calm, encouraged me to breathe. Grabbing him by the shirt collar, in desperation, I demanded drugs.

I gave in. I wanted to go as natural as possible but the pain was unbearable, even with my high tolerance for pain. However, much to my dismay the anesthesiologist, who had a foot long needle all ready, said, "Too late."

The doctor told me to breathe and wait until I was dilated more to push, but I cried, "Oh no, I am pushing now, it's coming out!" (I didn't know if it was a boy or a girl, wanted to be surprised). And within a few moments out she came. It took longer than I anticipated for the doctors to place her on my belly.

I started to worry she might be missing a finger or a toe or worse, after the complicated pregnancy and the scare my mother gave me that the baby could be born with serious issues. When I was ordered on bed rest, my mother gave me the worst case scenario about how my baby could be born with "major malfunctions." Even though I know she was trying to be helpful in her own warped way, it scared me so.

When they finally connected my baby and me in that inaugural moment, my first thought was, "She's purple." My baby was born with jaundice, but after a few days, thankfully, it went away. She was a healthy 6lb 6oz baby girl. Those last weeks in my womb was when she gained the weight she needed to be healthy. She knew.

Childbirth is such a painful experience. You think you never want to go through it again, but you do, like falling in love. I always said there's nothing worse than the pain of a broken heart, but like childbirth the pain disappears the moment you hold that child and eventually your heart desires to fall in love all over again.

I think that's the miracle of our soul, it is always looking for the experience of love and creation, no matter how much pain we have gone through. The painful memories fade away and all we can remember is the sweetness of love and the possibility of new life.

Eugene picked out her name: Aiyana. It's Native American Indian, meaning *eternal blossom*. Her middle name is Natalia, for *peace*.

We were a happy family for a short period of time. He was the proudest father. He took her everywhere with him: to work, to the gym, to dance rehearsal, even when he was just hanging with his boys. She was the light of his life.

***Alive and Breathing

After about six months, however, things started to shift. He started to stay out later and later at the clubs and sometimes wouldn't come home till early morning. We fought all the time. Eventually, after six months he moved out. It wasn't that we didn't love each other or care about each other, we did very much. We were so young and impulsive and didn't have the adult capacities to be in a healthy relationship. Looking back now I see how we both brought so many wounds and pain into our relationship.

Eugene was an anomaly. He never drank alcohol or did any drugs which shows such strength of character as a dancer in the entertainment industry. I admired him for that, but was naive. He should have been on medication for depression. He was hospitalized for an overdose after he tried to take his life over a break-up with his ex-girlfriend before he met me. He told me about this experience, and emphasized he was ok now, that he was strong and didn't need the medication. I believed him without questioning.

Our relationship continued to go downhill. At Christmas that year he proposed to me and when I turned him down he began to unravel.

He became desperate. One night he tricked me into going out to dinner to make peace and talk about our daughter. He told me he was taking me to his friend's restaurant in Nassau County. I got in his car and we drove for a long time until I saw a sign for New Jersey.

Realizing we were no longer in New York, I started to get nervous. I asked him where his friend's restaurant was. He responded with an attempt to cover up his plan because his plan that night was not taking me out to dinner, rather taking my life.

We ended up at a rest stop off the Palisades Parkway in New Jersey. I demanded he take me home, but he refused. He had found out I was dating someone else, and that's what set him off.

I was trying not to go into complete panic mode, trying to stay calm even though I was petrified. I was trapped in his car and became like a wild animal then. My adrenaline kicked in, and out of sheer frenzy I kicked the windshield, thinking I could escape. It shattered but not enough to escape.

Fear like that coursing through your veins paralyzes you. At least that's what it did to me. He put the passenger seat all the way back, jumped on top of me and began choking me, saying, "I'm going to kill you, then myself, and our daughter will grow up without any parents, and it will be all your fault."

It happened so quickly, I didn't have time to fight back. I didn't even have time to cry as the horrifying, debilitating thought that I may never see my daughter again went through my mind, then blackness, lights out.

I'm not sure how long I was unconscious, but I awoke and I was still alive. I saw Eugene sitting upright in the driver's side with a scarf wrapped around his neck and the other end in the window, gagging. He was trying to hang himself from the window in the car. I screamed, reached over, removed the scarf and set him free. As he was catching his breath, I quickly unlocked the car door and escaped.

Dark and late at night, I was relieved to see another car. I ran over and knocked on the window. There was a man sitting alone. I begged him, "Please help me." My cries and pleas fell upon deaf ears. He sat looking straight ahead, never turned his head to look at me, not once. Feeling helpless and not knowing what to do at this point, miraculously, a police car drove up. Looking back now I am sure it was my guardian angels looking after me, Archangel Michael to be exact. I explained what was happening to the police officer. At that point we learned our daughter had an extremely high temperature and we needed to get back to her asap. I don't remember how we got this information because we didn't have cell phones back then. It must have been Eugene's beeper.

The police officer unfortunately could not take me back because he had to stay in New Jersey within his jurisdiction. He explained to me that the only way to get home to Long Island was with Eugene. He assured me that he talked to him, and he promised to get us home to our daughter safely.

I'm not sure what the police officer said to Eugene, but it snapped him out of his delusion. As crazy as that seems, I had no other choice. It was the only way I could get back home to my baby. She was sick, and she needed me. Reluctantly, I got back in the car with him.

Trying to remain undisturbed and reposeful I sat there breathless. The only thing I could think of was my daughter and getting to her as soon as possible. Whenever he would start to go off about who I was dating I would bring the conversation back to Aiyana. I kept refocusing him on the responsibility toward our sick daughter.

We got to the house safely, thank God, and we took her right to the emergency room. She had a temperature of 104 degrees and was fading in and out of consciousness. After all I had just been through, the hospital staff was questioning us like we were criminals. Why? Because Eugene was black I thought? It turned out she had chicken pox, and she recovered.

I had no choice but to file a police report and get a restraining order after these events. This did not make Eugene happy at all. He was no longer able to visit our daughter. He also had to have supervised visitation.

The restraining order did not stop his desperation. One day after work I went to the daycare center to pick up my daughter and much to my shock she wasn't there. Heart in my stomach, "What do you mean?" I questioned the daycare provider.

"Eugene picked her up," she blankly declared.

Oh my God. This is not good, not good at all I am thinking. Trying to keep it together, I ran home. When I stepped into my bedroom, I was jumped on from behind, my scream muffled by the arm around my throat, and was thrown down on to my bed.

I wasn't sure who it was, it all happened so fast. Luckily my neighbor downstairs heard me scream and nervously called out,

"Stephanie, are you ok?"

The perpetrator eased off his grip and told me to say yes that I was fine or he was going to kill me. It was Eugene, which was both a relief and a dread at the same time. I didn't know what to do, but I had to make a decision in a split second. I knew this might be my only chance for help, so I said as composedly as I could but with a tint of, "please help me," sprinkled in it:

"Yes Donna, I am fine."

She replied, "I don't like the way you sound. I'm coming up."

It worked! To my relief, Eugene immediately let me go, escaped out of the living room window on to the roof and disappeared.

Stunned and terrified, I called the police again. They didn't seem too concerned about what was happening, even though Eugene left two sets of thick ropes behind with a suicide letter, blaming me again. Maybe domestic violence was something they see all the time, but I remember thinking they really don't seem like they care about me. It was the one time in my life that I didn't feel protected by the police. Again feeling the race thing.

***Terror

Now the worst part. Where was my daughter?

By now there was a warrant out for Eugene's arrest, although I didn't have confidence in the law enforcement at this point. Every day seemed like an eternity. I was in a state of numbness, the fear overwhelming that I may never see my daughter again. I don't know how I functioned, I just did. I continued to go to work at the investment firm I was with, going through the motions of normalcy. I felt like I was in one of those awful Lifetime drama TV shows, only I was the star. My co-workers who knew about my crisis tried to be supportive, but what could they do or even say?

The next contact from Eugene came with a new twist two days later at work. "I am going to kill our daughter so you will never see her again, and then I'm going to kill myself," he said indifferently. Then he followed up with: "This is all your fault," and hung up.

I have to keep it together. I kept thinking *this is not happening. This is a nightmare and I will wake up soon.* Feeling helpless, I prayed silently with every breath that my daughter would be returned back to me safely.

My daughter had been gone now for three days. Eugene's next call was such a relief to my heart, "I'm going to leave Aiyana at my aunt's house in Queens, then I'm going to kill myself." I wasn't sure how to feel at this point. I don't think I felt anything actually because I was in a state of shock; however, I noticed something different in his voice.

He had been threatening he was going to kill himself for months now, and to be honest, I didn't believe him. I actually retorted one time, "Go ahead and kill yourself already!" I was fed up with his manipulative behavior to get my attention.

I knew how much he loved our daughter. It never occurred to me that he might actually go through with his threats. As a mother, no matter how much I was suffering, I could never fathom doing that to my child. His tone of complete resignation caused me to pause.

"Eugene," I said tentatively.

"What?" he replied, with a cold indifference. Deafening silence.

"Nothing," I replied and hung up.

That was it, that was my last interaction with him. Surprisingly, after all we had been through and the fear and shock I was in, I had the urge to say, "I love you." I held it back because it caught me off guard to be honest.

What I've come to learn is that this feeling of love that cropped up even after all I had been though with him was my soul. The soul only knows love. Even in the midst of turmoil and great suffering, it is possible to feel love and to be love, even when all around us appears as the opposite.

Of course I didn't realize it then. I just thought I was crazy.

I left work, on a mission to bring my daughter home. Scared to death and afraid to get behind the wheel, I asked my cousin to drive me to Queens. As we got close to the aunt's house I saw a flashing light show of ambulances, police cars and fire trucks. Heart in my throat, I felt slight relief as we drove past the blaring light scene and approached his aunt's house.

Maybe this had nothing to do with Eugene, I thought. I knocked on the door. His aunt and uncle were home and happy to see me. Completely oblivious, they told me Eugene just left for a walk.

All I cared about was holding my daughter again. I walked in the house with so much anticipation in my heart, looking around for her. She ran to me with a big smile on her face and jumped into my arms. The first deep breath I had taken in days made its way into my lungs. I tried to God not to cry but the tears rolled down my face. I thought *don't let her see you cry and* stopped them.

I held her so tightly. *I'm never going to let you go* was all I could think. So happy to have my baby back I didn't care about anything else, until I heard a knock on the front door and men's somber voices. The detectives came over and asked me to identify a body. Still holding my daughter in my arms, I instinctively turned my body to shield Aiyana. The image of the Polaroid made me gasp in horror.

Eugene had hung himself on the neighbor's fence with the scarf that my grandmother gave him that year for Christmas. HIs face looked deformed and twisted; his eyes bulged out. I wish they never showed me that picture.

All those flashing lights down the road were for him after all, I realized as my stomach sank and my legs almost gave out. Holding my daughter in my arms prevented me from falling to my knees. I did everything in my power not to break down and cry in front of my daughter who was smiling and happy, not aware of the horror that was happening. I was grateful for that. *Keep it together* I chanted over and over.

He left a painful "good bye" letter in her diaper bag, blaming me for everything. I saved it for years (not sure why), along with some of his things I intended to give my daughter. Thank God something in me declared, "You are not taking the blame for this." Deep down I knew the truth, <u>I could not take the blame for another person's actions.</u>

Never the less, there was this persistent guilt that kept nagging at me, "If you told him you loved him, that might have changed things. Maybe it would have given him hope, and he would still be here for your daughter." I was second guessing myself, something I lived with my entire life until I processed it through a spiritual retreat about five years ago. At least I thought I did, but the guilt and shame had already seeped in and damaged my psyche.

***Getting Up

The memories of this time period are spotty. I was in a state of shock for the most part, and I didn't have anyone in my life for emotional support: not my family, definitely not his family or his friends. They all blamed me actually.

The co-worker I was close with, who gave us Aiyana's bassinet and who I turned to for comfort, said to me, "I'm sorry to have to tell you this but Eugene is going to Hell. That's where souls who commit suicide go." She was Catholic and that's what they believed. Thanks for that. Helpful, really.

My Jehovah's Witness neighbors downstairs who came up and saved me took away my hope that at least Eugene was an angel now watching over us. They sat me down in their apartment shortly after this tragedy and told me Eugene was asleep, like in a coma, and would not wake up until the second coming of Christ. "When is that going to happen?" I asked. No answer- didn't look promising.

I know people were trying to be helpful, but all they did was scare me and made me believe less in religion than I already did. Neither belief felt right or true to me.

The couple of friends I did have from college lived in other states. One day a few of them came to Long Island for an intervention since I had been lying in bed depressed. Ahh, what else was I supposed to do? I got really annoyed at one of my girlfriends who thought I needed to "get over it" and go out again. Really? That's compassionate.

I continued to lie in bed falling into a deeper pit of despair and darkness, thinking if I just laid here and never moved eventually I would wither away and die. I don't remember how I took care of Aiyana, if I even did, or how long I was in bed for. I vividly remember my two year old daughter walking over to me, putting her hand on my shoulder, smiling and saying in her sweet innocent voice, "It's ok Mommy." It was like she knew something. Those words resonated in my heart. My two year old daughter was comforting me! This wisdom from a heavenly two year old sure beat the wisdom my adult friends were giving me.

At that point I said to myself, *You have a choice, you can lay here, wither away and die, or you can get up and take care of that little girl.*

So...I got up. And everyday after that. It wasn't easy.

Sometimes in life just getting up and showing up is about all you can do, and sometimes that is all you need.

I tried to only cry when my daughter was napping or sleeping, but the pain overwhelmed me that it had nowhere else to go but out in heart-breaking sobs. I grieved at the thought of my daughter without a father and raising a child alone. At the same time, I was grateful that we were both alive. I decided to focus on a second chance at living. Focusing on the silver lining seemed like my only salvation.

That juncture in my life of rising up after being brought to my knees was one I was going to experience two more times, something I could not imagine back then. The one person who was my inspiration to keep getting up was my daughter.

***Perseverance

So I got up and went to work: no therapy, no counseling, no group support- just work, work, work and take care of my baby. I was in survival mode, working at an investment firm making $22,000 a year as an administrative assistant. Living on Long Island with a small child was expensive, and I didn't want to depend on WIC (welfare for single mothers or food stamps) which I was on, so I studied on my own, earned my Series 7, and became a licensed financial consultant.

My days were exhausting, as were my nights. I brought my daughter to day care in the morning, went in to work early, studied from 8-9 am, then worked from 9-5pm; on my lunch hour I would exercise. Physical exercise kept me sane. I would go for a run or sometimes I would even roller skate in the parking lot of my office. Looking back now, people must have thought I was nuts. I didn't care if I was sweaty the rest of the day; being strong and in shape was more important, and it was my only "me" time. I'd then pick my daughter up, rush home, make dinner, play the mommy role and study more. No matter what every night I read to her as I put her to sleep, falling asleep next to her in her tiny bed before she did though. The life of a single parent; I never had a break.

I was so determined to do right by my daughter. On my only week of vacation I went in to the office everyday, locked myself in a room and studied from 9-5pm. It was studycation and a sacrifice because this was the last career I wanted to have. I had to convince myself that learning about options and reading the prospectus of a mutual fund was exciting and interesting.

On top of that, my beautiful daughter was a challenge to raise. She was diagnosed with ADHD (Attention Deficit Hyper Disorder) and ODD, (Oppositional Defiant Disorder). The school psychologist insisted Ritalin would be the answer. She persisted for years until one day I looked her in the eye and said, "Dr. S, I appreciate all your efforts to help my daughter in what you think is the right thing for her, but just know that I WILL NEVER PUT HER ON DRUGS." She never bothered me again after that.

I preferred to deal with Aiyana's unruly behavior than numb and medicate her. By the time she was a teenager she outgrew the ADHD anyway. There was also concern that she would suffer from depression like her father, that it could be genetic. I refused anti-depressants for Aiyana well. Besides medicating her didn't make sense to me, her brain was still developing. That's what I call Mommy radar.

Between my stressful career, my repressed emotions, the anger, pain and guilt I was carrying that came out as yelling and screaming, I had to raise a defiant, hyper child whose automatic and immediate response to me was, "NO." Our house was not too peaceful, to say the least.

I did what I had to do for my child, however. She was the priority in my life now. I became successful and worked my way up in a man's world.

***Toxic Shame

In addition to the guilt and grief, I discovered a new version of shame. I felt embarrassed being a single mother. I felt ashamed when I took my daughter for a walk in the neighborhood and saw nuclear families living in their home with the white picket fence. I felt shame just taking her to the park. I didn't know where these belittling feelings came from, but if felt awful. It didn't help that we lived in an all white suburban neighborhood and my daughter was a mix of races. We definitely weren't cookie cutter people.

This stigma was not something I imagined. Racism existed even in my own family. My grandmother refused to let us use her cabana in Long Beach because she "didn't want to be the first to have a black person at the beach," she informed me one hot summer day. She also had to get permission for us to go to family dinner at the Country Club because "Blacks" were not allowed yet. This was in 1994 in New York!

Aiyana and I rented a tiny one bedroom apartment for eight years, that was all I could afford. My daughter had the bedroom. I slept in the living room which posed as my bedroom and gym as well. There was a couch, tv/entertainment center, my bed, a dresser and a recumbent stationary bike, all crammed in one room. But I made it work. I continued to grind away, sacrificing my dreams and happiness as a financial consultant to take care of my daughter.

***Knuckle Up

A silver lining that came from Eugene, besides my daughter, was a new best friend. One of his only friends who didn't blame me quickly became an angel in our lives. She and her boyfriend, who was Eugene's best friend, stepped up to the plate and watched over us for years. They were a light in our challenging lives. A couple of years had gone by and she didn't want to see me alone anymore, thought it was time I dated so she set me up with a co-worker from the gym. It turned out that the best thing I learned from this boyfriend was how to box.

One night at a club in Brooklyn after one too many drinks, he got possessive and angry and accused me of flirting with another man. Although that didn't happen, he didn't believe me and proceeded to hit me upside the back of my head as we sat in his mustang convertible arguing.

My boyfriend was a golden glove boxer, 220 pounds of pure muscle! The punch took me by surprise. As I was coiled over with my head on my lap, rage building, I came up in a fury and gave him a right hook to his nose. With blood gushing out of his nose, he looked down at the blood, looked at me, looked back at the blood in his hand and then started to smile. He was in shock, yet impressed.

*** Getting Up Again

So when I met my fiancee (I will refer to him as Soulmate#2) after this last boyfriend, I thought this new relationship would be my saving grace. My daughter, eight at the time, took to this man, called him "Daddy" right from the start, which made me happy. We upgraded to a two bedroom apartment with our own back porch and yard. My picture perfect nuclear family with the white picket fence was coming together. No more being alone. No more feeling like a loser. My happiness was riding on my daughter's happiness, but little did I know that hers was riding on mine.

This was my second dark night of the soul. The second time I would be lying on the floor contemplating whether the pain in my heart would be too much for me to live with and thinking how much easier it would be if I just closed my eyes and never woke up. This was also the third time I was hit in the face by a man. I knew this had to stop. This was my wake up call.

Sitting in our living room the next day, I told my daughter that Daddy was not coming back. She screamed, "No!" and ran into her room. To me there was no greater agony to my heart than hearing my daughter cry over losing another "Daddy."

Aiyana constantly talked about her biological Daddy and questioned how he died. It was disturbing because I had to lie to her every time. I made up a story that he got a virus and went to the hospital and then died. It worked for a few years until she started asking me what kind of virus. She was a very inquisitive kid and I didn't know what to say. Then I was paranoid that whenever she got a cold or virus she would think she was going to die. I didn't know what to do.

***Daughter

As much as Aiyana was sad over losing another Daddy, she was more concerned about me however. Noticing I was losing weight fast, she turned to me one day sitting on the couch together and said, "I won't be sad Mommy, if you aren't sad." Another turning point in my life as I realized the powerful affect I had on her.

It reminded me of the time when she was two years old. We were in the living room, I was having one of my adult temper tantrums, picked up my sneaker and threw it across the room. Aiyana went over to her her little sneaker, picked it up, looked at me, smiled, and threw hers across the room. She was initiating me! Her innocent expression, " Are you proud of me?" said it all.

(I learned later in my personal growth studies that children learn by watching and imitating others, downloading information into their spongy brains without a filter, almost like hypnotism in the theta cycle of the brain until the age of seven or so. I wish I knew this information when I was raising her!)

To this day she always calls me out on things. It's kind of annoying actually because she's usually right. She'll say, "Mom you're being a hypocrite." It was never about what I said to her, it was about what I did. Her insight was part of my inspiration to change my behavior, not just talk about it.

She was and is an unbelievable young woman. She was always picking me up and making sure I wasn't sad. She would write me little love notes and leave them everywhere for me. When we went to the supermarket she would disappear and return a few minutes later, after I had a heart attack of course, with a flower, a little teddy bear and a love note to ease my broken heart.

I carried a burden though. How do you tell your child that their parent took their life? How would that not make them feel like they weren't worth hanging around for? That would surely ruin her self-esteem. I felt helpless that no matter what I said, it wouldn't matter. I didn't want her to feel abandoned like I did my entire life. However, I knew I would always be there for her and do everything in my power to be the best Mom I could, especially after all I had been through since my entrance into this world.

My daughter, Aiyana, was my inspiration to heal.

***My Beginning

I came into the world in an unusual way. I was born on March 9, 1969 in Pleasantville, New York in a jail to my biological mother who was a heroin addict. My biological father was "unknown" since my mother engaged in sexual activities for payment. This information was kept from me until I was 17 years old, however. I have no recollection of my mother.

I became an orphan when she gave me up for adoption at birth. I was placed in a foster home through the Guardian Angel Home in Brooklyn until I was 4 years old. I want to believe my mother really wanted me, but didn't have the means to take care of me.

I have hardly any memories of those years with my foster parents. I only know what my adopted mother told me years later. She said I was undernourished, weighing about 26 pounds at four years old. When they picked me up to take me home, they had new shoes for me to wear that were a few sizes too small. Apparently, my feet were being crammed into shoes that didn't fit. I never had a bath in a bath tub, always washed in the sink. Supposedly, my foster parents were older and couldn't bend down.

I didn't eat much because my gums hurt and my baby teeth were rotten from in utero neglect, but no one realized this until my adopted family took me home. My dentist wasn't sure my second teeth would come in. My smile revealed a mouth of silver caps.

"Chipmunk cheeks" became my nickname as I would stuff food in my mouth at the dinner table, ask to be excused, go into the bathroom, spit the food out in the toilet and flush it down. I thought I was being clever but little did I know my mother was on to me. She used to make me sit at the table until I finished my food.

One time when we were out to dinner I made myself throw up on my plate so I didn't have to eat. My mother pushed aside the throw up and made me eat the rest. She would also serve me my dinner the next morning for breakfast. The list of foods I liked to eat that came home with me from the adoption agency were french fries, pasta with "gravy" and chocolate. (I'm still down with the french fries and chocolate).

Our car was nicknamed the "comet vomit" after my upheaval on the day my unfamiliar family brought me home on the Gotcha Day, August 14, 1973. I threw up all over the back seat, all over my new mother and my new brother. Not a good way to start blending in to the brand-new family.

I have a clear memory of the day the social worker from Guardian Angel Home came over to check on me with my new family and say good-bye. It was my first *conscious* memory of feeling abandoned. I remember the feeling clearly. I was standing at the top of the stairs in my new home with my new family in the suburbs of Long Island, scared and feeling helpless thinking to myself as she waved good-bye, ***Don't leave me***, as she walked out the door. ***That became my mantra for most of my life.*** I was four and a half years old at the time.

***Mothers

Five years after I was adopted, at the age of nine, my parents got divorced. This came as a big shock to me, and my mother moved out. I didn't want her to leave me. She was the only person in my new family I wasn't scared to be around. I vividly remember the day she left. I was in bed, crying, feeling helpless again. She brought me a vanilla shake and said good-bye as I cried, "Don't leave me!" as she walked out the door.

I lived with my Dad, who was an intimidating man and my two older brothers who weren't adopted. After my mother moved out there was a whirlwind of mother figures coming in and out of my life. My father remarried twice. The first one to my aunt, my mother's sister. Pause to take that one in...

The shocking announcement came one night when my aunt and two cousins were over. We were watching, *That's Incredible*, an old TV show. My Dad turned off the TV and said, "Kids we have something even more incredible to tell you. Your Aunt/Mom and I got married." We (my two brothers and my two cousins) all looked at each other in disbelief. How do we explain this one to our friends?

They moved in with us and my aunt became my step-mother and my cousins became my step-brothers. Now I had to contend with four boys and a new step mom. I liked her better when she was my aunt though. As my step-parent she didn't treat me as nice as she did her two boys. Her sons got much better treatment than we did, which caused jealousy and more conflict in our household.

I was happy in one regard because I loved my cousins. They were nicer to me than my brothers, so I aligned with them. Whenever I was scared, which was often, I would go downstairs into my cousin Chad's room and ask him if I could sleep on his floor. We called it, "bunking out." Usually my other cousin Bryce would come in and "bunk out" too. Those were good memories.

It turned out my father never actually married my aunt; it was a lie, one of many I would hear in my life. This new dysfunctional "Brady Bunch" family disbanded after a couple years, and they moved out. My step-mother turned back into my aunt and my step-brothers back into my cousins. Our family gatherings were always interesting, to put it mildly.

Next came Nelcia, a live-in nanny from Jamaica, who was quickly dismissed after my father found out she was smoking marijuana with my eldest brother. My Dad hired Josephine next, the complete opposite of Nelcia. Nelcia used to play Reggae music and teach us how to dance on one leg. She enjoyed laughing and goofing off. Josephine, on the other hand, looked like the woman on the Aunt Jemima syrup bottle but without a smile. She was big and intimidating with a loud booming voice that you could hear blocks away when she called us to the house for dinner. We did not mess with Josephine.

After a couple of years of live-in nannies, our neighbor moved in. Supposedly she and my Dad fell in love, news to me. She was from California and 30 years old, I was 15, and she was 15 years younger than my Dad. It was an impressionable time in a teenage girl's life and she made a significant impression on me. I was so craving a female ally in my life.

At first, our relationship was great. I was so happy to have a "big sister." She took me shopping, took me for facials, manicures and pedicures, all the girlie things I never did growing up with my father and all boys.

My brothers, however, had a different take on her. They thought she was a gold digger and was trying to kill our father by fattening him up. They ate out a lot, and they ate very well. A typical home cooked meal by my step-monster was a big hunk of the best cut of steak, about 6 ears of corn on the cob slathered with butter, potatoes and two bottles of wine, followed up by a Carvel ice cream sundae. They both became obese at one point. The name of my Dad's boat was *The Whale,* and it seemed they were going for that look.

They moved in to the apartment in the side of our house, where my father's in-home office was. The doors were always closed and locked. We were never allowed in. If I needed my Dad I had to walk up to the side of the house, up the dark stairs to the door, knock and wait. He would open it slightly and talk to me through the crack. They had a lot of secrets and a life that was separate from ours.

There were traits about my step-monster that I looked up to and admired, like her free-spirited self confidence. She taught me to "always ask." This lesson has stuck with me to this day. I watched her receive what she wanted even when she was confronted with "no" at first. She always persisted and almost always got her way.

"You never know, until you ask," she used to say.

However, she was the female version of Jekyll and Hyde. One minute she was nice and loving to me and the next she would be scolding me. I didn't realize that she was an alcoholic like my Dad. I ran away for a period of time and lived with my best friend in high school. I couldn't take the madness of our house.

One day she came up to my high school to bring me home. My boyfriend happened to be there that day as well to take me back to my friend's house. High school was hard enough without having my crazy step-monster and boyfriend on each side of me, pulling my arms out fighting to bring me home in the hallway; dysfunction at its best.

When she was drunk, which was often, especially after Bloody Mary's for breakfast, she would launch into her unstable emotional moods which would end with her chasing me around the house, screaming and trying to attack me. This erratic behavior only made me angrier and tougher. I was a bratty teenager and wasn't putting up with her crap.

She brought her brother and mother to live with us for a while too and they also had drinking addictions. Her brother gave me the creeps and slept in the bedroom next to mine. It was not a comfortable way to live. I don't know if she ever loved my Dad. I hope she did.

I'm not sure if my father's demise was because of her. There are always two sides to the story, three actually, plus my father was a grown man and could make his own decisions. She stuck with him for seven years, then left. My father lost everything: his law practice, houses, boat, cars, money and his health. Then, my father wound up in jail.

*** Father

I was never close to my adopted father. Actually, I grew up with the fear of God of him, due to his drinking, temper, and his back hand with the heavy college ring on it which I received many times across my face. My father was an intimidating man. He could scare anyone silent with just his voice. As an attorney working and traveling around the world, he was never home. When he was home, he wasn't present. His body might have been there, but his mind was somewhere else.

My dad told me, which may or may not be true, since truth was elusive in my family, that they adopted me because they always wanted a girl. My father had prostate cancer and couldn't have any more children after he had my two brothers. I was his Father's Day present. He used to say to me, "We *had* your brothers, but we *chose* you." It made me feel somewhat loved and wanted in the unstable chaotic environment I grew up in.

***Chink

"Sticks and stones may break my bones but names will never hurt me." One of the many socially accepted sayings we are brainwashed to believe, but is a total lie. It was something I repeated over and over to myself growing up as I heard the racist slang: Chink, Chink, Chink, Jap, Jap, Jap being shouted at me. Words can hurt, just as easily as they can heal. Words can also leave scars, which they did to me.

I bore the torture of my oldest brother who would holler, "Chink" at me over and over until I ran into my room and cried in shame. At summer camp, although I never told anyone, there was a boy who used to torture me behind everyone's back yelling "Jap" at me over and over. I had no idea why he would say that. It was so awful, I hated how I looked. These words damages my self-esteem and scarred me for life. My brothers never stood up for me when kids teased me either, and that hurt me more.

I found this short story from an email from my Dad:

A group of frogs were traveling through the woods, and two of them fell into a deep pit. When the other frogs saw how deep the pit was, they told the two frogs that they were as good as dead. The two frogs ignored the comments and tried to jump up out of the pit with all their might. The other frogs kept telling them to stop, that they were as good as dead. Finally, one of the frogs took heed to what the other frogs were saying and gave up. He fell down and died.

The other frog continued to jump as hard as he could. Once again, the crowd of frogs yelled at him to stop the pain and just die. He jumped even harder and finally made it out. When he got out, the other frogs said, "Did you not hear us?" The frog explained to them that he was deaf. He thought they were encouraging him the entire time.

This story teaches two lessons:

1. There is power of life and death in the tongue. An encouraging word to someone who is down can lift them up and help them make it through the day.
2. A destructive word to someone who is down can be what it takes to kill them.

Be careful of what you say. Speak life to those who cross your path. The power of words... it is sometimes hard to understand that an encouraging word can go such a long way. Anyone can speak words that tend to rob another of the spirit to continue in difficult times. Special is the individual who will take the time to encourage another. ~Author Unknown

***Almond Eyes

It was brutal looking different. I was so sensitive. I ran away and hid in shame in my bedroom, crying my almond eyes out. I didn't understand why everybody made fun of my eyes. I never told anyone, just kept the feelings hidden and started building a shell around my heart. Enduring this form of bullying was the start of my "toughness."

My other brother and I were a little closer, maybe because we were so close in age, only 9 months apart. Although we used to physically fight with each other, I knew he cared about me. When we were older and went out he had an infamous way of introducing me to people. He said, "This is my sister, Steph." Then people would have a confused look on their face because I looked nothing like him. My brother had blond hair, blue eyes and fair skin. He then said, "We're Siamese twins, but she got all the Siamese." It always broke the ice and made people laugh.

That was the silver lining my brother gave me. That and when Eugene committed suicide, my brother was the only one who seemed to care from my family. He was overseas in the military but took the time to write me beautiful heartfelt letters that I cherish to this day. Those letters were gold to me.

My mother got remarried two years after she moved out, when I was eleven years old. They had another child, my step-sister, Shannon, who I adored. My mother also found her calling in life, the fire department, to which she was dedicated. I grew up at the fire house on the weekends when we stayed with her. During the night, the radio would go off and she frequently would have to run out to a call. She would sleep a lot during the day from the stress of it all.

Needless to say, she wasn't too available for us either. It seemed like her career and new relationship were her priority. After my mother moved out I felt abandoned all over again and held it against her most of my life. I'm sure that was part of the reason we never had a close relationship but I also never felt she was a mother to me. In my eyes she was not there for me in any way. (Since then I have forgiven her- I realized she was just as wounded as I was). Still, when you are a young child it is a major wound and loss.

When my mother and step-father bought a house, the plan was to make the basement into three bedrooms for my two brothers and me. That never happened. The basement became a storage unit for their stuff.

My step-father was a nice man and I tried to get along with him, but he was another adult in my life with a drinking problem. When we came to visit and stay for a weekend we ended up sleeping on the pull-out couch in the living room that was stuffed with his used tissues. It was a cramped, tiny house and none of us had our own space. It was awkward, but I tried to make the best of it. I never felt like I fit in anywhere.

My obsessive neatness started then as well. My mother was not neat, and to live in chaos was stressful to me, even at the age of eleven. On the weekends when we came to visit I spent the whole day cleaning her kitchen, so when she came home from work she would notice it and give me praise. It was my way of getting her approval, love and acceptance. Even though my mother appreciated my cleaning she would rant that she could never find anything after I cleaned since I threw things away. I can't stand clutter, either can angels. Cleanliness is next to Godliness.

Feeling like an outsider inside my family, I pretty much raised myself. I always knew I was different. My adopted family was Caucasian, Irish, German and French, with blond hair, blue eyes and fair skin. Even though I was different looking (exotic according to many people), I felt like an ugly duckling. I was a mix of nationalities but never knew which since my adopted parents didn't even know.

I remember hearing my parents say I was Polynesian or Philippine. I felt like they said that because it was less Asian ("Oriental" back then) and more "acceptable," which made me feel more insecure. Adoption wasn't common at that time, and it didn't help that we lived in an all white middle-upper class neighborhood. There was only one other Asian kid in my school. We were in the honors acceleration classes together, of course.

***The Ugly Duckling

People would stare at me and ask me the same questions, and still do to this very day, "What are you? Where are you from? Are you Chinese? Are you Japanese?" Ugh, it was irritating. Didn't people know there were other Asian nationalities besides Chinese and Japanese! At first I used to say I was Polynesian, but nobody knew what that meant, including me, so I changed it to Philippine. That seemed to appease their curiosity about me.

It seemed like everyone else was more concerned with my nationality than I was. I really didn't care much at all. I felt like just saying, "I'm from God." (which is the truth).

All I cared about was looking less like I did and fitting in with everyone else. This was also a trait my daughter picked up. One day after school when she was twelve years old, she told me she wished she looked like Danielle, who had blond hair and blue eyes. That was the end of living in Kings Park, a predominately white neighborhood. We moved from the

North Shore of Long Island across the island to the South Shore where there was much more diversity.

When my daughter and I visited Hawaii, it was the first place that felt like home to me and where I belonged. One day while shopping I asked the price of something and the woman replied, "I give you the resident price." First of all, I didn't know there was tourist price and a resident price, but I didn't care; I was so happy that she thought I was Hawaiian.

At last, I thought, *I found my roots, my people?* I started telling people I was Hawaiian when I got back home. It seemed more socially acceptable and brought less feelings of shame to me. It turned out that I felt that way in a lot of places I traveled to: Argentina, Brazil, Spain, Portugal, Hawaii, Italy, India, Mexico, even Africa. I felt more at home there than I did on Long Island. People didn't stare at me in these other countries like they did in the United States. People just assumed I was one of them.

In Egypt it went so far that a boy ran up to my Dad shouting, "My Queen, my queen, my queen! I will give you 1,000 camels for her." My Dad jokingly replied yes, and I went into a panic until I realized my father was kidding and would never sell me for camels.

That was the positive side to looking and being different. I felt like I could morph and blend in to almost any culture and I liked connecting to other people. I felt comfortable around all types of people and in all types of settings. This quality of being mutable and adaptable has come to serve me well.

By then, though, I had a complex, and it wasn't good. It was complex! The damage was done and my self-esteem was deflated. I was on the softball team in high school, and the boys used to yell to me when I was up at bat, "Open your eyes!" It was humiliating.

By the time I was fifteen years old I decided after watching an Oprah show that when I turned eighteen I would get surgery that would give me an eyelid to make me look less Asian so people would stop making fun of me. I began to save up my money but never followed through. Instead, I just continued to try to look less Asian by perming and dying my hair and wearing a lot of eye makeup.

It wasn't just my eyes that were the object of mockery, my body was as well. I was bow legged which my brothers took complete advantage of any chance they got, mimicking the way I walked and swam. They called me "Bubble Butt" as they said I must be part black, referring to Janet Jackson. I know your siblings are suppose to tease you, but for my sensitive soul, it was overkill. It only made me feel even more self-conscious.

Ignorance of my nationality, my ancestry, and lacking any baby pictures or conventional memories, gave me such a sense of alienation that I felt like I never belonged anywhere.

It never really phased me about not having any baby pictures until one day about three years ago I was at a client's house and she was so excited to show me the photo album she had made for her daughter's twenty-fifth birthday. It was filled with pictures of her and records of all her accomplishments from birth to present. She was so proud of it and her daughter.

I smiled on the outside but inside I felt complete heartbreak at the realization that I didn't have one baby picture of myself, but worse, I never had anyone in my life that cared for me like that. There was a hole in my heart that felt so vast. I wondered if it would ever be filled, if anyone would ever love me like that.

My saving graces were exercise, music, sports, dance, and anything physical. That was my form of stress and emotional release. I was a tom boy to the core. My Dad pushed me to get into modeling in high school and I refused. "I just wanted to play sports," I implored. I refused to wear dresses, play with Barbies (that were all still in the box at the back of my closet), and only wore boys jeans. I loved a physical challenge. Having all brothers kept me active. We always were playing tennis, going ice skating, skiing, playing basketball or hockey, skateboarding or riding bikes.

I played field hockey, basketball, softball and was a cheerleader all throughout middle school and high school. I also danced. When I was twelve years old I would go into my room, turn on the music, dance and work out on my own, no DVD, no You Tube. I never needed motivation to move my body! Music and exercise were the only things that made me feel good.

Unfortunately having low self esteem and an addiction to my body image- the only thing that gave me a boost in confidence- left me susceptible to bulimia in high school. I thought it was pretty cool that I could eat whatever I wanted, throw it up and not gain a pound of weight. I was self conscious about my looks and never wanted to be fat or out of shape. I thought *if I have an ugly face at least let me have a nice body.*

Since eating sweets seemed to comfort me, I thought I had the best of both worlds. I didn't know any better back then. It wasn't until my boyfriend caught me throwing up Thanksgiving dinner at his house and read me the riot act that I stopped. I knew deep down that it was unhealthy, and being a healthy athlete was important to me.

There was a boy in my high school who gave me my first memorable compliment. He said to me one day, "You weren't just born, God created you." It was so different to have someone praise me. He probably never knew what an impact that statement had on me and that I remember it to this day. Thank you David.

***Where the Heck Am I?

As a child, I felt misplaced in a harsh world. I saw the world differently, thought differently, felt things very deeply. I was sensitive and had no one in my life that supported me or even understood me. Being brought up Catholic, the religion classes and receiving my confirmation in the church just made me more confused. I didn't understand what God was, who Jesus was and what the point of religion was. I didn't know there were other people like me. I used to look up at the stars at night, my heart aching, whispering *I want to go home.*

I sat up in our 200 foot pine tree and contemplated how I could heal the world or sometimes would walk to the beach by myself and sit on this rock in the middle of the Long Island Sound and think about what happiness felt like or what love really was. **It felt like those were two things missing from my life.**

My survival tactic for my sensitive heart was, "It could always be worse," I used to ponder, "I could have been adopted by drug dealers, or been in an physically abusive household or lived in the ghetto and had no food. At least I'm getting a good education and have traveled around the world." "I may not have a lot of love and support but I have food, clothing and shelter." I always looked for the silver lining.

I cried when I read the newspaper or heard the news, or even just saw someone else crying. I was so sensitive and compassionate, I thought something was wrong with me. I questioned why there was so much suffering in the world. It didn't make sense how some people lived so lavishly while others needlessly suffered. Then I would wonder how people could ignore it when it hurt me so much. To this day, when my daughter and I watch TV, she turns to me and says, "Oh my God, Mom, are you crying, again?" "It's a cartoon, Mom" or "It's a commercial Mom, really?"

Anything endearing or touching would invoke the tears to flow. When I watched *The Passion* by Mel Gibson (which I watched most of it with my eyes closed and my ears plugged with my fingers) I sat in the movie theater until it emptied out then started bawling like a baby. I had no idea where these deep sobs were coming from. I was traumatized. My date had no idea what to do, poor guy. Thank God he was a kind soul.

Even though it's a blessing, the modern world we live in does not promote compassion or empathy. It is looked upon as weakness. I used to think that something was wrong with me, but now I know something is wrong with the world. Empathy, compassion and understanding are the only things left that's going to save humanity and our world.

***My Mother is a What?!

In spite of feeling misplaced and unwanted, I managed to get straight A's through high school and college graduating Magna Cum Laude with a double major in Spanish and Humanities from Providence College. Good grades, sports and school were a pleasure. They distracted me from the emptiness I felt inside and the lack of stability and security at home.

My send off to college by my father was when I learned about my biological parents. I never knew anything about myself. I was in the dark for my entire childhood, lost and confused about who I was and where I was from.

I remember the night distinctly. My father sat me down on the couch, something he rarely did, and said to me, "Peenup (his nickname for me; Peanut really because I was so little when they adopted me), I want to tell you about your biological mother."

Nervous with anticipation, thinking I would finally understand who I was, he continued, "Your mother was a prostitute and a heroin addict. She was Italian American. We don't know anything about your father."

What?!?!?! Not expecting that I burst into tears, (which I never did in front of anyone). My father didn't do anything to comfort me: no hugs, no hand holding, no continued conversation, no way to process my feelings, no therapy; that was it. I am sure he was intoxicated at the time. Whatever little self-esteem I had managed to salvage was now gone.

"My mother is a prostitute," stayed etched in my brain and sank deep into my psyche. Not the best way to send your vulnerable young daughter off to college.

PETAL 2

Angel Intervention

***Martin Luther King Jr.

So there I was, alone and lost at Providence College In Rhode Island, a Catholic school unbeknownst to me at the time I applied. I picked the college because it was on another "island," as silly as that seems, and it was close enough to home if I needed to come back but far enough away to not get visits from my family often. I had no guidance or help picking a college obviously, which was odd considering the one thing my father pushed on all of us was college.

Growing up, my father always told us that no matter what happened he had money for our college tuition put aside for us. That's all we ever heard. That was the one thing I could count on, so I thought. Until I was pulled out of class freshman year to the bursar's office and was told I couldn't return to class because my father didn't pay my tuition.

Embarrassed and shocked. Another bomb! He told me he lost my tuition in the stock market crash of 1987 which was probably another lie, and to go down to the Dean of Minority Students and see if I could get a scholarship. I responded indignantly, "But I'm not a minority!" I called my mother and she said the same thing. It seemed like everyone knew something I didn't.

I never thought of myself as a minority. I grew up in a white family in a white neighborhood and thought I was one of them. Just the word, *minority,* brought up uncomfortable feelings of shame and inadequacy. With no other choice however, I put my pride aside and humbly went down to the minority office. (We're all majority under God.)

Apprehensive as I thought I might be expelled from college, I sat in front of a large, intimidating man, whose dialect was so heavy I had no idea what he was saying. Overwhelmingly relieved, he told me I qualified for a full Martin Luther King Jr. Scholarship that covered my tuition and books which he gave to me on the spot! I had to take student loans out for room and board and work part time as a Student Athletic Trainer for spending money. I was on the high honor role through high school and Dean Simpson told me I just had to maintain my GPA, participate in the minority activities and also do volunteer work, something I grew to love.

I'll always be grateful to Dean S. He saved me. I realize now he was one of the angels God planted in my life. Sadly growing up in an all white community I didn't know much about black history or Martin Luther King Jr. then. Fate would have it years later in my awakening, a Martin Luther King, Jr. quote became my new mantra, thanks to finding it in the Oprah magazine that my dear friend, Susie from college bought for me:

"Use me God, show me how to take who I am, who I want to be, what I can do and use it for a purpose greater than myself."

***MTV

This was my introduction to a whole other world, the world of minorities. Ironically, I had to go away to a Caucasian Catholic college in Rhode Island to meet black and Spanish people! It was the first time in my life that I felt like I fit in. And I was desperate to feel accepted and fit in somewhere.

One night I was at a club by myself, not to meet people or drink, but to dance, something I did often. I caught the attention of some of my fellow friars who were black. The next thing I knew I was being approached to be part of the PC Friars Basketball Dance Team. It was an honor because there was only one white girl on the dance team and the rest were black.

With that boost of self confidence in my dancing skills, one day when my girlfriend asked me to audition with her for MTV I agreed. They were in Providence looking for people to be on their show for their famous spring break episode.

The first part was the dance audition, which I passed. The second part was an obstacle course on stage, doing silly and embarrassing things like barking like a dog after we took a shot of alcohol without any hands. All of these things in front of a big crowd of course. I made it through that as well.

The last part of the audition was to go on stage and do something for one minute to entertain the crowd. They gave us no time to prepare either. I panicked but suddenly thought of the sign language class I was taking. For the final project I signed to the song, *I Need You Tonight* by INXS. My teacher loved it and gave me an A, so I decided to do that in addition to a little dancing. I told the crowd my dream was to be a singer, and I had a special song I wanted to sing for them. Instead of singing, I signed it.

It was a huge hit! It was unique, creative, and I overcame my stage fright performing it. I was in, and off I flew to Daytona Beach, trip fully paid for by MTV. With back stage passes and many perks I felt like I was a celebrity. I met many famous artists and performers. My favorite was meeting LL Cool J and taking a picture with him. It was so much fun.

When Downtown Julie Brown interviewed me I said something on TV that I wish I could take back. When she asked me what my philosophy in life was, I replied, "Life is too short to dance with ugly men." Even Downtown Julie Brown was taken aback, I think. At the time I thought it was cool and funny, but now I think how awful it sounded. It hurts me to know I said that. This goes to show how lost I was.

I was nervous when I had to tell my teacher, a Catholic nun, that I would be missing class because I won a trip with MTV to be on the spring break episode. Much to my surprise my nun teacher was excited for me and told me to have a good time! When I returned, Providence College put me on the front page of the school newspaper with an article about me and my trip. It was definitely a boost in my self confidence; although I defaulted back to my "mother is a prostitute" mantra and made some bad choices on that trip that I regretted.

The desperate need for acceptance always lurked in the background of my being which led me down the path of promiscuity. I was looking for love in all the wrong places, with all the wrong men. I didn't even enjoy sex. I didn't have orgasms, I didn't even know what they were. My first orgasm didn't come until I was in my mid thirties. The men I was with were just using me because I let them. My warped sense of self thought sex meant that they wanted me.

Thank God for my college roommate. We couldn't have been more contrary. She was the "Virgin Mary," and I was "Mary, the prostitute."

Every Sunday after my wild weekend of sleeping around and partying it up she would try to convince me to go to church with her, like that was going to help. I already thought I was going to Hell, so why bother? My holy friend was persistent though and never gave up on me. I had my most embarrassing moments in college. She bailed me out on many different occasions. I had no idea what a mess I was. Sorry Bissa. And thank you.

I did attend church with her a few times, but what left a lasting impression on me was volunteering. One day she convinced me to go to the pool with her to help disabled people exercise. It was one of the most gratifying experiences I had of my life. I didn't realize at the time that a seed was planted for me to serve the world in a greater way.

***God's Voice

Besides the lasting friendships, another gift that came from college was my experience of other cultures. In my junior year I studied abroad in Salamanca, Spain. Spanish was my major, along with Humanities, because I had no freakin' idea what I wanted to do with my life and absolutely no guidance. I just thought if I could speak Spanish, I could have an "in" anywhere.

Traveling abroad and backpacking through Europe rooted the taste and passion for travel which my Dad first planted in me. It was one of the best experiences I had in my life. My dear friend Susie and I bought a Eurail pass and backpacked all over Europe for a month.

It was my first lesson in traveling lightly. I ended up literally tossing out of the train window, my hair dryer, my extra shoes and clothes with pleasure. I had no choice since we walked everywhere, stayed in hostels and my backpack was a beast of burden.

Each one of our friends were studying in a different country, so that's how we picked our destinations. We visited Portugal, Spain, France, Italy, Switzerland, Germany, and the island of Tenerife. We also visited my cousin/step-brother and Susie's boyfriend who were *coincidently* stationed in the army together in Vicenza, Italy.

Even though I studied Spanish for four years in high school and four years in college, it wasn't until I lived in Spain with a Spanish family and had a Spanish boyfriend who didn't speak English, that I became fluent. This was one of the sweetest and most rewarding experiences of my life.

My Spanish family and I became very close. I couldn't believe it when it was time for me to go back to the states they asked me to stay and live with them. I must have exuded an "orphan of the world, adopt me vibe." I was touched and honored. I grew to love them so much as well. Torn with indecision, I knew in my gut that I needed to go home, even though Spain felt like home to me too. The night before I was leaving to go back to America was the first time in my life that I heard *God's voice.*

I had just said good-bye to my boyfriend, ran home crying hysterically, was lying in my small bed in my small room in the pitch dark, crying my eyes out, when suddenly I heard a deep commanding voice, ***"No te preocupes mujer,"*** which is Spanish for "**Don't worry woman."**

I stopped crying immediately, got very quiet and said, "Hello." I didn't know where the voice came from. My Swedish roommate sleeping in the bed next to me didn't stir.

The next morning at breakfast I asked if she heard anything in her sleep. She replied that she did not. I then asked her if she knew what, "*No te preocupes mujer*" meant, and she also did not. I told her that she said that to me in her sleep last night, but deep down I knew it was not her. I just didn't know it at the time that God was speaking to me.

It was one of the most practical and important wisdoms I realize now that God has ever said to me. I don't know how or when I became a worrier. I was only 21 years old, but I guess I worried enough that it warranted an audible and straightforward message from Spirit.

***Homeless

I went back to the States and graduated from college but didn't have a home to go back to. One weekend when I was home visiting from college, my Dad told us to hurry up and pack up our rooms, that the moving truck was coming and we were moving to our home in Florida. Once again I was being uprooted and the rug pulled out from under my feet. I loved our home and community. I remember as I was packing a box I just started throwing up.

So after college I went back home to Long Island and stayed with my aunt, the one who was my step-mother for a few years. This lasted only a short while because this was when I met my daughter's father, Eugene. Leaving Brooklyn and in between homes, he had nowhere to stay so he ended up on my aunt's couch. At first she was very nice and accommodating but after a couple of weeks she couldn't handle that scenario, and I don't blame her.

Off we went. We lived in my car for a while, surviving on peanut butter and jelly sandwiches. I had a tiny Ford Escort at the time. This was my first experience living out of my car. At 22 years old, everything is more like an adventure, not a burden, until I realized how cold and uncomfortable it really was, even with blankets. The romance was gone. But this challenge did prepare me for future experiences.

We finally found an apartment and after about a year of working miscellaneous jobs and dancing for entertainment companies on the weekend, I had enough. *This was absurd* I thought, *all that money and education and this is what I am doing with my life?* So I decided I would get serious and get a "real" job. I called up my friend from college, who lived in Jersey City and asked him if I could stay with him for a few days while I went into Manhattan to "pound the pavement."

***The Purple Plaid Suit

I bought the *NY Times,* read through the Help Wanted section and circled anything that looked promising. I put on my only suit and hit the streets. I was twenty three and the limiting thoughts had not yet taken over my mind. I was fearless.

Since cell phones had not been created yet, I walked around with an old fashioned paper map with no idea where I was going. I had to actually talk to people and ask for directions. I went from one temp agency to another. I felt like I was selling myself short, after all I graduated Magna Cum Laude from a good private college and agency after agency kept giving me typing tests and dictation tests. I did everything they asked, one after the other, all day long.

Disheartened and about to call it quits, I walked into my last agency. The young man that interviewed me seemed to be more interested in me than the others. He confirmed that I spoke Spanish fluently, one of the benefits of living in Spain, and then asked me if I was good with numbers? I said, "I'm half Asian, of course I'm good with numbers," trying to break the ice which he didn't find very amusing. He made a phone call, then asked me, "Can you go for an interview now?"

"Of course," I replied.

He proceeded to look me up and down and asked me if I had anything else to wear. Surprised at his question, I replied, "No." He told me it's not professional for women to wear pant suits. I was wearing the only suit I owned which Eugene's mother bought for me, so it was special. It was not just any pant suit, but a fleece purple plaid pant suit that we found in Brooklyn at one of those sidewalk shops hanging up outside. I thought I rocked it, but looking back now it's one of those, "I can't believe I wore that," admissions.

The woman who worked at the next desk overheard our conversation, walked over to me and said, "Come with me." We went into the ladies room, she took off her black skirt and told me to give her my pants, which I did hesitantly. Then she told me there was a Woolworths around the block and to go buy a pair of stockings, which I did. I interviewed on the 84th floor of the World Trade Center *and got the job.*

I returned to the temp agency and we switched clothes. I don't think I expressed enough gratitude to this angel who God placed in my life. I call this **Angel Intervention, or AI.** I was beginning to realize how serendipitous things flowed and how I was being watched over all the time, even though I always felt alone.

I had no idea what a stock or a bond was but was soon going to learn. I started as an administrative assistant and worked my way up to operations manager within a year. I am a quick learner.

Getting that job was divine intervention because I found out I was pregnant. My boss Paul, another angel in my life, helped me get health insurance so I would be covered for my pregnancy. He saved me, big time.

I was home on maternity leave when the first basement bomb went off in Tower One in 1993. Our office was ruined and we had to relocate to another building within the financial center. I went back to work six weeks after I gave birth.

One of the toughest and most unnatural things to do was to leave my baby with strangers at a daycare center. The first one we found returned her smelling like cigarette smoke with a bruise on her forehead. Then we found another place with a woman who became my friend, and that is where she stayed until she started school. I found a new job at Meryl Lynch on Long Island closer to home. I am grateful that I left the city when I did.

***The Discovery of Self-Help Books

Even though the financial industry was the last career I ever wanted, there was a silver lining ironically. This materialistic path led me to the world of personal growth. The first self-help books I was introduced to were by Robert Kiyosaki, *Rich Dad, Poor Dad*. I found these books so interesting I read all the rest of his books.

I bought a cassette player for my car and listened to Zig Ziglar on cassette tapes driving to and from work. Even though at the time it was to increase my sales, it also motivated me and helped me to feel more positive. I was given the book, *The Greatest Salesman in the World,* by Og Mandino that left an impact on me and led me to his other books. *The Greatest Miracle in the World* brought me comfort and inspiration, which I gave to all the people in my life.

These financial self-growth books led me to stumble across the book, *The Seat of the Soul,* by Gary Zukav. I read it even though I didn't really get it. I intuitively knew these metaphysical concepts and spiritual ideas were important. A seed was planted. At the time I had no idea how significant this was.

During one of my bookstore outings I discovered a significant book: *You Can Heal Your Life,* by Louise Hay. I only bought it because the cover was colorful and had pretty red hearts all over it. In the end it changed my life and became my new bible that I gave to all my friends. Although I didn't quite grasp these new Eastern concepts being raised in the West, something resonated with me.

I bought the cassette tapes that went along with the book and played them at night while my daughter was sleeping. I learned it was one way to reprogram our subconscious mind. I didn't realize at the time that it wasn't her subconscious that needed reprogramming, but mine! Who knows? Maybe that's why she turned out to be such a wonderful young woman now.

***Jail

At this point my father had been incarcerated for about a year. It was my first time visiting someone in prison and not really the scenario I imagined in my mind when I had my first child and introducing my father to my future husband. (We had planned to get married after Aiyana was born initially). We were both nervous and intimidated, shielding and protecting our baby from the steel cold scary environment- not sure if this was the right thing to do. At least I knew my Dad, dressed in all orange, couldn't say anything about Eugene being black. My father was an identical twin, which I used to get confused when I was a little girl. His brother, my uncle, came to the hospital when my daughter was born. It was as close to a father that I could get.

I never got a straight story as to why my father went to jail and then had to flee the state of New York. I did read about my father in the newspaper shortly after. The story he told me did not match up with the story in the newspaper, no big surprise there. All I knew was we lost everything. Again, I had no one to depend on but myself.

Since my father was banned from New York, he flew to Florida until we lost that house too. Then we lost all of our possessions which were in a storage unit, and he ended up "finding God" and becoming a deacon of the church; ironically, facilitating mass in prison.

Perhaps it's true that the healthy way for adults to grow is that the first half of life the focus is on material things, amassing wealth and security, then the second half of life is about getting rid of it all and seeking deeper meaning.

It's no surprise that my dad lost all his material possessions; after all, his affirmation every time we pulled the Porche or Mercedes Benz into the garage from an outing was, "Back home and broke."

My father was obviously not up on metaphysical quantum physics, but he demonstrated perfectly how your thoughts create your reality.

"Your beliefs become your thoughts,
Your thoughts become your words,
Your words become your actions,
Your actions become your habits,
Your habits become your values,
Your values become your destiny." (Ghandi)

It seemed my dad was on the fast track to spiritual maturity. He had amassed wealth, status and material things, lost them all, including his identity and recreated himself anew.

Then he suffered a massive stroke and never recovered. He chose not to partake in physical therapy because as he said, "They don't know what they're doing." He might have "found God," but he was still a stubborn arse and a drinking fool. His life became saturated with a "poor me" attitude and end-less emails. He lost his ability to walk, so he was confined to a wheelchair living at the computer in a room with a friend that was kind enough to take him in.

Unfortunately or fortunately, my father took religion to the extreme. He became a radical born again something...not sure what. He was always trying to shove Jesus down my throat. He would end every phone call or email with, "I hope you are taking Jesus into your heart, Peenup, or you will burn eternally in Hell!"

I'm pretty sure Jesus didn't endorse that message. God forbid I mentioned Buddha or any other enlightened masters that walked the earth. That never went over well with him.

God always takes care of his children. There were many angels looking over us. The man I was dating at the time Eugene committed suicide stayed in our lives. I never asked him to and he certainly didn't have to. He was the first honest person who was straight up with me and didn't play games. He was the rock that we needed. He was and still is a blessing in our lives. <u>There is always a silver lining. We just have to look for it.</u>

***My Angel Mechanic

When you go through trauma the brain's survival tactic is to block things out, including the good memories. I completely forgot about this special angel until the last minute as I was turning over my final manuscript. This person deserves a place in my book.

I don't remember how I was referred to Greg, but when you are a single parent under extreme stress with a car that doesn't run too well, a good mechanic is sometimes more important than a husband. At least that's how I felt. My used Nissan had seen better days. Once when my sister-in-law dropped me off somewhere and had to drive my car home, I left these instructions:

1. Do not drive over 55 mph or car will start shaking...a lot
2. Do not open the passenger side door, it does not open
3. Do not make left turns or car will stall suddenly

The last one was key if you were in a busy intersection! If a left turn was needed, I would have to find a way to get to my destination by making right turns only. Driving was an adventure for me, needless to say.

When Greg came into my life he was a God-send. This man would come to my house with his girlfriend, take my car, (his girlfriend drove his car back), bring it to his shop, do an oil change or whatever needed to be done, drive it back to me and only charge me minimally for parts. I don't think he ever charged me for labor. Who does that??? Earth angels do!!! I lost touch with Greg when I upgraded to my first brand new car, but I really hope he knows how much I appreciated him. Thank you Greg.

***Body Building

Becoming a female financial consultant in a man's world was not as easy task. I encountered sexual harassment and double standards regularly. Determined and hard working though, I climbed my way up from Abaco International to Meryl Lynch, Bear Sterns, Smith Barney, Citibank, and Bank of America, where I became a fully licensed financial consultant covering a territory of bank branches and customers.

I knew this was not my dream, but I made the best of it and always kept a grateful heart. At the same time I became a personal trainer and started body building, thanks to my boxer boyfriend. At 30 I entered my first all natural body building show in 1999. It was a great experience that taught me how to transform my physical body in six months with good old exercise and diet. I won Best Poser in that show. I competed in two more but with another trainer after we broke up.

One of the things that got me over my stage fright was a quote from the fitness model who inspired me to start body building. She said, "People don't care as much about you as you think they do." I got it.

People are too caught up in themselves to be thinking about you. That helped me to be less self conscious on stage and in life when I had to get up in front of an audience.

I used to do what I called the jiggle test. I would stand naked in front of the mirror and jump up and down. Whatever was jiggling, that wasn't supposed to be, had to go. Bye bye carbs, "Bread makes you spread" was my mantra. I was working out three times a day. Yet I was wise enough to know when to stop. I saw how this way of life could become an addiction very easily. It reminded me of a girl I went to college with who was a slave to her body image and low body fat. She use to ride on the stationary bike while squirting Redi Whip whip cream into her mouth. My strong inner voice knew that if anything had the potential to become an addiction I needed to stop.

While I was competing though I was dedicated and committed, like I am with everything I'm passionate about. When you want something badly enough, it's never about is there a way? There's always a way. It's about how badly do you want it?

In the morning before my daughter woke up I would do my first round of cardio on the recumbent stationary bike I crammed in my tiny apartment so I wouldn't have to bring her to the gym two times a day. Or while she was sleeping early in the morning I would jump rope outside on the sidewalk or run around the block a jillion times so I could keep running by the apartment to hear her in case she woke up.

On my lunch hour I went to the gym to meet my personal trainer, do my weight workout, ate lunch in my car, worked the rest of the day, picked up my daughter, went home, ate dinner, homework, dragged her to the gym; to the babysitting room where I would do my final round of cardio before bed.

I didn't share this with anyone at the bank because even though I had more freedom since I covered a territory of multiple branches, I didn't want to take advantage since sometimes my lunch hour was longer than an hour.

My secret got out of the bag (or shall we say the suit) one hot summer day during a horrific heat wave that coincided with broken air conditioning in the bank. All the employees were disrobing their suit jackets; everyone except me. I was wearing a sleeveless dress under my suit jacket that day, and I was hesitant about revealing my secret.

My co-workers kept staring at me quizzically, saying, "Why don't you take off your jacket?" Finally, dripping with sweat, I gave in. Trying to act inconspicuous but it was impossible. Their facial expressions were priceless. "What the heck are you doing?" they asked me as they stared at my arms. I had guns and they were no joke.

***"We were born an original; don't die a copy." ~Unknown

I didn't care what people thought, especially the other parents. The moms would shoot me dirty looks as their husbands drooled and ogled over me at meet the teacher nights. I already had people staring at me so this wasn't any different. I definitely didn't fit in with any other parents, so standing out even more didn't bother me. No PTA for me. I was the only mother picking her kid up from school on roller blades in a baseball hat. I was showing my daughter how to be her own person and a non conformist at an early age.

I was leading two lives and in my heart I knew that if I stayed at the bank any longer I would suffocate. The financial industry wasn't what was in my heart to do and as much as I was grateful for the education and experience, I knew it wasn't my calling. I was more interested in people than their money.

Even with all my exercise outlets, the pressure of having monthly sales quotas and being a single Mom with all the pain and hurt still repressed within me was too much for me to handle. I was angry, stressed out and hardly home for my daughter. When I was home, unfortunately she received the brunt of my stress. This was no way to live.

All I wanted was to be able to put my daughter on the bus in the morning and be there when she got home. I wanted to have time to bake cookies with her and just be "normal." I wanted simple and stress free.

I was so stressed out, one day my eye started to twitch when I got stuck in a traffic jam on the Long Island Expressway. It twitched for a month. I knew I had to make a change.

***Gymgirl

"Always be a first-rate version of yourself, and not a second rate version of someone else." ~ Judy Garland

I resigned in the summer of 2000, ironically the most lucrative year at the bank. My manager shocked, asked me why I was resigning. I replied, "To follow my dreams." Surprised but in respect of my decision, he told me I had an open door to come back.

My co-workers and friends all thought I was crazy. I was giving up a six figure income with bonuses and benefits. Trust me, there were many times that I questioned myself. It was a struggle financially being a single mom and I thought about going back to work full time in that industry many times. But I had to follow my heart.

I got a job at Gold's Gym and blossomed. I turned in my business suit for a sweat suit and was so much happier. I became a certified personal trainer and taught every class from kickboxing to rebounding to body sculpt and Pilates. I lived at the gym and was in my glory. Even my license plate said, GYMGIRL.

I am not my body. Imbalance happens when we are focused only on the physical though. I yearned for inner confidence and true security. Even during exercise, my only form of stress release, I was still a reactive bundle of stress yelling at my daughter for something and immediately my neck and back going into spasm. Thank God I had a good massage therapist who always made an opening for me. (Thanks John)

Inside I still craved love and acceptance. I went from one toxic relationship to another like a wound-seeking missile. Until I started to know who I really was, a spark of the divine Goddess, and truly loved and valued myself, I would keep attracting men into my life that were only interested in my body. My body was just the tip of the iceberg, there was so much more underneath. Hidden was the jewel.

(photo credit: J.M. Manion)

***Yogagirl

This career change from financial consultant to personal trainer and fitness instructor served it's purpose however, as another step up the ladder toward my spiritual growth. I had just finished teaching a kickboxing class and in came Bruce, a yoga teacher to teach the next class. I didn't know him very well. He asked me if I knew what yoga was. Oddly, I did not. I had never heard of it, which seems strange to me now.

He handed me a piece of paper and said, "Take this, I think you will like it." It was a weekend teacher training certification for level one yoga. I went on a whim, having no idea what to expect. When I was there all I could think was, *this is what I'm supposed to be doing*. That was in 2001, a pivotal turning point in my life.

Bruce was another angel in my life (I know for a fact that he has no idea), because that yoga certification changed the entire course of my life. It felt like it was the missing piece of the puzzle. I was hooked. I changed my license plate from GYMGIRL to YOGAGIRL and from that point on the focus of my fitness life was yoga.

I still continued to be well versed in the fitness world and stayed active in martial arts, weight lifting, triathlons, swimming and everything else physical, however, yoga had my attention and devotion. Over time I realized yoga was much more than a physical practice to keep your body in shape and this was what actually drew me to it, I just didn't know it yet.

This was the beginning of my "awakening," yet I had no idea it was also going to be the start of my breaking apart. I rarely talked about my feelings, in fact I wasn't even aware I had any I was so shut down and numb. Who has time to think about feelings when you are a single Mom just trying to survive?

I did however bring my five year old daughter to therapy after she was expelled from Kindergarten for shoving a boy into a book shelf and telling him to "Fuck off." I have no idea where she learned that? Oops, my bad. My daughter resisted it, like I did when my father made me go at seventeen when I ran away. I just sat in Dr. Doobie's office in silence. I couldn't get past his name.

PETAL 3

Waking Up

***My Poker Spine

RIGHT AT THE time I discovered yoga, I had also met Soulmate #2. I went back to work in the financial industry at Roslyn Savings Bank since my Series 7 and insurance licenses hadn't expired yet and money was an issue. There was a big pay difference between being a personal trainer/ yoga teacher and a financial consultant and he got laid off.

I'm selling my soul, but it's temporary, I told myself. Back into the dungeon I went, sacrificing my dreams for money.

Shortly after I went back to work my back gave out, or more like my back just decided one day it had enough. I woke up in the middle of the night in January 2003 with searing, excruciating back pain. This pain was familiar as I felt something like it after an 8 hour aeroboxing certification a few years earlier, but that was from over use; it was nothing compared to the pain I felt now.

The problem was when I went back to work as a financial consultant I stopped working out and exercising. For almost a year I just sat at my desk and stopped taking care of my body. This was a huge wake up call for me.

I found out I had multiple herniated disks in my lower back and neck amongst many other spinal issues, including arthritis and degenerative disk disease. On top of that my chiropractor at the time said I had a poker spine. I asked him what that meant. He said I had the straightest spine he has ever seen-not a good thing when we need the curves for protection from impact. After x-rays and MRI's I actually found out my spine wasn't just straight, I had reverse curves in my cervical and lumbar spine! Ugh.

The spinal doctor dropped a bomb on me when he said I had the spine of a seventy year old. Not the best way to deliver the news. I burst out in tears in his office. My physical health was everything to me, I was only thirty three.

I would be doing something simple like loading the dishwasher and my back would go into spasm and I'd be crippled in agony. It was not just painful but scary. I didn't know what would set it off.

One doctor told me never to run again; another one told me running would help my lower back by bringing blood flow to the disks. This contradictory information from two top spinal doctors in New York inspired me to take my healing into my own hands. This was the beginning of my education into prevention, health and wellness: not just body, but mind and soul. I learned how to take care of myself. Neither extreme, intense exercise or sedentary lifestyle were healthy for spinal injuries. I had to learn how to exercise for *my* body.

I also learned that most of the time back pain is caused by repressed emotions and past resentments that we are hold onto, in other words, emotional baggage. Injuries or illnesses are shouting, "Pay attention to me, Wake up!"

I had my first direct experience with this concept of mind/emotion/body connection when I was practicing my yoga routine to stretch and strengthen my back. I went into pigeon pose, a hip opener and burst into tears. I had no idea I even wanted to cry; it just came out of nowhere.

Surprised but feeling relief as I let the tears flow, I felt my body becoming lighter as I let go and just cried.

***The Hips Don't Lie

I learned later in my metaphysical studies that the hips are where we hold emotional baggage. It made sense to me. This happened a few more times during my yoga practice in the beginning. The two poses that stand out vividly were shoulder stand and wheel pose, which are inversions and back bends. As I released the pose I also released tears and sobs of stored negative energy.

I was still in the infancy of my new education into wellness and holistic health so I wasn't sure what was happening, but now I know that we hold "our issues in our tissues." Our cells have memories that are released during healing practices such as yoga. Got emotional baggage? Practice yoga. This is one of the reasons that yoga is such an effective tool for healing.

I knew that this health setback was supposed to happen. It forced me to slow down and take care of my health in a new way. I was more conscious of stress levels and how they immediately affected my body. I learned how to breathe and move in a way that was right for my body. Instead of panicking every time my back went out and being dependent on the doctor, I learned how to heal myself. I became my own doctor.

***You Can Heal Yourself

As I started to wake up and heal my body, mind and spirit, I used affirmations and mantras as I was practicing yoga. They came from my bible, *You Can Heal Your Life*, by Louise Hay. The premise behind this book is that pain is blocked energy, often caused by psychosomatic emotional imbalance in our thought patterns.

The probable cause of the issues in the upper back was stemming from a lack of emotional support, feeling unloved, and/or holding back love, (no surprise there). The new thought pattern and affirmation: ***I love and approve of myself. Life supports and loves me.***

The probable cause of the lower back pain was fear of money, lack of financial support. The new thought pattern and affirmation: ***I trust the process of life. All I need is always taken care of. I am safe.***

At first, I didn't fully understand the power in these affirmations and beliefs, but saying them made me feel peaceful inside, so I thought *why not?* I repeated them, whispered them, chanted them, sang them some days! I added them into my yoga/stretching routine in the morning and it seemed to help tremendously.

A student once asked an enlightened spiritual yogi what the difference was between feeling good and God. He replied by holding up his hand with his thumb and index finger touching forming the number zero.

If we don't feel well in our body, how can we feel well in our life? Nagging pain keeps us on edge and not fully present. It's hard to be happy when we are in physical pain. Healing our body is a priority on the spiritual path. I know many spiritual people who would just as well forget about their body, since it's not "who they are." However, our body is our temple, it's home to our soul. Ignoring our body is not a more enlightened way of being. We spend more time fixing our cars than fixing our body, remodeling our homes than taking care of our bodies. Those things are important, however, we can't ignore our human body and expect to live up to our potential. If you don't have your health, you can live in a castle with all the luxuries in the world and it won't matter if you're sick and you can't move.

Sitting was the most painful position for my back, so as a result I worked part time at the bank and then had to stop completely. My back pain was another sign that this career wasn't for me. I filed for partial disability but thanks to the non helpful insurance companies, they denied my claim. I hired an attorney, which cost me thousands of dollars and they still denied me. Unfortunately, not being able to work, not having health insurance and having to support my daughter by myself, I accrued high credit card debt and had to file for bankruptcy. This experience left me with a new shame-financial shame. Financial pain is real and it feels awful.

***F'in Angry

Before I left the financial industry all together, however, another angel appeared in my life. An intriguing woman opened an account with me at the bank. When I asked her occupation, I was surprised when she replied, "I'm an astrologer."

I was always drawn to astrology, the science of the planets and stars, even though I didn't know much about it and never met anyone that did it full time as a career. She asked me my date of birth and from that one fact she gleaned two thing: both my parents were born on cusps of signs, which they were, and that my daughter would be in a family with just one parent, which she was. How she knew that I had no idea, but it prompted me to save her card in my wallet.

Besides the physical pain and financial anxiety, I was having relationship challenges, going from bad to worse. Soulmate #2 had convinced our couple's counselor that I had several mental disorders, including bipolar, and convinced my daughter I had anger issues which I did, but was in denial. I would scream at him, "I'm not angry, mother fucker," then storm into our bedroom and slam the door. You know it's a bad sign when your boyfriend buys you a punching bag for your birthday instead of a pretty necklace!

The only real disorder I had was not healing myself. I was walking around wounded, filled with toxic emotions, angry with a fierce Italian temper (I loved to blame my temper on the Italian in me) and in denial that anything was wrong with me. That was an explosive combination.

I never physically abused my daughter, although I did break a wooden spoon on her butt once. (I learned that from my mother, who use to beat my butt with the wooden spoon). This alarmed Aiyana's therapist who warned me next time she would have to call social services and report me. We went though a few scares where I thought I might lose my daughter to the state. You know it's bad when you are working out at the gym and recognize the guy next to you because he's a police officer that has been to your house.

Sometimes what can be even more damaging than physical abuse however, is the emotional and mental abuse. My lack of self control of my words and anger bruised her emotionally. Yelling and screaming at my daughter was killing her spirit. Although I apologized to my daughter in person and in a letter years later, it took me many years to *forgive myself* for this.

***Angel Blanche

So one day at my wit's end, I pulled Blanche the astrologer's card out of my wallet and called her. I asked her if she remembered me since it had been a year since she had come into the bank. She replied, "Of course," like she was waiting for me to call. I asked her what an astrology reading was like. I'll never forget her reply.

She said, "Honey, one and a half hours with me is equivalent to two years in therapy!" Sign me up! I was in.

Blanche opened the reading with, "In all my life doing astrology charts, I never saw one like yours." My stomach dropped, was that good or bad? She said I had a very unique chart, and began to explain. For the hour and half I pretty much sat there with tears streaming down my face and my mouth agape. I learned so much about myself then. The only thing I didn't want to hear was when she told me not to marry Soulmate #2; I wasn't ready to hear that advice at the time, but she was right.

Blanche was another catalyst for my healing, *another angel God sent me.* She told me I pretty much raised myself and I was sweeping all my feelings under the rug, to which I agreed, and that I wasn't dealing with my feelings appropriately. She said I liked to wear blinders like horses wore. I also liked to wear rose-colored glasses. She said my chart was like a see-saw, everything was opposite each other and in extremes. I had to learn how to walk the middle way and find balance.

She also told me I came into this life to experience compassion and it was my destiny to lead and inspire large groups of people through public speaking and emphasized not just large groups, but the masses. I said, "Impossible, I will never be a public speaker." She told me it was my destiny. "It's right here," she kept saying, "in your chart."

Then her countenance changed as she looked me in the eyes, leaned in and said, "I bet no one has ever told you how to be a good parent." I shook my head. Blanche said, ***"If you want to be a good parent you have to be a happy camper."***

Well that was news to me! I have to be happy? I only thought of my daughter's happiness. I never thought to think that my happiness was also important.

***Happy Camperness

So began my search and my journey into my happy camperness. I became a happiness seeker of true joy. I continued on my yoga path and completed a 500 hour yoga teacher training. I studied, read and went to every workshop I could on yoga, parenting, healing and improving your relationships. I studied Buddhism, *A Course in Miracles, The Bible, The Bhagavad Gita, The Yoga Sutras,* Quantum Physics, *The Secret,* the Law of Attraction, *Think and Grow Rich,* Eastern medicine and wellness, nutrition, Reiki, Thai Yoga Massage, studied Universal Spiritual Laws, did past life regression, hypnotism, drum circles, yoga retreats, meditation retreats. I chanted my heart out at Kirtans.

I trekked across the country to California multiple times for work-shops and yoga trainings, even trekked across the globe to India, the mother-land where yoga originated to study and learn astanga yoga with the Beloved Pattabhi Jois before his passing. Into the concrete jungle of Manhattan I ventured to find inner peace and healing with Omega, a holistic institute, and various other well known teachers. I completed a 40 week in home spiritual St.Ignatius retreat, took workshops at Kripalu in Massachusetts, went to Florida for health and yoga retreats, and more. I was an open sponge, a spiritual seeker, committed to learning everything I needed to heal myself.

Dear Blanche gave me an affirmation to repeat before bed and when I awoke in the morning that I saved to this day: ***"I have absolute faith my higher self is supplying me with perfect health, happiness and abundance."***

I had no idea what an affirmation was or what my higher self was back then, but I went with it. That's the thing about awakening on the spiritual path: Some things you get right away, and some concepts take longer to seep in, depending on how many walls you have up. I had many, which I thought were there to protect me.

There was some truth to that, however when we protect ourselves by closing our heart, we also close our heart to receiving and experiencing the good too. When we think love instead of feel love, our life becomes artificial and superficial and we become numb, which was how I lived my whole life.

***Angel Gen Togen

Out of all the different philosophies, Buddhism resonated with me the most. As I started out on my yoga teacher trainings, which were mostly about the physical body through this particular organization, I simultaneously studied Buddhism, which is the science and study of the mind. I found the Dipamkara Meditation Center through an online search one day looking for a church or spiritual community that my daughter and I could join, besides Catholicism.

While there are many beautiful aspects about religion, the only thing I walked away with from Catholicism was confusion and a fear of burning in hell every time I cursed. And I had a potty mouth, so I was convinced I was going to hell. As an imaginative child I sat in my room and actually contemplated, shaking in fear what hell would be like because that's where I was convinced I was going after dropping the "F" bomb all day long.

Somehow I knew deep down that this wasn't what religion was supposed to be about. So when a meditation center came up online, my curiosity arose.

Kismet had it that the day I called for information the resident monk Gen Togden, who later turned out to have a significant effect in my life, was teaching a special class that night on parenting. I really was not planning on going, I had to get a baby-sitter and had reservations just like we all do when we try something new for the first time.

But God had other plans for me. Anne, the woman who answered the phone, would not let me get off the phone. She said it was not his typical class and one he would probably not be teaching again. She was persistent that I attend this class. It was so uncanny that I made it happen, *angel intervention again.*

I got a babysitter and brought my journal and sat on the floor at the feet of this brilliant, funny, wise, compassionate man/Buddhist monk. I was in awe. Every molecule in my being was smiling. I knew I was in the right place at the right time. This was the first time I heard someone say that I could have inner peace. I didn't even know what inner peace was, but something deep inside of me knew I needed it, and needed it bad.

***The Search

Now I was in search of **happiness and inner peace,** they were like two long lost friends, finding their way back home. I knew that there was another reality out there and I was determined to find it. What I finally came to realize after almost fifteen years of searching was that the healing I was looking for and the peace and happiness I was in search of, was right inside of me.

"**All that you need is within,**" was one of the first spiritual concepts introduced to me at a yoga class.

Could it be that simple, I wondered? That statement resonated with me but I couldn't quite figure out how to find it. The reason I didn't understand this truth was because there was so much blocking the way. Consequently, I learned that the spiritual journey is not so much about getting anything more, but about letting go and releasing all that is blocking your true light within.

This wonderful metaphor from Debbie Ford's book, *The 21 Day Consciousness Cleanse* describes this concept: "In 1957, a monastery in

Thailand was being relocated, and a group of monks was put in charge of moving a giant clay Buddha. In the midst of the move, one of the monks noticed a crack in its surface. Concerned about damaging the statue, the monks decided to wait a day before continuing with their task. One of the concerned monks came to further examine the giant statue. He shone his flashlight over the entire Buddha. When he reached the crack, he was astonished to see something reflected back at him. His curiosity aroused, the monk got a hammer and a chisel and began chipping away at the clay Buddha. As he knocked off piece after piece of clay, the Buddha got brighter and brighter. After hours of work, the monk looked up in amazement to see standing before him a huge solid-gold Buddha, a priceless treasure the likes of which never been viewed before. Historians believe the Buddha had been covered by clay by Thai monks several hundred years earlier, before an attack by the Burmese army. The monks had covered the Buddha to protect it so it wouldn't get stolen. In the attack all the monks were killed, so it wasn't until this day that the real value of this great treasure was discovered."

Like the Buddha's clay covering, our outer shell serves to protect us from the world, while our real treasure, our soul, our light, and our truth lies within to be uncovered and discovered. While mankind has the technology to send man into space we are still working on discovering the universe within ourselves, our innate spiritual genius, our DNA (divine natural ability).

Conquering inner space is what the yogis that have come before us have done. There are numerous yogis, saints, avatars and enlightened beings, some well known and some not, that have walked the earth to teach and remind us of all we once knew. Even *we've* had lifetimes where we "knew who we were." That is why Socrates said, "Learning is remembering." We lived our lives with the knowing of our divinity. Now we are here to wake up and remember our divine nature, once again.

"Don't you know yet? It is your light that lights the world." ~Rumi

***Pain in my Neck!

Divine timing had it that Buddhism came in and Soulmate #2 went out. Broken but also open and ripe for healing, this was the beginning of my "waking up." My new sleeping partner became the book, *Faith*, by Sharon Salzberg. I found comfort in her words- it is what helped me to keep going.

I knew that in order to move on in a healthy way I would have to forgive him. Forgive him for everything, including hitting me. **Better not bitter** became my mantra.

I sought counsel with a Buddhist teacher. Their advice was to do five nice things without anyone knowing, chant OM MANI PADME HUM daily during meditation, and do the Tonglen meditation: taking someone else's pain and sending them love. This purifies karma. The Tonglen meditation works very quickly, if you can get to that space sincerely and honestly. It's not for everyone though. If they hurt you and you haven't gotten past the anger and resentment, it will be challenging to do this meditation. Timing is everything. Or if you are an empath you might already be taking on their pain, so be mindful. Once you do though, miracles abound.

It was a process just to get to a place where I wanted to forgive him, but finally one day after doing this meditation for a couple of weeks, I wrote him a letter. During the cathartic writing process, I went from anger and blame to understanding and compassion and then finally to forgiveness, forgiveness of him, not the action.

When I finished the letter I felt free, like I just released a huge burden from my back. I sat up straight and turned my head to the side. I felt no restrictions and more surprisingly, no pain. I turned my head to the other side and the same thing. This was the first time in six months that my neck didn't hurt. I was pain free! It was a miracle. I turned on the radio to the song lyrics, *I Can See Clearly Now the Rain is Gone.* This is what we refer to as **Divine Validation**...communication from The Universe.

FORGIVENESS SET ME FREE.
From the book, *The Game of Life and How to Play It*, by Florence Shovel Shinn (1910): "Every disease is caused by a mind not at ease. I said once, in my class, 'There is no use asking anyone, What's the matter with you?' We might just as well say, 'Who's the matter with you?' Unforgiveness is the most prolific cause of disease."

(OM MANI PADME HUM: "The mantra Om Mani Pädme Hum is easy to say yet quite powerful, because it contains the essence of the entire teaching. When you say the first syllable Om it is blessed to help you achieve perfection in the practice of generosity, Ma helps perfect the practice of pure ethics, and Ni helps achieve perfection in the practice of tolerance and patience. Pä, the fourth syllable, helps to achieve perfection of perseverance, Me helps achieve perfection in the practice of concentration, and the final sixth syllable Hum helps achieve perfection in the practice of wisdom." ~Dilgo Khyentse Rinpoche)

For the next five years I studied Buddhism with a fury, read every book, and went to every class and workshop I could. I stayed home in bed one day and read cover to cover, *Awaken the Buddha Within,* by Surya Lama Das. I almost signed up to become a Buddhist teacher and even had thoughts of becoming a Buddhist monk. Deep within, however, I knew that becoming a monk would be an escape from finding myself, not the other way around.

***GURU: GEE, YOU ARE YOU, and it's a good thing!

The word "educate" in Latin means "to draw out". There is a saying in yoga, "Om bolo sat guru bhagavan qi." It means: the true teacher lies within. That is what the path of yoga or any authentic spiritual teaching will bring you back to, your inner teacher. Our personal truth, which is our unique self-expression, will only be found once we investigate and discover it within the deepest recesses of our being.

On my spiritual quest for happiness and inner peace I met many seekers that had a guru. In my world, the word "guru" floated around a lot, but I never felt drawn to seek one. While it might have been right for others, I knew it wasn't my path. I knew inside I was my own guru and that depending on someone else for my inner peace and happiness would prolong my search for something outside myself.

There are times in life when a guru can be a saving grace. However for me, I looked to everyone as my guru. As a student of the universe I try to learn something from everyone, whether it be a best selling author, a child, a new yoga teacher, even a homeless person on the street.

An unexpected teacher came into my life for a brief time a couple of years ago. She was an in-home health care aid from Jamaica who lived in the apartment downstairs from me taking care of old man Joe, riddled with Parkinson disease. It was no easy job as Joe's condition worsened and she would have to pick him up off the floor. Joe was 220 pounds of dead weight and my friend, Lorna was about five feet tall and 100 pounds. Sometimes she would call on me and ask for help but it was still a struggle between the two of us. She didn't have a car so she was stuck in this tiny studio apartment 24/7, alone, taking care of Joe who was barely living.

One day I told her I might be jumping rope in the morning as I was starting the Insanity workout program and asked her if that would be ok, to which she responded, "**Yea mon, nothing bothers me."** That was some serious dharma- words of wisdom from my neighbor. It was true, Lorna was always smiling. Even with her circumstance- stuck in that tiny apartment all day and night with nothing, not even conversation and company, sending money home to her family in Jamaica with barely anything left for herself, and having the overbearing task of taking care of this man, who was a stranger really. I'm sure she didn't read and study as hard as I was, but she didn't need to. She was just naturally happy. Lorna was my idol. Gurus come in all shapes and forms.

As a serious student of life I am open to learn from everyone, including and especially Mother Nature. From *Return of the Bird Tribes* by Ken Carey:

> "In every moment the Great Spirit communicates to all creatures everything they need to know. Through ten thousand billion agents—angel, elemental, animal, vegetable and mineral— through the vast and subtle network of living design beyond the weather, before the wind, the truth is ever being transmitted

into this world of form. It is up to each one to sense how that truth translates to him or her in each moment of the day. And this is as true for humans as it is for any other creature.

The process is not complex, the sensing and translating is not done with the mind. It is an automatic process that occurs spontaneously below the level of thought when judgement subsides and allows perception to simply be, a natural process that takes place effortlessly when your mind relaxes its cultural interpretations and trusts you to experience the natural clarity that is always present-when you are present."

***Petty Tyrant

Thanks to Buddhism and Gen Togden, when I changed my perspective of my daughter from an annoying defiant pain in my butt to my teacher, things started to shift for us. It turned out that I didn't really need to go anywhere to become enlightened. After dragging her to Buddhism classes and meditation classes which she barely tolerated, I realized that it was me that needed the teaching, not her after all.

In Carlos Castaneda's book, *The Fire From Within*, the character Don Juan exhorts that one that has a petty tyrant is lucky and if one does not have a petty tyrant to begin with, one must go seek one out. This was a new concept for me... perceiving annoying people as my teachers.

"My child is my teacher," was a much different vibe and energy from my perceived need to control her. My ego calmed down and our communication improved. She felt my energy shift as I treated her with respect. I started to really listen and honor and validate her feelings. Children are more sensitive to energy when they haven't been burned and numbed by the world and still have their intuition intact.

My daughter could sense the slightest bit of hypocrisy, which unfortunately was rampant in traditional schooling. Almost every year Aiyana had a problem with her teacher and she would end up being transferred to another classroom. One time that sticks out in my mind, I was called down to school because she didn't just run out of the classroom, but out of the school building. Something or someone set her off.

After they retrieved her, the teacher and class were evacuated and there she was, sitting face to face with the principal. I walked in, he threw his hands in the air and said, "I don't know what to do with her. She won't listen. I give up. She's all yours," and walked out.

It was a sight to see! My eight year old unconventional daughter going head to head with the principal, who lost the battle. She did not fit in with the disingenuine system, inheriting her intolerance for hypocrisy from me.

As I started to shift and view my daughter as my teacher and released my need to control her so she'd conform to my standards and societal standards, the power struggle subsided. Don't get me wrong, it took time, many years. I still read every parenting book I could get my hands on and tried every reward/punishment tactic I learned about. It was a challenge parenting such a strong willed independent being, but she taught me so much.

> "Traditional medicine generally holds that stress is the cause of many human disorders and illnesses. The problem with this diagnosis is that it doesn't accurately address the source of stress. It looks to blame external circumstances, without realizing that all stress is internally generated by one's attitudes. I must emphasize again that it isn't life's events, but one's reaction to them, that activates the symptoms of stress. As we've already discovered, a divorce can bring about agony or relief; and challenges on the job

can result in stimulation or anxiety, depending on whether one's supervisor is perceived to be a teacher or an ogre." ~*Power vs. Force,* Dr. David Hawkins

*** Our Children are Our Greatest Teachers

We are not responsible for anyone's soul growth but our own, and that includes our children. Our children are their own souls. We are their *guardians,* not their *owners.* Children have their own blueprint, karma, journey and reason for being here. The best thing we can do is be an example to them, not try to control them into doing what we think is best for them. Easier said than done. There's a reason people say you are only as happy as your least happiest child. It's hard to let them go and watch them fall down and suffer, but sometimes we must or we will continue to enable them and they will never grow up. Raising independent, happy productive children is a fine line and balancing act-one that is different for each child as well. If no one modeled good parenting, how do you learn?

Often times we have unresolved issues from our childhood or we live our unfulfilled lives through them. Both are counterproductive and adverse to their happiness. Our wounds get triggered over and over again by our children and all of our relationships until we heal ourselves. Once we decide to make inner peace a priority and stop the conflict with our children, our family, our co-workers and most importantly ourselves, we will no longer have conflict. As my perspective changed, peace came. Healing our home is just as important as healing the world I have learned.

"There is no single effort more radical in its potential for saving the world than a transformation of the way we raise our children. They must grow up to be adults with only a fraction of our neuroses, or the world is in serious trouble. This is not the time to mimic our parents. It is a time to reverse the trend.

We have a chance to rewrite history, to parent them as we wish we had been parented. And thus does our own reparenting occur. We release the past as we release the future.

> Children are not children. They are just younger people. We have the same soul at sixty that we had at forty, and the same soul at twenty-five that we had when we were five. If anything, children are wiser. They know more than we do, and have at least as much to teach us as we have to teach them. How dare we try to fit hem into our boxes and make them play by our rules, which are so very, very stupid? How dare we tell them anything when we live in a world so obviously backward? And how ungrateful and irreverent we are to listen so little and watch so casually when angels themselves have moved into the house."
> ~ Marianne Williamson

***Heal the Hole, Heal the Whole

You don't have to be a spiritually aware person to see what's going on in the world, on a macro and micro level. We are in a time of profound pain and profound change. There is a shift happening, more and more people are feeling a "divine discontent," and starting to realize that "things" will not bring happiness, true happiness that is. People are beginning to wake up to a stirring within and heed the calling of their souls.

We are becoming aware that we are conscious co-creators of our life, becoming empowered and living from what feels right in our hearts rather than what's repeating in our minds. We are becoming aware that change on the outside must first happen with change on the inside and to make a positive difference in the world we must first heal ourselves.

> "If there is peace in the heart, there will be beauty in the character. If there is beauty in the character, there will be harmony in the

home. If there is harmony in the home, there will be order in the nation. When there is order in the nation, there will be peace in the world." ~Lao Tzo

***Reframing

Good conditions are nice but they don't help us to grow and evolve. My dear yoga teacher, Mokshapriya, said once in philosophy class that if your life is full of challenges and adversities you are an advanced soul who was looking for some adventure and growth in this lifetime! A life without chaos is boring to the soul. Certainly this could be a helpful way to re-frame our thoughts and beliefs!

It's the adversity in our lives that shape our destinies. We can accept them and transform them into teachings of love, wisdom, patience and compassion, or we can resist them and suffer. As Buddha says, **"Pain is inevitable but suffering is optional."**

When we accept the good and the bad and stay with a middle way attitude of non judgement and acceptance, our whole life becomes our spiritual path. Yoga becomes more than an hour in the yoga studio on your mat, but every moment of your life is an opportunity to practice.

Here is a wonderful Buddhist parable illustrating the power of reframing:

> In a small village, the story goes, lived an old farmer. He awoke one morning to discover that his horse had run away. The news circulated through the town, and his neighbor paid him a visit and offered condolences, saying, "What a shame."
> "Maybe yes, maybe no," said the farmer.
> The next day, the horse returned, bringing with it five wild horses.
> "What a blessing," said the neighbor.

"Maybe yes, maybe no," said the farmer.
The following morning, the farmer's son tried to ride one of the wild horses, was thrown, and broke his leg. "What a shame," said the neighbor.
"Maybe yes, maybe no," said the farmer.
That evening, high-ranking officials from the army arrived, enlisting every able-bodied young man and taking them off to war. The farmer's son, however, was left behind.
"What a blessing," said the neighbor.
"Maybe yes, maybe no," said the farmer.

Reframing takes quite a bit of practice and then some. It is challenging to find an equanimous state of mind when we are drowning in emotions of fear and anxiety. That's why practicing yoga helps us. We learn how to retrain our nervous system by learning how to steady our mind by concentrating on steady and equal breathing patterns while holding arduous poses. It's body, mind and emotional training all wrapped up in one.

Here is another reframing prayer that came from an email from my father, more applicable to modern times:

> Heavenly Father, help us remember that the jerk who cut us off in traffic last night is a single mother who worked nine hours that day and is rushing home to cook dinner, help with homework, do the laundry and spend a few precious moments with her children. Help us to remember that the pierced, tattooed, disinterested young man who can't make change correctly is a worried 19-year old college student, balancing his apprehension over final exams with his fear of not getting his student loans for next semester. Remind us, Lord, that the scary looking bum, begging for money in the same spot every day (who really ought to get a job!) is a slave to addictions that we can only imagine in our worst nightmares.

Help us to remember that the old couple walking annoyingly slow through the store aisles and blocking our shopping progress are savoring this moment, knowing that, based on the biopsy report she got back last week, this will be the last year that they go shopping together.
Heavenly Father, remind us each day that, of all the gifts you give us, the greatest gift is love. It is not enough to share that love with those we hold dear to our hearts or not to just those who are close to us, but to all humanity. Let us be slow to judge and quick to forgive, show patience, empathy and love.

This prayer I took to heart since I was that single mother and patience was not my greatest asset!

***Changing Paradigms

In Buddhism there is a saying that became my new mantra, replacing the "Everyone always leaves me," **"I will become a Buddha for the benefit of all."**

Being a "Buddha" means an awakened soul or enlightened being and it is available to everyone. It is similar to being the "Christ." Jesus became the "Christ" when he rose above the illusion and saw all beings as equal. Jesus saw the truth of the world, that we are all One and that "an eye for an eye" just makes the whole world blind. If we really want to save humanity we have to apply love and forgiveness even to those who persecute us. We all have the opportunity to become the "Buddha" or the "Christ" in this lifetime, and it doesn't matter what religion you are affiliated with. Love has no religion.

The first part of this saying is key, "I will become," means you have to do the work and heal yourself first. This is the part that we tend to avoid because it means we have to look at ourselves and take responsibility for our actions and our life, all of it. It means you can't play the victim role anymore and blame others. It means waking up to the realization that you chose your life and continue to choose it every second of the day. It means you have to forgive yourself for everything, including the not so stellar things you have done. And most importantly, "I will become" means **self-love.**

I know many "spiritual" people who are stuck. They're unable or unwilling to go deep and look within, flitting from workshop to workshop, class to class, but never fully participating in the change. They get stuck in their heads, living from intellect and from a false sense of superiority from having spiritual knowledge. The spiritual ego is another trap that keeps us imprisoned. When our mind becomes crammed up with spiritual knowledge there will be no room for living from the heart.

> "Sacred writings are beneficial in stimulating desire for inward realization, if one stanza at a time is slowly assimilated. Otherwise, continued intellectual study may result in vanity, false satisfaction, and undigested knowledge." ~*Autobiography of a Yogi,* Paramahansa Yogananada

***Spiritual Distractions

In the midst of my awakening, I'll never forget one day what my friend said when he came over and walked into my bedroom, "Coming to your house is like going to a seminar."

Beaming inside, I took it as a compliment. I made my environment a reflection of all the change I was trying to accomplish, not really comprehending then that changing the outside (my environment) was not going to change the inside (my consciousness).

There was a time I couldn't leave the house without my protection crystals, my books, my angel cards, special bill in my wallet, or my crystal jewelry. While these outer things can provide a degree of help and protection or reminders, they are not the cause of change. Be wary not to depend on outer things to give rise the inner change. Only *you* and your *beliefs* can promote change and growth.

From the profound book, *Power vs. Force* by David Hawkins, M.D., Ph.D.:

> "When I first encountered kinesiology, I was instantly amazed by the potential I saw. It was the "wormhole" between two universes-the physical, and the mind and spirit- an interface between dimensions. In a world full of sleepers lost from their source, here was a tool to recover that lost connection with the higher reality and demonstrate if for all to see. I proceeded to test every substance, thought, and concept I could think of, and had my students and research assistants do the same. Then I noticed a strange thing: Whereas all subjects went weak from negative stimuli (such as fluorescent lights, pesticides and artificial sweeteners), students of spiritual disciplines who had advanced their level of awareness did not go weak as ordinary people did. Something important and decisive had shifted in the subjects' consciousness-apparently as they realized that they weren't at the mercy of the world, but rather affected only by what their minds believed. Perhaps the very process of progress toward enlightenment could be shown to increase man's ability to resist the mutability of existence."

(Dr. David Hawkins was in WW 2, medical school, psychiatry, agnostic, fatal illness and at 38 was about to die, in last anguishing moments thought was if there was a God, and cried out to God, if you do exist, help me now and completely surrendered. when he came to he had a Presence around him and within him, that stayed with him for months, he basically was experiencing his God self only, or the Infinite Oneness, it replaced his small ego self.

He saw that all of mankind was motivated by inner love, but simply became unaware, living their lives as sleepers unawakened to the perception of who they really are.

He discovered or rediscovered a way to measure human consciousness through kinesiology, which is now a well established science, based on the testing of an all-or-none muscle response stimulus. A positive stimulus provokes a strong muscle response and a negative stimulus results in a demonstrable weakening of the test muscles.

Dr. Hawkins treated thousand new patients every year and saw that the origin of emotional sickness lay in people's beliefs that they were their personalities. He has since transitioned from the physical body, but left an indelible mark on the world).

The **power of your belief is stronger** than anything- any piece of jewelry, crystal, mandala, mantra. That's why many people start off doing and saying affirmations and nothing changes, then they give up. It's because for change to stick it has to be believed down to your soul, for those science minds, down into your subconscious. It has to become you.

When we open up to the new world of spirituality there can be a lot of distractions. We can go to a class, workshop, seminar, online class, every day of the week. There is no shortage of classes and things we can learn right from our own living room... chakra balancing, singing bowl meditations, sound healing, essential oil workshops, past life regression, angel card workshops, polarity rebalancing, rebirthing, the list goes on.

While they can be beneficial tools to help us on our road to self realization, if we are not careful, we can get caught in the trap of always being a seeker. This can be a way of avoiding the real work. The real work is discovering for oneself who one really is. Like Morpheus says to Neo in *The Matrix,* "It's not about knowing the path, it's about walking it." All knowledge comes through experience. Without experience we cannot understand or learn anything. But we need the knowledge first. "The truth shall set you free," can only happen when we lose our opinion that's getting in the way so we can re-member what the Truth with a capital T is.

> "Don't keep searching for the truth, just let go of your opinions."
> ~Chinese Sage-Chuang Tzu

***Self Knowledge

> "All type of knowledge means ultimately self knowledge." ~Bruce Lee

In order to learn anything new or to recall wisdom from within, we must have an empty mind. I heard once that Bruce Lee would pour coca cola into a glass and say to his students, "How can I teach you anything new if your mind is already full like this glass of Coca Cola?" He would pour out the soda, then refill it with water, and tell his students to have a clear mind like the glass of water.

We have many possessions, and not just material goods. We have possessions of the mind: preconceived ideas, spiritual pride, opinions, prejudices, negative limiting thought patterns and world views, academic distinctions, degrees, attachment to material organizations and status, etc. All of these pre-conceived beliefs prevent us from discovering the most important knowledge-self knowledge-who we really are and what this earth gig is all about. Ignorance comes from a closed mind and too many opinions. You know what they say about opinions? "Opinions are like assholes, everybody has one."

"Most people, and learned people especially, have all kinds of knowledge that does not in the least affect or improve their practical lives. Doctors know all about hygiene, but often live in unhealthy way, notwithstanding; and philosophers, who are acquainted with the accumulated wisdom of the ages, and assent to most of it, continue to do foolish and stupid things in their own personal lives, and are unhappy and frustrated in consequence. Now, knowledge such as this is only opinion, or head knowledge, as some people call it. It has to become heart knowledge, or to be incorporated into the subconscious, before it can really change one.

> The modern psychologists in their efforts to "re-educate the subconscious" have the right idea, though they have not yet discovered the true method of doing so, which is by scientific prayer, or the Practice of the Presence of God." ~Emmet Fox, *The Sermon on the Mount*

The most important education is the one that is left out of our schooling systems: tapping into the intuitive tools we already possess within, learning about universal laws of science and spirit, and understanding who we really are and why we are here. Fortunately, thanks to the internet, there are thousands of schools and teachings available online as the Age of Awakening has begun.

> "When you operate on the basis of your so-called knowledge, you are operating without divine foundation. Belief in your own knowledge is not belief in God. Trust in your own knowledge is not trust in God. No matter how much you learn within your present framework of finite knowledge, it will never be even one step closer to an understanding of God, the universe, or yourself. Knowledge, as you presently understand it, will never bring you closer to Life." ~Ken Carey, *The Starseed Transmissions*

***Angel Weston Jolly

It's not easy to look at yourself honestly, most people won't or don't until a major life crisis happens and even then many people resist. That's the ego in self-preservation mode and that's when pride can get in the way instead of serving us. Pride can keep us in denial and seeing the truth about ourself. I was one of them for many years. My pride and ego self-preservation didn't allow me to see my part in the pain and suffering I created as well as see the beauty of my soul. And the universe says,"You are either going to learn the hard way through pain and suffering or you can learn the easy way through letting go, trusting and surrendering to the higher power, but eventually either way, you will learn."

One of the first compliments I received from a man that didn't want anything in return was from Weston Jolly, another angel in my life. I was attending my first workshop with him, walked in, he looked at me and exclaimed, "Wow, you're drop-dead gorgeous!" Not expecting that I said nothing in return. My self-esteem was still damaged, and I was lost and insecure on the inside. I didn't feel pretty. I wasn't ready to receive it or believe it, although it felt good.

Weston is a gifted intuitive medium and during this transformative workshop he honed right in on me. The question he posed to everyone in the group, "What is the repetitive pattern that shows up in your relationships and in your life?"

When it came my turn I said, "Rejection." He shook his head, "Something more."

I said timidly, "Abandonment." "Bingo," he replied.

He turned away then doubled back and looked at me with wide eyes. "Wow!" he said, "On a scale of 1-10 for passion, you blow the ten away. Your passion is off the charts!"

Weston was the first person to recognize that in me and see my true self. I had so much depth, intensity, and passion as Weston called it, but never let it show. I didn't even know what it was. On the *outside*, I seemed to have it all together; on the *inside*, I was still a lost soul.

Can you see me now?"

I longed for someone to see me; not the hurt abandoned girl, but the powerful, beautiful goddess. Weston saw the real me, not the masked me. "Just be beautiful you," was his advice to me in every session I attended with him. Even though I didn't know how to do that yet, it felt so good to be in his presence. That's the key to holding the space for someone's greatness to emerge, to be the one awake; who recognizes another's light, even when they are asleep to it.

The hardest thing for people to see is themselves. You are love.

Another short story from my Dad's emails: *The Rose Within*

"A certain man planted a rose and watered it faithfully and before it blossomed, he examined it.
He saw the bud that would soon blossom, but noticed thorns upon the stem and he thought, "How can any beautiful flower come from a plant burdened with so many sharp thorns? Saddened by this thought, he neglected to water the rose, and just before it was ready to bloom... it died.
So it is with many people. Within every soul there is a rose. The God-like qualities planted in us at birth, grow amid the thorns of our faults. Many of us look at ourselves and see only the thorns, the defects.
We despair, thinking that nothing good can possibly come from us. We neglect to water the good within us, and eventually it dies. We never realize our potential.
Some people do not see the rose within themselves; someone else must show it to them. One of the greatest gifts a person can possess is to be able to reach past the thorns of another, and find the rose within them.

This is one of the characteristic of love... to look at a person, know their true faults and accepting that person into your life... all the while recognizing the nobility in their soul. Help others to realize they can overcome their faults. If we show them the "rose" within themselves, they will conquer their thorns. Only then will they blossom many times over." ~ Unknown

***EGO: Edging God Out

"Love is who you are. The ego is something you have." ~Me

In the spiritual world, the ego usually gets a bad rap. With an acronym of Edging God Out, how could it not? But Spirit doesn't live in the clouds,

Spirit is right here, in you, in me and in everything. Without the ego we would not be an effective force on the earth plane and we wouldn't be able to function as a human being. It's important to understand however, that while the ego is necessary for us to be here, it cannot run the show anymore. We need to keep in mind that we *have* an ego, we *are not* an ego. Once we have that understanding, everything shifts.

I look at the ego as two parts: healthy ego and unhealthy ego. When everything becomes, "it's all about me," we are in the unhealthy version of our ego. An example of this I learned from my favorite Buddhist monk, Gen Togden. He was the first one to connect the dots between depression and unhealthy ego for me. He offered another perspective when he said depression is selfish because you are only thinking about yourself. Wow, how true is that statement! We get so caught up in our unhappy thoughts and sad story about ourselves that we identify with the feeling that comes after and say, "I am sad or I am depressed," and that becomes our reality. The thought comes before the feeling, not the other way around. I do believe there could be a chemical imbalance as well, but regardless we need to get control over the detrimental negative thoughts we obsess over.

When our ego keeps us stuck in an old fear or limiting thought pattern and we are afraid to change or step out of our comfort zone because we are afraid of what people might think about us, we are in the unhealthy part of our ego. My first lesson about Mr. Ego keeping me stuck happened about ten years ago during my studies of the *Science of Getting Rich* with Bob Proctor. He was coaching me one on one for a period of time and invited me to be on his global conference call with hundreds of people listening. It was an impromptu interview on how I healed my back and neck, using some products by a Japanese wellness company, Nikken, along with yoga. I was nervous.

My angel friend, Pat Barry, coached me down from the fear-of-speaking-ledge. He said, "You are so nervous because you think this is all about you. It's not about you, this is about others, something bigger than you. You don't know who will be on that call and be touched or affected by your story." As soon as he said that, something inside of me shifted, and I relaxed.

Ever since that Pat Barry speech, any time I have to speak in front of large group of people I think about what he said. Even after teaching yoga for sixteen years I still get nervous. Another time I was in California at a huge marketing convention with about 1,000 people. Pat said he wanted to interview me then have me go on stage and do a headstand. I said ok and sat down to wait, thinking *what did I just get myself into?* While I was sitting my knees and legs would not stop shaking. *Great, how am I going to do a headstand like this?! Ok, this is not about me, remember.* I took a deep breathe and asked for back up from "On High" and went up there.

On stage now, calmly panicking as I set up for this headstand because it's a make-shift stage that moves! *You gotta be kidding.* So now I'm shaking on a moving stage and have to do a headstand. *This is perfect* I joke with myself. Oh and I forgot to add, I was dressed in nice slacks and a button down shirt, no yoga attire. Without thinking I just did it. I went up smoothly, held it, heard a lot of applause then exited just as smoothly, sweating profusely. Phew! Thank you God. That was a comfort zone buster for sure!

> Once I remember this is not about me, I am just the channel, my knees stop shaking, I relax and become a more effective messenger. Taking the spotlight off ourself allows our true essence to shine and our authenticity felt. "It's not about what you have that is your greatness, it is about what you can give." ~Yogi tea bag

The healthy version of the ego is when it takes on role of employee to the boss-soul and acts and creates with the highest of intentions for the highest good of all. I like Patanjali's explanation of the ego from *The Yoga Sutras of Patanjali:*

> "The Self will always be falsely represented by the ego until our ignorance is removed. I often refer to these two "I"s as the little "i" and the capital "I." What is the difference? Just a small dot, a little blemish of ego. The capital "I" is just one pure stroke, just as the highest truth is always simple and pure. What limits us and makes us little? Just the dot. Without the dot we are always great, always the capital "I."
>
> "All the practice of Yoga are just to remove that dot." ~Translation and Commentary by Sri Swami Satchidananda

On the other side of the unhealthy ego spectrum I know many spiritual people with good intentions who ignore their own needs or feelings, as they feel it's "their ego," and not very high or spiritual. We can't ignore ourself and think we are going to be holier or more enlightened that way. Our needs and feelings matter as well. If something or someone is causing us discomfort, it's usually an issue that needs to be addressed, not ignored. The world does not need more martyrs; it needs more teachers.

***Spiritually Naked

As you start to awaken and realize you need a little tweaking, it's still not easy to change. Change can be challenging and uncomfortable. Since we are creatures of habit and comfort many of us choose not to make the effort and stay in our comfort zone. However, <u>life begins when we step out of our comfort zone.</u>

We come out of our comfort zone and take risks every day without even knowing it._Inspirational speaker and author, Tony Robbins first brought this to my attention. He said of course we take risks- every time we get in our car and drive we are having faith that the double white line in the road is keeping us safe as we drive by cars at 60 miles per hour.

Maybe we can take that same risk and faith and apply it to other areas of our lives as well.

When I was new to the spiritual path I thought I could change my subconscious self-sabotaging thought patterning by doing things completely opposite. For example, I would walk in the out door at the supermarket, and walk out the in door. At the boardwalk on the beach I would run counter to the direction that everyone else was running and walking. I don't know if that did anything for me on any level, but I do know I aggravated a lot of people.

I was willing to try anything. I was committed.

When Weston asked me if I could be more feminine at the end of one of our sessions I walked out confused as to what that really meant. I started wearing more skirts and dresses, thinking that would make a difference. I had no idea what the concept of "feminine" really meant.

It wasn't until later in my spiritual studies that I realized what he meant and I had one of those A-HA moments. That is how spiritual knowledge works. We hear a concept one or two or twenty times by different people in different ways, then one day it clicks and makes sense. Enlightenment happens. Spiritual seeds and practice, like exercise, is *cumulative*. Nothing goes to waste, no matter how many times you stop and quit, then re-start again- like the Ragu spaghetti sauce, "It's in there."

The timing of when that happens is different for every single person. We cannot force "awakening" to happen. We just need to remain open and receptive, which is what the feminine energy is about.

In another session with Weston our topic was on being "spiritually naked." So when I was approached to do a couple of different naked photo shoots, I said, "Sure why not!" I figured naked photo shoots would hasten my healing and enlightenment; still type A, trying to reach nirvana and inner peace as fast as I could.

I don't think it did anything but help me to get over being naked in front of people I didn't know. In my head the entire time I kept chanting, "I am not my body, I am not my body," as I pranced around naked like a fairy. It was one of those things looking back when you cringe and say, "I can't believe I did that." It seems I have a lot of those moments.

***Serenity

The spiritual path, the Hero's Journey, a concept first introduced by the legendary Joseph Campbell, is not an easy path to walk. We hear a calling and leave the known to venture into the unknown. We encounter challenges and crisis, death and rebirth, revelation and finally transformation. It's called a Hero's Journey for a reason, it's not for the faint of heart.

Along this journey we might find there are some things that are hard to change and that is where we have to practice acceptance and compassion for ourselves. Kindness toward ourselves goes a long way. Self-condemnation and beating ourself up does not serve us, what so ever.

There will be some things we want to change, but find it difficult. That's when we call upon God, or Spirit or the Universe (whatever term you feel comfortable with). The point is to call upon that something for help.

The Serenity Prayer brings me back to the peace in my heart every time I read it: ***"God grant me the serenity to accept the things I cannot change, courage to change the things I can, and wisdom to know the difference."***

If you don't believe in a higher power you won't be able to change. You might have a temporary change but not a lasting one that transforms you from the inside out. We can't do it alone. We were never meant to do it alone. (And there are a lot of unemployed angels just sitting around waiting for you to ask for their help. Free will is our gift from God, so if we don't ask they won't intercede).

"Ask and you shall receive," has proven true in my life. What I learned is the help always comes, it just might not be in the package or timing we imagined.

***Divine Peeing

About ten years ago I experienced my first Polar Bear Plunge with a group of Franciscan priests on the North Shore of Long Island where I grew up in Mt. Sinai. My intention behind the icy plunge was to purify and cleanse myself dedicating it to Jesus and all of humanity. I thought *if Jesus could sacrifice and suffer the way he horribly did for all of us, then I can jump into the freezing cold ocean.*

I ran into the ocean in my bikini on January 1st, jumped in, dove under and exploded up screaming. I had no idea that when water is that cold it feels like the opposite of cold, like your skin is being burned. I ran out, sat on the beach wrapped in blankets, proud of myself that I was brave enough to go through with it, feeling cleansed and alive.

I had a dilemma though. I had to pee really bad and there was no way I was going back into the frigid ocean. Normally I can pee anywhere outside, I'm not self conscious when it comes to that. I have mastered the art of discretely peeing in public. When you drink as much water as I do, this is the consequence.

Mastery or not, I had a problem since the beach was an open area full of priests in long robes: not a friendly public peeing place. I walked over to the bathrooms which I was sure were going to be locked and they were. My bladder was ready to explode!

Out of nowhere a man appeared dressed in a leather jacket, looking like he just got off his Harley. He asked me if I needed something. I replied that I needed to use the bathroom, trying to not look desperate. My sister-in-law had joined me at this point. Without answering me he walked over to the bathroom door, whipped out a serious industrial sized keychain, found the right key instantly and voila, opened the door.

We looked at each other in bewilderment and quickly went inside, now happy and relieved. We agreed that it was weird how he appeared out of no-where. When we came out he was still there. We thanked him profusely and asked him what his name was. He replied Matthew. Next thing I knew, just as he appeared out of the blue, he disappeared.

> "Ask and it will be given to you; seek and you will find; knock and the door will be opened to you. For everyone who asks receives; the one who seeks finds; and to the one who knocks, the door will be opened." ~ Matthew 7:7-8

Some of you might be thinking why God would waste time worrying about my bladder? Doesn't He/She have more important things to worry about? Well, you either believe God is or God isn't. There is no half way truth. If God is, then God is in everything, everyone and everywhere... Omnipresent, Omnipotent, Omniscient. If all prayers are answered and God does not judge then yes, as trivial as you might believe your request is, God does not. Whether you believe that was a coincidence or divine intervention really doesn't matter anyway because according to quantum physics what you believe becomes your reality. I believe my angels were looking out for me that day, as they always do. It was just one of my many miracles!

***Bitch

Working as a diligent student of healing, I have literally transformed myself from the outside in and the inside out. About three years into my yoga awakening, I had lunch with the personal trainer, who trained me for my body building competitions (not the ex-boxer). Noticing how different I was he said, "Wow you've changed, you seem so peaceful now."

I was very pleased with his comment, being the good yogi I was and working as hard as I was. *But wait* I thought, "How was I before?" I inquired.

He replied, "A cranky bitch on no carbs." And according to my philosophy I shared with Downtown Julie Brown on MTV, I was definitely a bitch. I even wore a baseball hat in college that said, "BITCH" in bold silver lettering and thought I was cool. Another cringing moment.

When I was fifteen years old, if someone said to me, "Have a nice day," my response was, "Don't tell me what kind of day to have." Yea, I said that.

I shouldn't have been so surprised at my trainer's observation. When I was eleven years old I was having a sleepover with my four best friends. We sat around in a circle and someone decided we would all take turns going around telling each person what they liked and disliked about each other. We were quite the open minded group of tweens.

I don't really remember what my friends said about what they liked about me because all I could remember is what each of them disliked about me. They all said I acted like a bitch with a bad attitude. They followed it up with, "We know you are going through tough times at home with your family situation and that's why we understand why you can act so tough and mean. We know on the inside you are really sweet."

I was a bully in middle school. I used to torment a girl named Barbi on our field hockey team. As she would start to run across the field I would trip her with my stick when she least expected it. I also used to make myself faint by hyperventilating on the field to torture my coach and send her into a panic to end practice early. I "called a girl out" once to the playground to fight her. I stole her pick from her back pocket and made fun of her Gold Digger jeans. I was one of those mean girls. I was not kind to myself, so I was not kind to others.

***Stuff in the Basement

In Rocky V his son asked him why he was fighting again and Rocky answered because he still had "stuff in the basement." I love that answer. I totally got it. It's our own inner demons that can fuel us to make changes in our life, if we are aware of them. When we let them go unnoticed, they find their way into our bodies. For me, the anger that I carried with me was unresolved hurt and pain from abandonment, which found its way into my back and neck and out on other people.

Usually we think of anger in a negative way. But like every emotion, it has two sides: positive and negative. Used in the positive, anger can help to make changes in our lives, it can light the fire under our butt to be productive and step out of our comfort zone. As long as we are not taking it out on other people, anger can be a powerful force and emotion.

When I was in middle school my nickname was RoadRunner because I ran so fast on the field hockey field and basketball court. That was because I was mad all the time. Now I run like a tortoise, but I'm very peaceful!

The only time I made it to the fast lane in swim practice was after an argument with my girlfriend when she was criticizing and judging my parenting skills. That's the one thing I go ballistic over. Never judge me about being a parent, I turn into a fierce lioness. It was the fastest I ever swam though!

Needless to say, when I began to study Buddhism, I signed up for every class and workshop I could on anger. One of my close friends observed, "You are quick to anger," which made me angrier. I needed to get to the bottom of why I was so angry and seethed with so much rage at times. I honestly thought I was defective in some way. I wondered how I could have such a big loving compassionate heart one minute, then be ready to explode the next.

Even after all those eight hour workshops I was still freaking angry! What made me even angrier was the response I got every time I told someone I was angry, "You're a yoga teacher, how could you be angry?" I'm still f***in human!

What I did learn which has proven instrumental in my life is one, to acknowledge and accept the fact that I'm angry and two, the *awareness to nip it in the bud.* The first feelings of impatience or frustration are the little embers, the beginning of the angry mind. It's like a dry forest waiting to catch fire. Even sarcasm is a form of anger. It's anger in disguise, just dressed less intimidating. Anger comes in all forms and manners. That is why meditating or having some sort of awareness practice is key.

I really had a lot of work to do: no more sucking my teeth, rolling my eyes, huffing and puffing, making sarcastic comments, those are all forms of anger; it's negativity expressed through the body. Practicing peace is like climbing up a ladder. It takes carefulness and patience to go up a ladder one step at a time, but one misstep and we fall right down to the bottom very quickly. That's how fast negativity and anger spreads.

> At least I know what my triggers are that create angry responses, so I prepare myself in advance or stay away from those situations when possible. If I'm hungry and tired and stuck in traffic or a long line, that's a bad combination for me, that's a forest fire ready to burst into flames. "The best thing you can do is get good at being you." ~Fortune cookie

***Life is an Echo

The sleepover that night with my friends was a wake-up call for me at eleven years old. They were a gift in my life because they told me the truth, even though it wasn't easy to hear. Noticed they said I ***acted*** like a bitch; they didn't say I *was* a bitch. They also delivered it in a soft, tender way with love; that is the only reason I could hear it and take it in.

Judge the action, not the person.

That's the problem too, we can't see ourselves. It's not like we walk around with a mirror in front of us. We are programmed to look outside ourselves, to judge the material world as a guide to our success. We don't grow up in the West with meditation and spiritualism, we grow up with consumerism, materialism and Bugs Bunny. I saw a bumper sticker the other day that said, "What would Scooby Doo do?" I guess we replaced Jesus with Scooby Doo.

If you don't have true friends in your life being honest with you in a kind and loving way you can always use your life as your mirror. Your life is a reflection of your inner being and inner beliefs. You can tell how well you are doing in your life by the outer conditions. I love Emerson's quote: "What you are shouts so loudly, that I cannot hear what you say."

Here is another short story that resonated with me that I share in my yoga classes: *The Mountain Story*

> "A son and his father were walking on the mountains. Suddenly, his son falls, hurts himself and screams: AAAhhhhhhhhhhh!!!
> To his surprise, he hears the voice repeating, somewhere in the mountain: AAAhhhhhhhh!!!
> Curious, he yells: Who are you?
> He receives the answer: Who are you?
> And then he screams to the mountain: I admire you!
> The voice answers: I admire you!
> Angered at the response, he screams: Coward!
> He receives the answer: Coward!
> He looks to his father and asks: What's going on?
> The father smiles and says: My son, pay attention.
> The man screams: You are a champion!
> The voice answers: You are a champion!
> The boy is surprised, but does not understand.
> Then the father explains: People call this ECHO, but really this is LIFE.
> It gives you back everything you say or do.
> Our life is simply a reflection of our actions.
> If you want more love in this world, create more love in your heart.
> If you want more competence in your team, improve your competence.

This relationship applies to everything, in all aspects of life. Love will give you back everything you have given to it."

YOUR LIFE IS NOT A COINCIDENCE, IT IS A REFLECTION OF YOU.

~Author Unknown

***Be the Change

My first gig on Fire Island six summers ago forced me to step up to the plate. Fire Island is a small barrier island, 30 miles long, that runs parallel to the South Shore of Long Island. It's my favorite place in the world. There are no cars on fire island, people schlep their stuff on little red wagons. You can get there by ferry or you can walk by beach, which I prefer.

I was hired by a women five days a week for the month of August for personal training and massage. It was a blessing for me as my bank account was in the red. When I got off the ferry with my massage bag, a well intended man saw me walking, looking lost, so he offered to take my bag on his bike and bring me to my client's house. He dropped me off and left. I was so grateful since it was about 90 degrees and humid, until I realized he dropped me off at the wrong house on the wrong side of the island! The street ran on both sides of the island, the bay side and the ocean side. I had no idea.

Gratitude quickly turned to attitude and it wasn't a good one. I had to schlep all the way back across the island with my massage bag. Even though it was only a fifteen minute walk, I was annoyed and frustrated that I was going to be late and covered in sweat.

Great, what I bad first impression, I thought. My client said she will stand out in the street and wait for me so I won't get lost anymore. As I got closer to her I tried to fight off the frustration and negativity, but was losing the battle.

Then I said to myself: "*You are coming to bring her healing and inner peace. How the heck can you do that if you walk up to her angry or with even the slightest bit of frustration. No one wants to be greeted like that.*" First impressions matter, as they plant the seed.

I took a deep breathe, let the tension go, shifted back into *being* the peace, and greeted her with a sincere smile on my face. She offered me a shower I was that sweaty, but I said I would just wipe off.

She turned out to be a lovely woman and I was so grateful for her generosity and kindness. We ended up hitting it off, becoming friends and staying in touch after the summer was over. I even had Thanksgiving dinner at her house the following year with my daughter. What made me happiest though is that I helped her find inner peace.

I have encountered this situation many times during my yoga teaching career. Having awareness of my old ways of reacting with frustration, annoyance and impatience helps me, as I remind myself of my role and my purpose.

Teaching yoga has been one of the most transformative careers I could have chosen. No coincidence there.

***Spiritual Armor

In my journey toward healing I *gradually* let go of the anger and resentments and found inner peace and contentment. My life shifted as I learned how to bring more balance into my life. I was an outright type AAA with daily to do lists that included time to eat and shower, I was that wound up. Now my to do lists are more casual and I have learned to not freak out when everything on them doesn't get done, which they never do.

One of the ways I learned to cope with my defiant teenage daughter who was not a morning person, was to wake up two hours before she did. The morning time was our battle ground, and I always regretted sending her off to school after fighting and screaming with each other. I was a guilt-stricken mess the rest of the day.

I was up at 5am with a morning routine that included yoga, an uplifting spiritual reading, centering and meditation, along with coffee of course. I needed that time to be prepared, calm and centered before the little monster, I mean my teacher, awoke.

From *Everyday Grace*, Marianne Williamson:

> "Most of us wouldn't think of beginning the day without washing the accumulated dirt from the day before from our bodies. Yet far too often we go out into the day without similarly cleansing our minds. And our minds carry more pollution than our bodies, for they carry not only our own toxicity but that of the entire world. We carry the fear, anxiety, stress, and pain not just of our own lives, but of our families, our nation, and millions all over the planet.
>
> Our greatest weakness is the weakness of an undisciplined mind. Time spent in morning prayer or meditation can save hours of tears shed later over something we have said or done. How many times have we said to ourselves, "How could I have been so dumb?" The answer is that we are not dumb, we were simply at the mercy of a frantic mind, not centered on its own sublime power. We were focused on things that are ultimately unimportant, while the deeper issues of life were left mainly ignored. These are the things that are bound to happen when we do not take time each day to purify our thoughts."

Dear God,
I give you this morning.
Please take away my despair of yesterday.
Help me to forgive the things that caused me pain
And would keep me bound.
Help me to begin again.
Please bless my path
And illumine my mind.
I surrender to You the day ahead.
Please bless every person
And situation I will encounter.
Make me who You would have me be,
That I might do as You would have me do.
Please enter my heart
And remove all anger, fear and pain.
Renew my soul
And free my spirit.
Thank you, God,
For this day.
Amen

Just as I was AAA personality, my daughter was AAA oppositional. If I said the sky was blue, she would say, "No it isn't," and believe herself. I'm not kidding. She resisted meditating and practicing yoga with me like everything else. One day, however, during her senior final exams she told me she was getting stressed and asked me if I would meditate with her. I almost fell off my chair.

This was an illustration of *being* the example versus telling a child what to do. "Do what I say, not what I do!" She saw me every morning in my room, sitting quietly meditating. I was getting in there somehow, even though she fought me every step of the way.

What also helped to bring balance into my life was scheduling downtime into my day. I made it a point not to fill every hour with work or an appointment and instead of squeezing in every errand on my to do list that day, if time was tight, I'd let it go. It seems like common sense but I was programmed to be productive. I made "me" time a priority and it has worked in my favor. Instead of feeling stressed out because I didn't get everything done I wanted, it actually did the opposite. I had more energy, better health, more peace of mind and still had plenty of money.

I also left more time driving in between appointments, because on the road is where I still lost my patience rather quickly. Plus having the license plate, **Yogagirl,** really forced me to stop flipping the bird at people.

One of the traits I regretfully passed down to my daughter was my road rage. I witnessed this wonder when she first started driving. Sitting in the passenger seat as I watched in dismay "little me" getting frustrated and shouting obscenities at the other drivers. In my mind, the catchphrase from Steve Urkel, *Family Matters* trilled, "Did I do thaaaat?"

Now when I am stuck in traffic, which happens often on Long Island, instead of getting frustrated and angry, I say to my angels, "Please get me to the church on time," take a deep breath and let it go. They haven't failed me yet!

***Inner Peace

When I found Buddhism I learned to prioritize "inner peace" and make the quality of my inner state of being at any time the most important thing. They kind of used the scare tactic reminding us that death is certain, the time of death isn't; therefore, we need to be in a peaceful state of mind when we die. According to Buddhism, at least my interpretation, your state of mind when you die determines what you reincarnate into. I was freaking out for a time praying I wouldn't be pissed off when I died and reincarnate into a bug and get squashed. I don't think that is what they meant but it certainly motivated me to be in a happy, peaceful mind-set as much as possible. Hey, whatever works!

Whatever we focus on we create. "Where there is no vision, the people perish." ~Proverbs 29:18 If we don't have a vision or direction then we are like a cork in the ocean, bobbing around susceptible to every little wave. First comes the vision or intention, then focus and attention, then devotion, then vigilance and perseverance, which equals reality.

When I made inner peace and healing my priority, I stopped doing things that brought me the opposite or created conflict: hanging out with negative people, going to loud busy places that didn't bring me peace, shopping malls, bars and nightclubs. The Bazooka Joe comic I saved from when I was eleven years old turned out to be a helpful reminder many times throughout my life: "<u>Better to be alone than in bad company.</u>" I learned from everything, including Bazooka Joe which was the start of my quote collecting.

***Sacred Solitude

I read once that women grow in the darkness when they are alone. I felt that was true for me, but only if I was able to get past the hysterical emotions first. The alone time nurtures our soul. We must first go within before we go outward. Otherwise we just get depleted, and I know too many depleted super women.

> "Sacred solitude is precious time to self review, to dive deeply into the Self and to rediscover the love within. In times of solitude balance is regained and we realize once again that love of self is not something that has to be earned anymore, it is a birthright.

Alone time gives us a chance to recalibrate and rediscover who we are. Love is a vibratory frequency, and we are LOVE."
~ Archangel Metatron through Tyberonn/Earth-keeper

Rumi, the great Sufi poet said, "A little while alone in your room will prove more valuable than anything else that could ever be given you."

And I say, "A little dance alone in your room listening to your favorite song will prove more valuable than anything else that could ever be given you."

Along with stopping the harmful things I was doing to myself, I became more aware about what I was feeding my mind and stopped singing songs that weren't in alignment with what I knew to be my truth. Gen Togden, my favorite Buddhist monk, first planted that seed. He used to warn us about listening to songs and music that enforced attachment and conditional love, which are most songs on the radio. Maybe belting out, *Love is Battlefield,* was why I was at war my whole life?

I fell in love with Indian music when I found Krishna Das. It took a white Jewish boy from Long Island to turn me on to Kirtan. It happened in Miami at an Omega yoga conference. I just finished a kick ass class with Baron Baptiste, was lying in shivasana in the dark with about 200 people and this soul stirring music blaring through the airwaves that I never heard before. I started weeping. The song kindled something deep in my soul that I had never felt before (my heart). "What was that?" I questioned the woman next to me when we got up. She said, "Krishna Das, you can buy his CD right outside." And that's exactly what I did and haven't stopped listening to him since that day in 2003. (The song is Baba Hanuman from the album Breath of the Heart)

Kirtan, which can be used as a form of meditation, is a call and response method of singing ancient mantras that are about God and love and joy. Kirtan uses the instrument, the Indian sitar, which is designed to open your heart chakra and bring healing to all the chakras. That's why it feels so good. You don't even need to know what a chakra is, just being in the energy of the music uplifts your soul. Krishna Das brought me back to my center of love every time I was confused and hurting, which was often. I am so grateful to him and his music and have shared it with so many people. I love you KD!

(Every living thing is surrounded by an energy field, which is affected by changes in our physical and emotional states. Our aura is comprised of seven layers. The chakras exist in the first layer of subtle energy and influence our physical, emotional and mental states. They act as conductors for energy to move through all the layers of the aura. There are seven major chakras along the spine, which most are familiar with, and then there are many minor chakras as well. As we ascend we will move toward twelve chakra system, explained in book two).

***Sing a Song

Music has been a healing tool for me. Whenever I was sad or feeling down I would just put on my favorite inspirational song and sing and dance in my room. Before I understood the science behind it, that I was going into the alpha state of my brain waves and raising my vibration, I just knew it made me feel good. To make affirmations even more powerful, sing them out loud while you are dancing. It works!

I am not *in* the Universe. I *am* the Universe. Uni meaning One, and Verse meaning song. One love, one song. Our universe is a song and just like an orchestra needs each musician, our song is needed to complete the song of the universe.

We are made of light, sound, color, and vibration. Each one of us has a soul song or an "electronic stamp" and that is how we are recognized by Spirit. Our energetic stamp or signature is made up of vibrational tones or frequency patterns we emit through our thoughts, emotions, and actions.

> "Energy is generated through frequency patterns of attraction. Thoughts, words, and emotions send to a certain band of frequencies into your auric field and beyond; thereby, your reality on the physical plane is created. The Universal Laws state that you must always experience what you create. When you are radiating frequencies of love all around you, the negative forces will not/cannot effect you." ~ Ronna Herman, Reference & Revelations

That's why LOVE WORKS.

***Bring Me Om

Sufi saying: "When you have the gift of sound, you need no other, for the world becomes a living mantra." Mantra is a Sanskrit word meaning, "The thought and sound that liberates and protects."

Om is actually spelt AUM, and is chanted with 3 syllables...AAAAA.... UUUUU....MMMM

Om is not a word, it is a vibration or mantra that reverberates in all living things. It is the sound of creation beginning with the Supreme Creator-God. Om transcends time and space, it reconnects us to our higher states of consciousness and the matrix of Oneness where the individual merges with the Infinite. Om symbolizes the manifestation of God in form, which is who we are. In the beginning was more than the word, it was the sound, the vibration, the OM.

Om in itself can be used as a prayer. One of the reasons why chanting is so powerful is that stills our mind and opens our heart. Chanting raises our vibration, clears our chakras, realigns and harmonizes our physical, emotional, mental, spiritual, and etheric bodies.

In many other countries singing is as natural as breathing. In our country we are judged by our voice, hence reality shows like American Idol. If your voice is not that Hollywood worthy it's easy to become self conscious and put the kabashh on singing out loud. My daughter's first voice coach from a Harlem choir said to her at fifteen, "If you can talk, you can sing." Some people are natural born singers, like my daughter, and some of us have to work on it more and take lessons, like me!

> "I don't care if I sing off key, I find myself in my melodies, I sing for love, I sing for me, I shout it out like a bird set free." ~*Bird Set Free* by Sia

***Shopping Angels

All of these outer changes I was making were easy compared to stopping the negative thoughts that were plaguing my mind, especially over money. After I filed bankruptcy, I obsessed over my bills. Fortunately I watched the documentary, *The Secret,* based on the book, *The Science of Getting Rich* by Wallace D. Wattles (1910), and attended the Science of Getting Rich Seminar with Bob Proctor. I was pretty shocked to see that what occupied my mind most of the time was debt. It was the toughest habit I had to break.

When I heard Marianne Williamson say, "the Holy Spirit knows how much your rent is," I was so relieved. That was the first time the thought entered my mind that God was concerned with material things like my bills. It came at the perfect time because that's when we moved to the south shore of Long Island so Aiyana could go to a diversified high school and the rent increased $800. When I stopped worrying and trusted that God's got my back, abundance came and all the bills were paid. (It took me a long time to stop worrying however).

After the idea that God was concerned with my rent was planted, a new seed bloomed. Why not take God shopping with me? I know this is where I lost some people but I can tell you from experience that there is a fashion angel for sure that knows your style.

When you go from body builder to yogini your body changes drastically. Since I am a bargain shopper I went to my favorite TJ Maxx, walked in and pretty much right in front of me was a rack of shirts, all different, cute, unique, my size and on sale. *Wow,* I thought, *good job God.* I ended up putting about 30 shirts in my shopping cart to try on and most of them fit.

Dilemma, usually nothing fits, today they all fit. *I really shouldn't be buying all of these shirts,* I'm rationalizing. I went up to the cashier anyway with my cart full. Noticing, she asked me if I wanted to apply for the TJ Maxx Credit Card.

I blurted out, "I wish I could get one but it would take a miracle." (Since I had filed bankruptcy a few years prior, it still was on my credit report).

The woman said, "Well, I believe in miracles."

She was speaking my language! "So do I!" I replied. I loved meeting people who believed.

The angel of credit cards approved me and that was a miracle. The first credit card since my bankruptcy and since then have built my credit back and now it's the highest it's ever been. This experience taught me besides God being the best shopping partner, not to worry about finances.

***God is My True Banker

When I went back to work as a Financial Consultant at the bank, every month we had a sales goal to meet. We got paid "drawer" style, meaning each month we received a paycheck but had to make sure our sales covered the paycheck. If we didn't, we owed money. It was stressful way to earn a living, especially as a single mother.

By the end of the month, I would start panicking. I would figure out how much more I needed in sales to make my quota, then go to work. Each morning I would do my centering meditation and end with the affirmation, "Use me God, connect me to someone who needs my services," something like that. Then within the last couple of days of the month someone would come in and open an account with just the right amount of investment that I needed to meet my quota. It happened without fail. I never had a month that I didn't meet my goal.

"In God We Trust," is printed on our currency, after all. When and how did we remove ourselves so far away from that idea?

***You Are a Hard Habit to Break

Still, with all of this divine experience and validation, my negative ingrained thought patterns still stuck around**.** Having the awareness is the first step, changing the pattern is where the rubber meets the road. I thought ex-boyfriends were hard habits to break! They pale in comparison to the obsessive negative thoughts about money I was parading around with! Twenty years to make it, ten years to break it.

> "You can't walk around saying you are rich and acting like you are poor." ~My higher self

I busted myself recently. Having been doing the work, all the prosperity programs you could think of; I still wasn't receiving material abundance, until one day I realized there was an inconsistency. I was saying one thing and doing another.

The Universe records everything. Every thought, feeling, word spoken, and deed goes out as vibration with our electronic signature imposed on it and comes back to us reflecting the same energy. It's known as: "Like attracts like," in the field of science; "You reap what you sow," in Christianity; in Eastern religions, "The Law of Karma," or the "Law of Cause and Effect." In metaphysics, this principle is described as, "the Out-breath and the In-breathe of God."

This unifying thread that runs through all the great teachings, also called The Law of the Circle, simply means that what we send out through our thoughts, feelings, words and actions must return to us. Therefore, at any given moment, our lives are reflecting the sum total of whatever it is that we created through our *past* thoughts, feelings, words and actions.

This simple truth, when one wakes up to it, can change your whole life. There's never really "doing something behind someone's back," including talking badly about them. When you do things in secret, it's never really "in secret." You can't think you are fooling someone or getting over on them, there is no hiding in the Universe. When we become awake and aware, congruous with our thoughts, feelings, words and actions, we become a student of the Universe and also more responsible and accountable. We cannot say one thing to the Universe and think or do something else. This is where integrity and impeccability play a role in our own lives as well as our relationships.

***Change your Beliefs, Change your Thoughts, Change your Life

When you are immersed in self-help books on the spiritual path it's easy to forget about the basics, changing your thoughts changes your life. I think part of the reason is because we hear it so often now that the truth becomes cliche. We stop listening when we hear things too many times, just like we did with our parents, good advice falling on deaf ears. In addition, there is so much information available at the touch of a button, it's easy to get swept away in it all. Sometimes we forget the basics- it doesn't have to be that complicated.

Be that as it may, if we check in with our self when we start to feel discomfort or irritability, it's usually because of our thoughts. When we're not paying attention we quickly revert back to our habitual thought patterns in our deeply worn brain grooves. They're subtle and insidious, sneaking up on you when you're not paying attention. When we let go of those thoughts, breathe and focus back to the present moment, everything shifts.

From *The Sermon on the Mount*, Emmet Fox, scientist, philosopher, spiritual teacher:

> "We make or mar our lives by the way in which we think. The great Law of the Universe is that what you think in your mind you will produce in your experience. As within, so without. You cannot think one thing and produce another. If you want to control your circumstances for harmony and happiness, you must first control your thoughts for harmony and happiness, and then the outer things will follow.
>
> If you want health, you must first think health; and remember thinking health does not mean merely thinking a healthy body;important as that is, but it also includes thinking peace and contentment, and good-will to all, for destructive emotion if the primary causes of disease.
>
> If you want material prosperity, you must first think prosperity thoughts, and then make it a habit of doing so, for the thing that keeps most people poor is the sheer habit of poverty thinking.
>
> However, habits of thinking are the most subtle in character and the most difficult to break. It is easy, comparatively speaking, to break a physical habit if one really means business, because action on the physical plane is so much slower and more palpable than on the mental plane. Our thoughts flow across the stage of

> consciousness in an unbroken stream, and so rapidly that only unceasing vigilance can deal with them.
>
> For this reason many people become discouraged with themselves and indulge in a great deal of self-condemnation because they do not very speedily change the whole current of thought over the whole area of their lives. This, of course, is a capital mistake and incidentally, self-condemnation being an essentially negative and unrighteous thought, tends to produce still more trouble in the old vicious circle.
>
> If you are not progressing as fast as you wish to, the remedy is -to be still more careful and to hold only harmonious thoughts. Do not dwell upon your mistakes but claim the Presence of God within you."

Until we know truly in our hearts who we are, like Emmet Fox says, "claim the presence of God within us," that we are all entitled to abundance in all things because we are all Beloved children of God. To take it one step further, we are God- we will still attract whatever program is lurking around in our subconscious. Whatever you believe will become your reality.

It all comes back to your thoughts, or as Zig Ziglar liked to say, your "stinking thinking." And that's one of the main reasons why yoga is so powerful and alchemical. The definition of yoga according to Patanjali's *The Yoga Sutras*: Yoga chitta vritti nirodahah: The restraint of the modifications of the mind-stuff is Yoga.

Chitta is the mind-stuff (consciousness), Vrttis are the waves and ripples (thoughts) rising in it, and Nirodahah means restraint.

Patanjali's definition of yoga is not complete for me. When I learned about it years ago something didn't quite resonate with me. So we quiet our mind, so what? It seemed to me there was something missing. What's the reason it's so important to quiet our mind? We need to quiet our mind so our heart can do the thinking- so we can hear our soul. Since all that we need to live an abundant, happy, prosperous, joyous life in within, it would make sense we need to stop the incessant unending noise chatter of the mind.

> "The bottom of the lake we cannot see, because its surface is covered with ripples. It is only possible when the ripples have subsided, and the water is calm, for us to catch a glimpse of the bottom. If the water is muddy, the bottom will not be seen; if the water is agitated all the time, the bottom will not be seen. If the water is clear, and there are no waves, we shall see the bottom. That bottom of the lake is our own true Self; the lake is the Chitta, and the waves are the Vrttis." ~Swami Vivikenanda

Why do we have such a hard time disciplining our minds and controlling our thoughts? Simply because we don't practice. If we want to play a musical instrument, we take lessons and practice for hours. Our mind is our instrument, the most powerful tool of creation we have. If we want to get good at meditation, controlling our thoughts, and creating the life we want, we have to practice.

It took me over ten years of practicing sitting quietly and stilling my mind, and I still have trouble sometimes. People tell me all the time they can't meditate. I ask them how long they've been practicing..they usually answer a few times. We've spent a lifetime living in the turbulent mind, it's not realistic to think you can control the mind after a few attempts. "Without practice, nothing can be achieved." (Patanjali yoga sutra #1)

Pablo Casals, the world renowned cellist, still practiced three hours a day when he was ninety-three. When asked why he still practiced at that age, he said, "I'm beginning to see some improvement."

I use to sit and *try* to meditate with a kitchen timer set for one minute. I couldn't even get to five seconds without having thoughts and they weren't good ones. I gave up over and over again, but went back to it, over and over again. I used to go to Buddhist meditation classes and fall asleep. It was embarrassing! Sleeping isn't meditation by the way. I had such a hard time in the beginning, but I persisted.

Let go, being again. Let go, begin again. Let go, begin again.

I learned how to train my physical body, the next part of my journey to real and lasting transformation was learning how to train my mind.

"The highest possible stage in moral culture is when we recognize that we ought to control our thoughts." ~Darwin

***The Mass Consciousness, Ugh!

We also must keep in mind that our mind and everyone's else minds are joined. That is good and bad. If we are trying to free ourself from the limited negative thoughts, part of the reason it's so challenging is because were connected to the collective mass consciousness. And the collective consciousness is not so pretty.

"The total number of minds in the universe is One. In fact, consciousness is a singularity phasing within all beings." Edwin Schrodinger, Quantum Physicist

So on top of conquering our own monkey mind, we have to deal with everybody else minds! Trying to pull ourselves up and out of the quagmire of the collective consciousness while simultaneously meeting the demands of our busy modern lives is no easy task. That's why Yogi Manmoyanand, after meditating for years in the Himalayas with his teacher, freaked out when his teacher told him it was time to go into society and become a householder and get married. He knew the concrete jungle was no joke compared to the peaceful life in the caves of the Himalayas. His book, *Sivananda Buried Yoga* is one I highly recommend if you want to learn about true yoga.

Hence, so many people choose to sleepwalk through life and remain ignorant. "Ignorance is bliss" is not really true. "Ignorance is the *illusion* of bliss," is more like it. Staying asleep to all that you are and all you can be prolongs the delusion, confusion and suffering. If you want your life to belong to you, you must have a spiritual practice and discipline. If you don't take the time to prepare, to put on your spiritual armor in the morning before you walk out the door, more than likely you will succumb to the negative, impatient, life-taking thoughts that permeate the world.

There are tricks you can do if you have trouble sitting still and clearing your mind. The one thing I noticed was that I had divine thought and inspiration when I was cleaning, doing the dishes, in the shower, running, dancing, driving, or walking my dog. I kept a pad of paper and a pen next to the shower and the treadmill and used the voice recording on my iPhone to capture the inspiration when it came.

Later I learned I was going into the alpha state of my brain waves by keeping the left side of my brain occupied with the task at hand which gave the right side of my brain a chance to be heard. The right side of our brain is where we can tap into our intuition and creativity as well as divine guidance and inspiration. Since I was left brain dominant most of my life, this was a great technique for me to use. I found that running and yoga not only gave me a boost of endorphins, happy feel good hormones coursing through my body, but the answers to a lot of situations in my life. While it wasn't a "no thoughts" meditation, it was meditation enough for me!

I also found this inspirational validation from Doreen Virtue's book, *Messages From the Angels:*

> "Ah yes, your relationship to oxygen. The very breath that you take at this moment is fueled by a desire to continue upon this path that you have started. Some may say that breath is automatic instinct, but from our perspective, it is a behavior that you engage in, as confirmation of your desire to stay upon the earth.
>
> Each breath contains information within its molecular structure. We imbue each molecule of precious oxygen with guidance and instructions. It is our chief means of staying in touch with you, and within you.
>
> Your breath is tantamount to a continuous meeting between us angels, your higher consciousness, and your Earthly self. It is a roundtable discussion, in which your next move is planned,

and then the next. All of this is based upon your intentions, you see. With your out breath, we are able to extract from you that which you no longer desire. And with your inbreathe, we imbue positive direction that holds you up in the face of apparent discourse.

When we encourage you to exercise, we do so partly to encourage this deeper form of breath. We know that you have noticed how many of your questions and troubles are answered at the conclusion of your exercise activities. That is because we are deeply transmitting to you along your exercise route. We are instilling you with comfort, guidance, and new perspectives on the situations at hand."

***Breath of the Awakening Heart

One of the most effective and least expensive ways, free actually, of finding inner peace is to pay attention to the breath. It's eye opening when we start to pay attention to our breathing during the course of the day... how often we are barely breathing or even holding our breath.

I never realized how important breathing was until I started practicing yoga. During workshops and trainings I attended I used to think it was annoying how the teachers would go on and on about the "breathing thing," then I became one of them.

We can live for three weeks without food, three days without water, but only three to four minutes without oxygen. It's the first thing we do when we come into the world and the last thing we do when we leave. <u>How we are breathing in between that first and last breath matters.</u>

The breath is a simple, inexpensive, accessible modality that brings healing to our bodies and minds. By simply changing our breathing patterns we can bring our nervous system into the parasympathetic mode in which the body does what it is designed to do: heal itself. That is why yoga is so effective regarding physical health; the combination of poses with pranayama (conscious breath work) shifts the nervous system from sympathetic to parasympathetic. Being in state of sympathetic nervous system (flight or fight) comes in handy when you really need the adrenaline, but to be in it constantly causes a cascade of damaging effects to the body by creating imbalances in the hormones and blood chemistry.

> "Everything is interconnected. Change your posture and you change the way you breathe. Change your breathing and you change your nervous system. This is one of the great lessons of yoga: Everything is connected-your hipbone to your anklebone you to your community, your community to the world. This interconnection is vital to understanding yoga. This holistic system simultaneously taps into many mechanisms that have additive and even multiplicative effects. This synergy may be the most important way of all that yoga heals." ~Timothy McCall M.D.

Right now, rub your hands together vigorously and feel the subtle heat or energy between your palms. Take a deep breathe though your nose down into the bottom of your belly relaxing your stomach muscles like a Buddha belly, place your hands on the crown of your head and slowly drag your fingers down your face, exhaling through your mouth like a slow leak in a tire. Take your time, exhaling twice as long as the inhale, letting go of the thoughts in your mind and releasing your face muscles. End with your hands crossed over your heart center and take another deep breathe in, this time into your heart. Feel your heart center soften and expand as you relax more. Stay here for a few more rounds of deep breathing, however feels good for you. Inhale love, exhale love from every pore of your being. Inhale light, exhale light. Inhale peace, exhale peace. Smile from your heart and let it pop out on to your beautiful face. All is well. And so it is.

***Steady and Happy

Since one of the things I learned from my first astrology reading with Blanche was learning how to find balance and walking the middle path, the breathe is one tool that helps me to stay aware and keeps me in the present moment. I can go from anger to peace with all the in between emotions in 60 seconds. I am a walking paradox of opposite emotions and have to learn how to navigate the middle. It makes sense that my astrological sign of Pisces is two fish swimming in opposite directions!

In yoga we refer to the concept of having an equanimous mind as **Stirham Sukham,** which means steady and happy. When we are practicing yoga asana or poses we engage our muscles, but if we tense them too much we create more tension in our body, which is counter to yoga. There is a happy medium of being aware and engaged but open and free flowing. This can be applied off the mat in our daily lives as well.

I find that my first response in relationship when someone hurts or disappoints me is to close down and run. It's my natural defense mechanism, as I'm sure for many others as well. However, I didn't want to be like the majority of bitter people that close their hearts and profess, "I'm done!" and walk away. Truth is we're never "done." As long as we're here on this earth, in this body, we'll never be done.

Each time that feeling comes up for me, now that I'm more aware, I stop myself and reflect before I respond or make any decisions. I set my default to discernment instead of defensiveness. I stop and ask myself: Are these *my* issues and neuroses or is this relationship causing me more discomfort and negativity than adding joy in my life? Or am I just not getting my way and shutting down to play it safe? Am I being too hard, too judgmental, too critical? Is it all about me? Most of the time the answer is yes; I have reverted back to my old patterns of insecurity and fear.

Too many times we make the relationship about what we can get out of it, instead of asking the question, "How can I give?" When we give to others we are giving to ourselves just as much. Giving opens our hearts to the natural love and compassion that's within us. When we give, we receive. It's a win win for all parties! What I have found is when I don't close down and stay the course, I learn more about myself, I grow, and become a mature spiritual adult. I call this making deposits in your spiritual bank account. Cha ching!

> "How often I have betrayed myself, forgetting-or, more accurately, resisting-the twenty minutes of meditation, the hour of reading, the spiritual meeting or recovery group that would prepare me for the roller coaster ride that always lies potential in an intimate relationship. Part of the problem is that we expect love affairs to always feel good. They don't. Actually, relationships don't feel good anyway. We feel good. Unless we are centered within ourselves, we cannot blame a relationship for throwing us off. No man can convince a women she's wonderful, but if she already believes she is, his agreement can resonate and bring her joy."
> ~*A Woman's Worth,* Marianne Williamson

PETAL 4

Breaking Open Again

***Angel Bob

SOMEONE ELSE THAT helped me get to know myself better was another astrologer, Bob Cooke. I met Bob back in the beginning of my journey when I was a newbie to all this stuff. I went yearly for a reading. I wanted to know why every time I told someone who was into astrology that I was a Pisces- sun and a Scorpio-moon, they cringed.

While I believe in the science of astrology, I take it with a grain of salt. Astrological forces have an influence over our lives, whether we believe in it or not, but free will still reigns supreme. Ultimately, we are the creator of our reality and our lives, but astrology is a wonderful self-help tool.

One of the things Bob made me aware of was that I had the gift of attracting "wolves in sheep clothing," so whenever I met someone he told me to call him with his date of birth. I felt like I was cheating in a way, but I listened to Bob because I didn't have much luck in the dating arena.

For example the last date I went on, my last to this day, was with a guy who had tattooed sleeves on both arms. Since I realized we didn't have much in common in the first sixty seconds we were together after he asked me what television shows I watched and I didn't watch tv, I asked him what his tattoos meant. His left arm was covered in skulls and crossbones, which was a fashion fad at the time, so I didn't think much of it. When he responded, "There was a time in my life when I had a pact with the devil," I started to get a little freaked out, and covertly began to inch away from him.

I went to his other tattooed arm, thinking *this arm has got to be better*, asking him what it meant. He said, "You don't know what misanthrope means? Look it up on your phone."

So I did and as I read the definition of misanthrope: "hatred for the human species," I continued to inch away from him even more hoping he wouldn't notice the fear that was building inside, praying he was not some serial killer and silently requesting the protection of my angel Michael. I excused myself to the bathroom. I knew I had to get away from this guy fast. Not the best taste in men, yea, I needed Bob.

Bob was right on the money, every single time too, about every guy I met, even when I didn't want to believe him. It never was good news either. Until one day I called Bob, gave him a date of birth and Bob asked me, "Where did you meet him?"

This was surprising. He never asked me any questions. It was usually, "You can date him but being with him is like watching the grass grow," or "He's good for a fling," or "The sex would be good, but don't expect him to commit to anything long term..." You get the picture. Finally after all these years Bob gave me the thumbs up! This was historic!

***Dreams Finally Coming True

I decide to go for it, and go for it did I ever. I ended up getting married to him, getting divorced, and crawling back to Bob with my heart shattered in my hands a year later, totally devastated. When Bob asked me what happened, I told him, "You gave me the thumbs up." He replied, "I didn't tell you to marry him."

And the learning continues…

Of course, I didn't marry my husband because Bob gave me the thumbs up. We were soulmates and we fell madly in love with each other. It didn't hurt having the approval from Bob either, I have to admit.

I met my husband, I will call him Soulmate #3, volunteering at a young men's group home on Long Island. He was a counselor there, and I was teaching yoga to the young men in recovery. In the summers he went to California to fight forest fires. The summer we met he never used his plane ticket and made it to California; we spent the summer at the beach falling in love.

I felt sure and safe that this was the person I could let my guard down with and trust, the first person at thirty eight years of age that I opened up to and let in. Part of the reason was because Soulmate #3 was a strict practicing Catholic. He was actually contemplating becoming a priest right before he met me. I changed his mind pretty quickly (wink, wink). He was probably one of the last men walking the planet at thirty seven that still believed in being with only one woman for his entire life. He was waiting to meet his bride.

I honored his request- because I didn't pressure him to consummate the relationship and we were deeply in love, he told me we were married on a soul level and wanted to give himself to me. So give himself to me he did and did and did, and we got pregnant. It wasn't planned but abortion was not an option for him, being Catholic. We were madly in love, and I always wanted another child so we decided to make a family. We got married in town-hall on February 28, 2008.

This was one of the happiest times in my life. I remember feeling like I finally belonged somewhere, with a man who loved me and would never leave me. The family I always dreamed about was coming true. It was so nice to be someone's wife, at last.

Soulmate #3 was also the first relationship where I felt comfortable and safe enough to experience an orgasm. I had problems down there, no, not down there, but up in my head. When I consulted my gynecologist about my non-orgasmic life, he did a thorough examination, which I passed with flying colors then gave me the number to a sex therapist. The issue wasn't my female body parts, thank God, the issue was in my head and fixable.

My non-orgasmic life was also fueled by inappropriate sexual experiences I had when I was nine and again when I was a teenager. It was something I never talked about but knew it affected me. The head, the heart and the vagina are all connected I've come to realize. They say the largest female sex organ is the brain, and I concur.

As soon as I found out I was pregnant I panicked and began exercising like crazy. I started bleeding a lot but continued to work. I'm not sure what propelled me to ignore my body and these signs. I should have been home resting with my feet up. Shorty after, I had a miscarriage. Even though I always wanted another baby, part of me didn't feel ready. I must have known something was off deep down.

Still, I was emotionally distraught and having conflicting emotions. Even though my doctor tried to convince me that it wasn't my fault, I felt responsible and guilty. One of my biggest dreams was to be in love in a healthy relationship and bring a child into the world. I felt like this was my last chance at thirty-eight years old to have another baby and I blew it.

***All Cried Out

Shortly after we lost our baby, we went to India together for a month to study and practice yoga. As soon as we got there we looked at each other and said, "What happened?"

India tends to do that to you. It brings up all your shit to detox, then leaves you stripped down and spiritually naked to bare your soul. There's no hiding your shit in India.

Everyone we met thought we were on our honeymoon. They had no idea (and either did I), it was just the opposite, the beginning of our decline. About two weeks after we returned from our trip to India, I walked into our bedroom to find his things gone. The rug was pulled out from under me, again.

Blindsided and feeling total abandonment, I went spiraling down. I drowned in my tears as I cried every day for a year straight, and I'm not exaggerating. The only time I had a little bit of reprieve from my heartache and misery was when I was teaching yoga.

I would cry in my car driving to the studio, get myself together in the parking lot, blow my nose, wipe the tears away and remind myself that I don't know who is going to be in class and what they are going through and that I have to be the one to bring healing and light and love to the class. So I would put my problems and heartache to the side for the time being and go in and be a channel for yoga to flow.

Sometimes the grief would be overwhelming and I would end up crying softly while my students were in Shivasana (final relaxation). As painful as this was, at the time I didn't realize how *powerful this practice was* for me. It showed me that when I wasn't making it "all about me," I felt relief. It taught me a lot about being selfless and being a conduit for God's love to flow through me. I taught my best classes when I was vulnerable in pain.

Even so, after class I went right back to the same mental and emotional torture questioning, *Why? How? Why? How?* How could I let this happen again? I thought if I can make a thirty-eight year old virgin Catholic run away and divorce me I must be a wreck still! I had a lot of work to do, even after seven years of consistent introspection and healing.

Why? That one little word can really make us stuck. Sometimes we don't know why, especially when it involves another person. Sometimes we just have to *accept*, without knowing why.

I was so depressed during this time of separation with Soulmate#3 my good friend said to me that I was lucky I can sleep, as she was going through woman life changes and having issues with sleep. I thought to myself, *not really lucky, the reason I am going to bed at 7pm and sleeping so much is because it's the closest thing to dying to me.*

When I spoke with my intuitive friend who can see chakras, she said compassionately, "Oh honey," and told me my heart look like someone took a shotgun and blasted a hole right through it.

It was then when I was lying in bed one night, I heard God's voice for the second time, **"You have so much love inside of you."** I wasn't sure what that meant exactly and how it could help me not feel so hopeless and depressed, but it was a silver lining that helped me get up out of bed.

***Fire

So when I went crawling back to Bob with my heart in my hands he very tenderly began to explain some things to me which helped me to see what happened. It made so much sense. In effort to keep as much private as possible I will not share what Bob told me about Soulmate #3 and our relationship, I will share only what he told me about myself.

While he concurred that I had a lot of anger or fire as he called it, inside of me, he also showed me the positive side of it. He told me I can turn that anger into something positive. He showed me that the benefit of being a deep person was that I can go where most people won't go and from that dark despair and sadness I can bring back a pearl of wisdom or a sign of beauty and light and hope for the world to see. He helped me to look at what I always deemed as imperfections and flaws as strength.

I gravitated to yoga and meditation because I am very spiritual in nature, that's the water sign in me (Neptune); but I can also go down to the valley where there's mud and blood and darkness; that's the fire in me (Pluto). According to Bob, "Pluto eats Neptune for breakfast."

He continued, I came into this lifetime to learn about myself through my relationships with men mostly, but they would usually end with Pluto blowing them up. *Great,* I am thinking, *this sucks. Yup, I can see that in every one of my relationships.* On a more positive note he did say that I will find real true lasting love, but later in life. *Ok I can deal with that. Thank God I won't be alone my whole life.*

He said that I needed a partner who can walk through the fire with me, not shrink or run away from it. I understand that now. I also understand that it doesn't give me the right to take my fury out on another person. That is where I have to do the work and control my intense emotions.

Talk about a paradigm shift. I never thought of myself like that. I always thought I was angry and defective. Bob showed me the beauty and grace in the so called imperfections. *Bob was another angel in my life.*

This so called relationship disaster with Soulmate #3 actually turned out to be a blessing in disguise bearing many gifts. I just needed to get through the emotional pain and heartbreak of it first to see them. After two years of grieving and a lot of spiritual counseling and work on myself, I began to see the light again.

Hence sparked my forty week St. Ignatius Spiritual Retreat. One of my soul sisters that owned the yoga studio where I taught, witnessing my struggle, nudged me toward this retreat. She was doing and thought it would be helpful. I resisted at first because the retreat used readings from the Bible. After having a not so positive experience with Catholicism, I turned it down. My angel friend convinced me to at least meet with her spiritual director.

The day I met with Valerie was another pivotal day in my life. She was another angel who guided me through some pretty dark times. She did not try to convince me to do the retreat, she just listened to my heart-ache, then read me a poem. As she was reading it, I started to weep. I cried because I knew this was exactly what I needed in my life and that I was in the right place at the most perfect time.

Let Your God Love You

-by Edwina Gateley, *Psalms of a Laywoman*

Be silent.
Be still.
Alone.
Empty
Before your God
Say nothing.
Ask nothing.
Be silent.
Be still.
Let your God
Look upon you.
That is all.
God knows.
God understands.
God loves you

With an enormous love,
And only wants
To look upon you
With that love.
Quiet.
Still.
Be.

Let your God-
Love you.

This was just the medicine my soul needed. Every day we had a reading, and not always from the Bible, spiritual exercises, journaling and meditation. Each week I met with my director, Valerie, and the first question she asked me was, "So, where was God in your life this week?"

I loved that question, it helped me to see that God was always in my life, even when I felt forgotten. It was life-changing for me. For the first time in my life I felt loved by God. It was no longer an intellectual idea or concept, I took God's love into my heart, along with this quote:

> "Prayer begins with the realization that I am loved by God as I am. God's love is based on nothing and therefore, is the most basic and secure fact in my life. I simply let myself be loved by God. This is not so much an activity of mine, but a passivity in which I let God's love soak in and permeated my whole being." ~adapted from "As Bread That Is Broken" by Peter van Breemen

This retreat was about walking in Jesus' footsteps for forty weeks from his birth to his death to his resurrection. I was immersed in his life and his teachings and went through what Jesus went through but as my lessons and learning experience in my life. It was then when I really got to know who Jesus was, why he came to the earth, and developed a relationship with him.

Jesus' message was one of the most important messages in the last two thousand years and also one of the most distorted and misunderstood. The most painted image in the western world is the crucifixion of Jesus; no coincidence there. But Jesus didn't come here so we can focus on his torture and death. There's enough of that happening in the world without Jesus having to do it too.

Jesus was about the resurrection. He said we will do greater things than he did. How do we do that? How do we resurrect our lost sad selves? Through love and forgiveness, for ourselves first and for others. Love yourself, love you neighbor. Spirituality doesn't have to be that complicated.

Forgiveness is the only way out of our Hell. Heaven is not a destination; heaven is a state of beingness in our minds and hearts right here, right now. Jesus was here to show us the way out. He was about the resurrection, and his message was that he is us, we are him, and we too will do just as many great things. He's not coming back to save us. We have to save ourselves.

For two years in a row on Ash Wednesday I had a dream that Soulmate#3 (my former husband) came back to me to reconcile. I was in his arms again feeling so happy, then all of a sudden the thought popped into my head, *If I go back with him, I will lose my soul.* Then I would wake up.

***Not Just My Soul, My Favorite Dress!

I was like Julia Roberts in *Runaway Bride* with the eggs. Her favorite eggs were whatever her fiancées' favorite eggs were, she never knew what she liked herself. My eggs were my clothes. I would morph my outfits into what my man liked and lose my style all together. What I wore was a form of self expression to me, it mattered.

Soulmate #3, being a conservative Catholic, gave me a hard time with my attire. Most of my wardrobe was spandex and tight form fitting clothes since

I was a yoga teacher and personal trainer. It's what I lived in. I never thought anything of it. He, on the other hand, would have preferred me to wear turtle necks in yoga class and a Burka; which he casually mentioned one day that he thought it was cool that women wore them and you could only see their eyes!

After experiencing the wrath of his opinion about my outfit one day on the way to the supermarket in the cute athletic spandex dress I was sporting, I submitted. He unhappily argued, "you can see everything." I decided to receive and wear the new clothes he started buying me following a complete overhaul of my closet, getting rid of anything that might spark an argument, which happened to be most of my wardrobe!

I'm ok with downsizing and getting rid of clothes, it's something I enjoy actually... except when it's your favorite dress. My favorite dress was one of those dresses you will never find again: unique, fun, colorful, comfortable and danceable! It was sexy but classy, one of a kind that not only fit me like a glove, both men and woman fell in love with me when I wore it! I felt like the dress was me. It reflected my personality to a tee.

I dropped it off, in addition to a huge bag of all my other argument provoking clothes at the nearest donation center which happened to be for Veterans. They probably never got such a dazzling colorful collection of clothes before. Whoever was lucky enough to find them, I'm sure made their day.

What I learned is losing ourself in a relationship is a recipe for disaster. Of course, we want to please our partners because in making them happy makes us happy. But where do we draw the line? I stopped going to drum circles and dancing because he didn't approve...that was one of the activities that brought me the most joy! Healthy boundaries was something I needed help with. I had to stop making my partner's needs paramount to mine and stop ignoring the red flags. It was my pattern, not surprising given my background, but I realized I needed to source my happiness from myself and God first before another person and be true to myself.

Easier said than done. How do we give of ourselves so completely without losing ourselves entirely?

I got a tattoo, of course. That's what everyone does right?! I got my first tattoo on the Good Friday after he left. I tatted my left ring finger with a band and married myself that day. It was my commitment to myself and God first. I swore to myself that I would never lose myself like that again. While it is natural for us to want to trust someone wholeheartedly, we also have to remember that they are wounded just like we are and have their own set of emotional baggage.

***Swim SoulFire, Swim!

After my tattoo I did something else spontaneously. I signed up for a really long open water swim across the Great South Bay in Long Island. Soulmate#3 had done an Ironman competition which inspired me to start triathlons. I participated in a couple of sprint triathlons after he left, thinking it would ease the pain of abandonment which they didn't, but brought me to a new chapter in my life which I'm most grateful for. What I found I liked the most about the run, bike, swim triathlons was what most people disliked: the swim.

I grew up on the Long Island Sound on our boat and in the water. My Dad had us get our boating license and certified in scuba diving when we were young. We scuba dove and swam in many places. My crazy life took me away from the water even with living on an island. I forgot how much I loved to swim and be in the water until I began triathlons.

So when I saw a sign in town one day for this annual charity swim across the bay, I said "Why not?" I was desperate to try to get my mind off Soulmate #3 and heal my heart. Anything that could help or even just distract me was a blessing. I sent in my application with $100 check and was accepted, having no idea this was a hard race to get into with a waiting list that only took the first 100 entries.

After I received the welcome letter and sat down to read what the swim entailed I started to freak out, *what did I just get myself into?* I could manage swimming around the sound or pool just fine recreationally, but to swim open water across the Great South Bay, almost six miles? The reality started sinking in that I needed to seriously learn how to swim.

Luckily, my friend Marc was a swim coach. I'll never forget my first official swim lesson at the YMCA. I swam *one* lap across the pool, gripping the edge, gasping for air, thinking, *holy shit that was really hard?*

"Ok, now swim back," he said. Panting, I asked, "Can I rest a minute?" "No, go now," he commanded. My sweet friend Marc turned out was not so sweet in the pool.

That was in February. Between him and the swim team, Open Water Swim, I became a part of, in July I completed the cross bay swim, nearly six miles. It took me almost four hours, but I did it.

I fell in love with swimming just like I did yoga. Being in the water was like coming home to my soul. Swimming was much more than exercise for me, the water returned a part of me that was long lost and forgotten.

> "I've been swimming all my life, you said, but I never saw these things. Ah, you swam, but never before without the fear of drowning. Lie back, and I will swim you home. The stars will guide us, the waves will carry us, and all our fear will slip away. Surrender now. the sea caresses. Together we will meet the sky, and find our love for everything." ~ *Enchanted Love,* Marianne Williamson

Swimming brought me through some challenging times when I was feeling the empty nest syndrome. I spent five months sitting home alone on the couch depressed and lonely after my daughter was gone, and worse when Karma left. My coach had this uncanny radar, texting me at my lowest times, "get to the pool," "come swim," and other encouraging reminders to get me out of my funk. It worked. Swimming saved me. It was not just the exercise of swimming that I loved, it was the community that I became a part of. My swim coach who became a dear friend, was another angel in my life who I will always be grateful for.

I took swimming seriously for the next three years. I completed the Cross Bay Swim two more years in a row. One year I signed up for an 5K ocean swim after completing the Cross Bay Swim. I think that year I spent more time in the water than out, morphing into the mermaid that I am. I was like Daryl Hannah in the movie, *Splash*. When I started to feel off or tired I would get in my shower and hose myself down with water, for real. On top of all the swimming, I took on a fundraiser for my coach's nanny's brother who lived in Australia. The thirteen year old boy was born with a debilitating disease and needed an electric wheelchair. That year we dedicated the proceeds of the 5K/10K Fire Island ocean swim to him.

Fueled by love, I got it all done: completed two long distance swims, organized and ran a fundraiser, and worked full time teaching yoga and doing massages. We were successful in raising the money for him and it felt great to tangibly help someone in need. As a thank you to our sponsors, I made a special card with the Starfish Story and a silver starfish medallion attached to it.

The Starfish Story: (adapted from *The Star Thrower*, Loren Eiseley)

One day a man was walking along the beach when he noticed a boy picking something up and gently throwing it into the ocean.
Approaching the boy, he asked, "What are you doing?"
The youth replied, "Throwing starfish back into the ocean. The surf is up and the tide is going out. If I don't throw them back, they will die."
"Son," the man said, "don't you realize there are miles and miles of beach and hundreds of starfish? You can't make a difference!"

> After listening politely, the boy bent down, picked up another starfish, and threw it back into the surf.
> Then, smiling at the man, he said, "I made a difference for that one."

I added to the card, "Thank you for making a difference in Nathan's life."

A couple of months after the fundraiser, I was on my daily beach run when I stumbled upon hundreds of starfish strewn all over the shore. I had never seen one starfish on the beach, now I was looking at hundreds. Most of them were still alive. I bent down, began picking them up and one at a time threw them back into the ocean. *This is just like the poem*, I realized as tears started rolling down my face. Although my coach showed his appreciation and I knew Nathan was grateful for what we did for him, I never received a thank you directly from him. He might not have been aware that was important to me so I tried not to let it bother me, but my sensitive heart felt it. For me, this was God's way of thanking me.

Karma, and all the good deeds we do, do not go unnoticed. We might not receive the gratitude or energy back from the same person but the Universe has a way of balancing it out. This was my gift. I wept in awe and gratitude as I saved as many as I could that day, one starfish at a time.

***False Growth with a Message

During the time my heart was recovering from my divorce, my annual gynecologist appointment revealed a growth in my uterus. I was told to come back in another week as they wanted to do a different type of test and minor surgery might be necessary if it was still there.

I tried not to become too alarmed or frightened, but the thought of minor surgery in my private parts was not something I wanted to experience again. I had one done a few years prior that brought me to the emergency room in excruciating pain. I decided I needed to heal myself, so I went home to Mama Hay, took out her bible and read:

> "Tumors are false growths. An oyster takes a tiny grain of sand, and to protect itself, grows a hard and shiny shell around it. We call it a pearl and think it is beautiful. We take an old hurt and nurse it and keep pulling the scab off it, and in time we have a tumor.
>
> I call this running the old movie. I believe the reason women have so many tumors in the uterus area is that they take an emotional hurt, a blow to their femininity, and nurse it. I call this the "He done me wrong" syndrome.
>
> Just because a relationship ends does not mean there is something wrong with us, nor does it lessen our self-worth. It is not what happens, it is how we react to it. We are each responsible for all our experiences. What beliefs about yourself do you need to change in order to attract more loving kinds of behavior?"

I sat stunned absorbing this insight. That was exactly what I was thinking 24/7, how "he done me wrong." I looked up the new thought pattern: "I lovingly release the past and turn my attention to this new day. All is well."

I chanted this all day long while visualizing the growth disappearing. The next week at my gynecologist appointment, they used a more specific sonogram, and lo and behold, there was nothing there! I had a clean slate of health!

From *Quantum Healing* by Dr. Deepak Chopra:

> "...the mind and body are like parallel universes. Anything that happens in the mental universe but leave tracks in the physical one...your body is the physical picture, in 3-D, of what you are

> thinking. We don't see our bodies as projected thoughts because many physical changes that thinking causes are unnoticeable. They involve minute alterations of cell chemistry, body temperature, electrical charge, blood pressure, and so on, which do not register the focus of attention. You can be assured, however, that the body is fluid enough to mirror any mental event. Nothing can move without moving the whole."

The same is true for all of existence...<u>anything that happens in the mental plane leaves tracks in the physical one.</u>

***Hurt People Hurt People

As I started waking up and discarding my armor, I realized from my relationships that I was attracting emotionally unavailable men into my life because I was emotionally unavailable to myself. I realized that if I wanted emotional stability in a relationship, I must first give it to myself. I learned if I wanted to stop hurting, I had to stop hurting myself; if I wanted to stop being abandoned, I had to stop abandoning myself. I would re-enact my childhood trauma over and over again until I healed that core limiting belief that no one wanted me and no one loved me.

I had the intellectual knowledge but hadn't integrated it into my heart. I still wasn't loving myself. Until I started truly loving myself and knowing I was worthy just because I exist and nothing more, I would not find the love I was looking for "out there."

> "Christianity with its teachings of original sin taught us we were flawed in our nature and we need forgiving. We lost our sense of divinity, and true balance was lost as we found it easy to give but difficult to receive, guilt and unworthiness seeped in to our psyche. We will continue to experience self denial and self

> rejection until we learn we are divine. Self love is an absolute on the path of healing, until you can love yourself and learn you are a flawless spark of God in the great Divinity you cannot truly love others or attain mastery." ~Metatron, earth-keeper.com

Because of the trauma of abandonment I suffered throughout my life, I was insecure inside and the only way I could manage it was to act in control. I couldn't blame my soulmates for leaving me like they did. I was just as much at fault and just as angry and violent- I just showed it in different ways. I was also still playing the victim role by blaming them. This is how we grow up to become spiritually mature adults. We take responsibility for our part in the relationship, do what we can to make amends and choose to do things differently in the future with more awareness. It doesn't always work right away, as I found out, but it's a process.

(For the purpose of my story about transformation I focused on the "challenging" parts of my relationships, however I'd like to state for the record that there were many positive beautiful aspects of each relationship that I cherish. I have no regrets. I'm grateful for each one. I am also grateful to the family that adopted me. We have our dysfunctions like all families, but I love them. They are my family).

***Trinity

At the end of my relationship with my Soulmate#3 we got a puppy. It was a bone of contention between us as he didn't feel we should get a dog. I promised my daughter that as soon as we rented a home that allowed dogs we'd look for one. So finally, after fifteen years, our landlord gave us permission. It was a big deal to us but my husband had no understanding and objected. After much heated discussion over this dog, we ended up getting one.

Unfortunately, when this eight week chocolate lab came home with us when we returned from India, and my husband left two weeks later, I was devastated and could not care for the puppy properly. My fifteen year old daughter helped but it was "teenage style," not enough. The hyper-active puppy needed a lot of attention. I was a useless wet noodle and in no mood to train a puppy. So we decided to find a better home for Trinity, which we did with a big yard and other dogs and children who were excited to have her.

The day we brought Trinity over to their house was a revelation for me. As I was holding her, about to hand her over, she finally stopped barking. I hesitated, feeling an overwhelming sense of guilt and sadness. I thought about changing my mind, but then my daughter nudged me into letting her go. Trinity just looked at me quietly with sad puppy eyes and we left.

I sat in my car distraught, surprised at my feelings and my reaction. After all, I only had this puppy for a couple of weeks. I thought we barely bonded.

***Forgiveness of My Biological Mother

The next morning running down the beach, I was thinking about Trinity and processing the situation when all of a sudden I stopped running, fell to my knees and started sobbing. It seemed the beach was where I did a lot of my healing. *This must be how my biological mother felt*, I thought. How was I supposed to have any type of relationship with a mother I never knew and what could I think about a woman when all I knew about her was that she was a prostitute and a heroin addict?

After having my own child I felt compelled to know more about this woman who carried me for nine months in her womb and gave birth to me. I realized we must have had some kind of bond. Since my adopted parents knew nothing except what they had told me already, I decided to write to the adoption agency. Following the legal steps of phone calls and paperwork, a couple of months later I received a letter in the mail with everything they had in my file. (This was in 2001, coinciding with the start of my yoga journey). Since it was a closed case, the adoption agency was only legally allowed to disclose non-identifying information, and that included for my foster parents as well. After reading and learning that the first years of a child's life are the most important in development, I wanted to reach out to them to say thank you for taking care of me. I lived with them until I was four years old. The adoption agency said if someone had a bad experience with their foster parents, they could retaliate, so it wasn't safe. Oh well.

When the letter arrived, I was so nervous…so many thoughts streaming through my mind…Would I finally fit the missing pieces together of my life? Would I finally know who my mother was? My father? Would I finally know who I am? I tore it open and began to read.

It broke my heart to read about my birth mother. I guess in the back of my mind I was hoping that my Dad was lying to me about her. I didn't want to believe what he told me was true. But sadly the letter backed up his story. Now it was real, whereas before it could have been one of the many lies my Dad told me.

Her story sunk into my heart like an anchor at the bottom of the sea. I cried for her, I cried for me, I think I cried for the whole world. I could only imagine the depth of her hopelessness, despair and suffering she had to endure to be in the position to use sex for drugs. What was worse? Some women out of desperate times use sex temporarily to make their lives better, but my mother used sex to make her life worse. I wanted to find her, hug her and tell her that I was ok, I was better than ok and that I forgive her and love her.

All this time I was harboring judgment, shame and self rejection. Whenever I was upset my thoughts always went to "my mother didn't want me," then, "my mother didn't want me (adopted mother)", then "nobody wants me," when I was in full blown pity party. I would cry so hard at the thought, it became my reality. This was pure toxic energy to my heart.

I realized she probably wanted me. There was a time a few months after I was born that she hesitated. According to the letter she was ambivalent about her plan of adoption. I was six months old and she was just released from prison when she visited me. My mother didn't sign the adoption papers until I was three after she visited me one more time. *That one little sentence from the letter was my saving grace, my silver lining.* That pause and indecision she had I'm sure was torture for her. I felt strongly that she really wanted me but she just didn't have the means or the ability to care for me in the way that a baby deserves, similar to how I had to give up Trinity.

After all, there is a bond that forms in the womb and she did carry me for nine months and bring me into this world. The labor lasted 11 hours and 30 minutes! That in itself is an act of pure love. Giving me up for adoption was an act of unconditional love, not abandonment at all.

As I knelt in the warm soft sand, my heart broke wide open. I walked to the water's edge and my tears became part of the ocean that day, this time with tears of understanding, compassion, forgiveness and grace.

Every time I read that letter my heart breaks just a little bit. It's amazing how it affects me so much even after all the work I have done. It shows me that no matter what we are still human and we still hurt.

***Karma

One year later, my daughter and I decided to try again with a dog. We went online and googled mini dachshunds. A litter came up from a rescue shelter in Pennsylvania. When I called and talked to the woman she said she was abandoned in the woods by her mother, which they know is mini dachshund, but the father is unknown.

You're kidding?! This is me in a puppy! I couldn't believe it! The woman didn't quite get my excitement even though I shared my story with her. Didn't matter, this puppy belonged with us. It was fate.

Karma quickly became my dog as my daughter ended her high school years and then went off to college. I rescued her but she really rescued me. She has saved me by the simple but ever so tough task of keeping my heart open.

Karma has become my best friend. She comes with me to my yoga classes and assists in my healing sessions with clients. She is a natural healer and is nothing but unconditional love. She is my soul-joy! Thank God for Karma. She is a truly a gift.

"Whoever said diamonds are a girl's best friend... never had a dog."

In a world where it's rare to receive unconditional love, loyalty and acceptance from another person, it is nice to at least feel it from another living being. While I think that it's beautiful to find that love in an animal, I don't think we should stop trying to find it or cultivate it in ourselves or another. After all, **we are here to love each other.**

***Never Not Broken

If we've lived long enough on this earth we have experienced some kind of loss. There's no escaping loss on the physical plane- whether it's loss of someone we love, our career, our health, our youth, our financial security or all of the above. Our heart has probably been broken not once, but numerous times, maybe even smashed into a million pieces. We can let loss close us up and numb us to life or we can let it break us open.

In our country we are not equipped emotionally and mentally for loss. Our motto is, "Put on your big boy pants and man up! Haste makes waste, gotta go back to work and get back into the swing of things. Get out there! Go get em! Stay busy, busy, busy."

There is a Hindu Goddess called the Goddess of Never Not Broken, "Akhilandeshvari," pronounced ah-kee-LAN-desh-va-ree. I resonated immediately with this deity. She symbolizes the power and opportunity to be broken open by loss, heartache and trauma.

It's normal to resist change but this Goddess whispers in our ear that with change comes liberation; liberation from our past, from our wounds, from our negative habits, and our stifling routines. However, she takes this one step further, and proclaims the real power and liberation is in staying broken wide open, allowing ourself to flow with the currents of life and recreate ourself anew each and every moment. Our vulnerability then, becomes our strength, not our weakness.

To be broken open for love takes courage, humility and gentle strength to go through the fire. But through the fire is how one must walk. We can't go around it, it doesn't work that way.

It's what we call in yoga, *tapas*, or the spiritual fire. Tapas means, "to burn or create heat." The more you fire gold, for example, the more pure it becomes. Each time it goes into the fire, more impurities are removed. It's the same with us, it is the burning away and purification of all that is inauthentic about ourselves, the lies and the stories we tell ourselves, the inner fears and insecurities, and the walls around our heart.

For my gardeners, just like with plants, in order for them to grow, be healthy and increase yield, the dead, damaged, diseased or non-productive tissue from the crop or plant needs to be pulled out. Some plants self-prune, which is called abscission. I like to think of parting from negative people or boyfriends as abscission, self-pruning. We have to be willing to give up part of ourself, the part that's no longer serving our soul's growth, so the real us can appear, the angel in physical form.

***What are We Surviving?

My dad used to say I was a survivor. That was it, nothing followed that statement. What was I surviving from? I can see how people in concentration camps were survivors. But what am I surviving? A lack of love? Peace? Understanding? Purpose? Can that be just as detrimental to our well being? to the world?

Being a survivor in the twenty first century has such new meaning now than it did a mere seventy-five years ago, when people were surviving concentration camps. I am a survivor, like we all are, from the disconnect from our true spiritual nature, growing up and living in a world that is so opposite from where we came from and where we will return. Now we are trying to survive the loss of meaning and depth to our lives; we are surviving the shallow, artificiality of the world that doesn't support our soul.

The sign I had on my wall for many years, "Tough times don't last, tough people do," served me for a long time, but I decided no more surviving. I knew deep down this is not why we are here, to suffer, endure, survive, then die. Was that what life was all about? It was time to thrive, to feel alive, to feel period. I was tired of being numb. I just wanted to feel happy, that's all I ever wanted. While you are on the path to awakening, however, it is easy to lose your way.

***Faith is when you close your eyes and open your heart.

It's hard to have faith when everything is uncertain. But that is the way faith is cultivated. You don't need faith when everything is going your way. That's not when faith is needed. Faith is something we might not be able to see or feel or smell or touch, but somewhere in the depths of our being it calls to us. It gets us off the floor when all we want to do is lie down and die, it get us to that yoga class that you know somehow you need, it pushes you gently to keep going, no matter how hard life gets, no matter what your circumstances may be, it is the voice that says, *don't give up, you can do it, help is on the way, just please don't give up. I know you are tired and I know you are scared but walk, walk with me, take one day at a time, one step at a time, one breath at a time, it will be ok.*

Faith brings out the best in us, our human spirit of perseverance and steadfast strength. Faith is knowing that no matter how bad things may seem or how awful or depressed you may feel, spring still comes, flowers still bloom, babies are still born and people still fall in love and marry. Faith is knowing the sun will still come up in the morning and angels will lie down with you when you rest at night. "When nothing is certain, everything is possible."

Faith brings the right people in to your life at the right time, along with the right book! When I first started reading self-help books *The Way of the Peaceful Warrior* by Dan Millman jumped out at me when perusing the shelves of the book store. It was the title that caught my attention. I found it to be so enlightening that I read it three times in a row, then took notes on it.

That is how I taught myself from books. I didn't want to be one of those people who read self help books and stayed exactly the same, angry and unhappy. I witnessed this first hand from a good friend. The first read I did was to get a basic feel for the book; the second read was highlighting and underlining; and the third time through I summarized the highlights in my journal. As soon as my pen hit the paper or my fingers to the keypad, the information downloaded into my brain. Writing was learning to me.

I loved this book so much, I went on to Amazon and checked out all Dan Millman's other books. I had them all, about five of them, in my shopping cart then hesitated. A pang of guilt came over me. Even though I was buying them used, money was tight. To appease my guilt I took one book out of the shopping cart and moved it to my wish list.

About two weeks later, at work at Roslyn Savings Bank, one of my clients that I hadn't seen in over a year walked in unannounced and placed a book on my desk. It was the Dan Millman book that I didn't buy, *The Laws of Spirit!!!* And you question a higher intelligence?

When I worked at Bear Sterns in Manhattan, the last book I thought I would ever get from a stockbroker who became one of my dear friends, was_*Conversations with God,* by Neale Donald Walsch. It sat on my bookshelf for ten years until one day I picked it up and couldn't put it down. I devoured it along with all of his other books. I fell in love with Neale Donald Walsch, his story, his books and his teachings. I felt like they were speaking directly to me. They have changed my life because they changed my perception about myself and the world.

This has happened to me with so many books. In 2008, my good friend and fellow yoga teacher gave me *The New Earth* by Eckhart Tolle. I started to read it but got stuck at the chapter on the ego (of course) and put it down. Eight years later I went back to it, read it, get it and think to myself *I can't believe I didn't like this book before.* I wasn't ready before; my state of consciousness was not ready to receive the message.

> "Awakening happens," in between pages, lines, words, moments, conversations, meditations, in between life. It's a continuous process and a sacred journey- not one to be rushed, but to be savored every step of the way **...** all of it, the good, the bad, highs and the lows, even the heartache and despair.

***Pop Spirituality

I wasn't one of the fortunate ones either that had a near death experience, life changing vision, miraculous event or spontaneous transformation happen in which my old paradigm was completely transformed in an instant. I also didn't grow up with yoga parents, have a personal guru or did hallucinogens or ayahuasca. I had the complete opposite. I had abandonment written into every chapter of my life from birth until now at forty-seven years of age.

What I've learned is that there is no one single recipe or solution to healing yourself and changing your life. We are all different and have our own karma to work through. Each of our journeys is unique and precious. I have friends that have experienced the Oneness and complete Nirvana and have seen the "other side," but still default back to their old patterns. Enlightenment takes not just knowledge, but the maturity, wisdom, mental and emotional strength and capacity to hold it.

There is this new culture emerging, I call it Pop Spirituality. It goes along with our cult, or culture that supports immediate gratification. There are so many people jumping on the New Age Heal Your Life Spiritual Bandwagon that it sort of demeans the journey and takes the sacredness out of it. While I believe that instantaneous healing is possible, I also feel that books with titles like Seven Steps to Instant Transformation can be misleading. They can make you feel even more like a failure if you go through the steps and are still stuck.

No one ever tells you in self help books that the process of healing your life and real change takes years and years of ups and downs, many challenges and trials and tribulations. It could mean getting your heart broken open and maybe even smashed into a thousand pieces over and over again. It could mean many dark nights of the soul. It's not pretty and it's certainly not easy. From my experience, lasting healing is like taking two steps forward and one step back, like the game we used to play as children, remember Mother May I?

But who would want to buy a book with the title, *"Healing Your Life, It's Painful, It Sucks, It Will Rip Your Heart Out and Smash It Into a Million Pieces and Question Your Very Existence."*

I remember one day sitting on the couch feeling proud of my-self because I got through a few nights without being depressed after Soulmate#3 walked out on me. I called my spiritual friend who was like a mom to me to tell her about my accomplishment. She, however, did not share in my enthusiasm, "Don't think you are there yet. You can go right back."

Total Debbie downer. I was annoyed at her, bursting my bubble like that. But she was right. I was right back down in the dumps the next week. We heal one part of our life then it comes back around to re-visit us and we get to heal it again and then it comes back around again, but only this time it's a little easier and then it gets easier and easier as we let go and release our pain and burden. Onion healing. Maybe that's why we cry when we cut onions?

***Send in the Clowns

> "Being gloomy is easier than being cheerful. Anybody can say 'I have cancer' and get a rise out of the crowd. But how many of us can do five minutes of good stand-up comedy?" ~P.J. O'Rourke

I have been a serious person my whole life, my sense of humor buried deep. I guess that's what happens when you are sensitive empath growing up in my world, just trying to survive and protect my big, loving heart. I even had "back up proof" that supported my belief that I was sad.

When I was pregnant, I had to see a hematologist because I have Thalassemia Minor, a genetic blood disorder, which the doctors did not uncover until I was 21. It took five years of doctor visits to try to find out why I was suffering from low iron and fatigue at such a young age. Most doctors just assumed it was anemia, and gave me iron supplements, which did nothing but make me constipated. It wasn't until I went to a doctor in Florida who asked me my nationality, and realizing I was half Italian, the lightbulb came on.

Apparently Thalassemia Minor occurs chiefly among people of Mediterranean descent, (and you thought only good food, coffee and romance comes from the Mediterranean). Thanks, Mom.

Thalassemia is caused by faulty synthesis of part of the hemoglobin molecule. The hematologist explained I actually have less red blood cells than the average person and the red blood cells are what transport oxygen to the cells. On top of that, my blood cells are shaped differently than the normal. I always have to be different.

When I first saw my red blood cells under a microscope at the hematologist's office and saw that they were shaped like tear drops, I thought *no wonder I am so sad, even my blood is crying.* And that folks, became my reality.

On a positive note, when my live blood was analyzed through microscopy twelve years later the nutritionist announced, "Wow, I have never seen white blood cells like this before!" Apparently my white blood cells were making up for my red. It turns out I have a kick-ass immune system. Way to go white! Silver lining all the way.

> "According to the overall way that we interpret the meaning of events, the same situation may be tragic or comic. Physiologically speaking, in the choice of attitude, one chooses between anabolic endorphins or catabolic adrenaline." ~*Power vs. Force*

***Kooky Angels

> "Seriousness is the glue that holds suffering together." ~Elizabeth Keiffer

As I started to heal an unexpected thing began happening. I started to laugh again. I found my sense of humor and actually began having fun. It was during one of my first angel readings that I became cognizant of my waking funny bone. When you go for an angel reading for the first time you don't really expect the guide to bust out laughing, this is serious stuff we're talking about, right? Still chuckling, she said my angels were just like me- quirky with a kooky sense of humor. Apparently they were having a blast entertaining her with silly antics, imitating me in a loving wacky way. She explained that our guardian angels can tend to take on our personality.

I don't think it's a coincidence that the word Light, being light, and having a light heart all mean the same thing. Being able to let go of the seriousness and finding humor even in the most tragic situations is a gift. I discovered how a *sliver* of humor even in the worst case scenarios can shift the energy and bring relief. I used to think that it was disrespectful and of course there is a time a place for humor and laughing, but it is an art to be able to lighten up the seriousness. Laughter heals. The way I monitor my progress in this journey of mine is whether I am laughing or not. In the end, it's all just temporary anyway. You gotta have a good time while you're here.

One of the best compliments I received was when I was suffering through my abandonment breakup with Soulmate#3. My close friend said, "I know your heart is suffering now, but you still have a sense of light about you." And most recently from one of my yoga students, "Truly thankful for having you as my teacher. I know you're in pain but you're still radiating so much light! I'm always shaking at the end of your classes from the vibrant energy that you fill the room with. Stay strong and trust the journey."

That's when you know you have arrived, *at least for now...* when you can still be light and a source of joy, even in the midst of extreme sorrow. Like Swami Beyondananda says, "If we take laughter seriously we can take seriousness humorously."

I make myself laugh more than anyone. I have a great time by my-self. I read once in an astrology book from my date of birth that I might be the most interesting person I will ever meet. Lord, I hope not. Still, I don't need to be entertained, my life is entertaining enough. After all the only person we are guaranteed to be with forever and through eternity is ourself! We need to like ourself, be our own best friend and laugh at ourself. I am constantly making silly jokes and comments and cracking myself up. I do start to get a little worried, however, when I realize not only do I talk to myself but I answer myself as well. That's starting to get borderline weird maybe.

> "We're all bozos on the bus, so we might as well sit back and enjoy the ride." ~Wavy Gravy clown-activist

No matter what your title, role, occupation, status, we are all in the same boat, we all struggle, we all have issues, dysfunctions, we are all a mess yet we are all perfect at the same time. That is the irony of the human-divine condition. Honoring all of it is the beauty of life.

*** The Open Secret

"Let's bring the fun back in dysfunction." ~ Lisa Gayle

In a way we have all experienced abandonment. I don't know of one person who has grown up in a perfect family. We live in a dysfunctional world and our families and we are a reflection of that dysfunction. Even the families I grew up with that I thought were the perfect "Brady Bunch" family only appeared that way on the outside. There was just as much dysfunction I came to learn later, it was only hidden.

During my divorce I found much comfort in Elizabeth Lesser's book, *Broken Open,* so much that I slept with it every night, hoping the words of wisdom would magically sink into my brain during my slumber. Just to know that other people are as messed up as me was a healing balm to my soul. Jalaluddin Rumi, a thirteenth century mystic poet whose writing is still just as potent and fresh today, refers to the masks we wear as the Open Secret, which shows up in our life from simple interactions to deep dysfunction. Our typical exchange of greetings goes something like this, "Hi how are you?" They say, "Well." You ask, "How are the kids?" They say "Great, everyone is well." "The job?" They respond, "Fine, all good." Then they ask the same questions back and you walk away thinking they have it all together and their life seems so perfect, what's wrong with me? Not that we want to hear everyone's dirty laundry, but it would behoove us to remember no one's life is perfect, everyone has their own issues and dysfunctions and deep down we know that.

When I was going through my divorce, I walked around like a wounded wet noodle, heartbroken and depressed. Only my close friends knew how I was feeling. With everyone else I did the ole cover up, "Fine, well, everything is good," smiling on the outside but dying on the inside.

One time though I was moved to open up with the truth to a Starbucks employee who was taking my coffee order. I was wearing a cheery sweatshirt to compensate for my dreary mood that said, "The Sun Shines for Everyone." Fake it till you make it, was the only thing at that point I was capable of doing.

She made a nice comment about it and I courageously replied that the sun didn't shine for me anymore, that I was going through a divorce and my heart was broken. Her sunny disposition immediately went solemn as she shared that she went through a similar experience and knew how I felt. She proceeded to give me a cup of coffee on the house with a genuine heartfelt smile and said, "Things will get better."

While I know this didn't cure my broken heart, in that moment I felt like the sand bag of sadness was a little lighter and I could breathe again. There was a crack of light that entered my heart, and knew that the sun would indeed shine on me again. If we could just string together these kind and tender moments where we are open and real and sharing in our trials and tribulations of our humanness then perhaps the world would not seem like such a cold, lonely and harsh place. When we are unguarded and vulnerable we allow others to be the same and in that moment the world is lifted to a little higher vibration.

*** Never Make Assumptions

A simple act of kindness and generosity can make a huge difference in someone's life. One of my first private yoga clients back in 2003 showed me the power of being present and kind. A few years had gone by after we stopped doing yoga but we remained good friends. One night at the dinner table after I had introduced him to my new husband, he proceeded to tell him the story of how we met and how we started yoga together.

I was on the treadmill at Gold's Gym and he was working out with the weight machines. I noticed him right away as he had taken a couple of my yoga classes, but that day I noticed he was wearing something unusual: sweatpants with very expensive looking Italian dress shoes. *Odd outfit to work out in* I thought. We made eye contact and he came over to me, asking me how I was. I was not good and told him so. (That was the time Soulmate #2 walked out on us). My openness prompted him to share his story of woe. We bonded, became fast friends and he hired me to come to his home twice a week to teach him yoga. Many times his three kids would join in as well. I became part of the family and spent a lot of time with them outside of yoga sessions as well.

He enjoyed telling this part of our story. Then he became somber and said to my husband that I saved his life. At first I thought he was kidding, but I realized he was serious as he went on to explain how he was going through a dark time with his divorce and three kids, his entire world crumbling down around him when I showed up. Speechless, I had no idea that I made that much of an impact. I knew he was struggling, but I didn't know how bad.

That's why we can never make assumptions about people. On the outside he seemed to be ok. He had material wealth and success, usually a smile on his face, but inside he was hurting, worse than I thought. We never really know what 's going on within a person.

That experience taught me so much. Besides never judging a book by its cover, it taught me about the power of kindness and going the extra mile, which I did with the books I brought him, the poems I read to him, the inspiration I imparted to keep him going. I was new to teaching yoga then and was constantly working on my skills as a yoga teacher. I realized that didn't matter as much as me showing up every Tuesday and Thursday morning at 7am at his house with a smile on my face and a caring heart. It's not about what you know, it's about who you are.

*** Your Presence is Enough.

That truth showed up in my yoga classes as well. Being a conscientious yoga teacher, I was focused on fitting all the poses I could cram in, with the different modifications for each student in one hour. I wanted my yoga classes to be pleasing for everyone, which is an impossible task I've come to learn. Then I received a message from my angels, "Just your presence alone is enough."

Oh what a relief! "Thanks God, needed that one." We become frantic when we think we have to do something or so many things to be worthy to make a difference. The fact is if you are the light, just by being you, your presence automatically uplifts and heals.

What I've come to learn is that my job at any given time as a light worker and citizen of the world is to be as present as possible, living from my heart and not my head, in harmony with my higher self, in harmony with God, being love and shining light. The logistics of how, when, who, where, is not my job. That is the Universe's job when I'm in alignment with my highest self, serving the greatest good of all. I also stopped trying to change people or change their minds. That is also not my job. Once I made this decision, I became more peaceful and took back energy that was needlessly being siphoned away.

My primary job is to be the light. My secondary job is through whatever means I am expressing my light with, whether it's consulting, waitressing, teaching yoga, cleaning houses, parenting, etc. Once the divine foundation is set, all else falls into place with ease and grace.

***Go the Extra Mile

The financial world served my soul as I took the advice to heart from, *The Greatest Salesman in the World*, by Og Mandino: Go the extra mile.

This is a rare practice in today's cut throat world where people are trying to get as much as possible with giving as little as possible, thinking they will get ahead this way. The opposite is true however.

When I first implemented this philosophy as a financial consultant, every time a customer opened an account with me whether it was for $500 or $50,000, I sent a hand written thank you card, a rare and precious practice. While I can't say if this had an immediate affect on my sales, I believe it helped. Give and give thanks, gratitude is the attitude. When I went back to work waitressing a few years ago, at the bottom of each check I would hand write, "thank you" with a heart and my name. It took time especially when restaurant was busy. A grateful heart creates abundance.

In any endeavor or business, the way to stand out and be a success is that simple philosophy, leave people with an increase; in other words, when you walk away from them you have imparted something to them and they have more than they had before they met you. It could be as simple as a warm smile or greeting, encouraging words, a positive wish or intention, a compliment, or an act of kindness. If you feel successful, you will leave them feeling successful. Happiness is contagious.

Everything we do, whether its investing people's money, serving their food, or showing up at their house for yoga, when it's done sincerely and with love, people feel it. In our superficial busy world of doing, it's nice to be recognized and seen and to feel like you matter. Kindness is contagious; it's the stuff people gravitate towards.

When I'm at a crossroads I encourage myself with: "Go the extra mile." It pays off every time. My life is full of blessings, love and kooky angels.

***God's Calling, You Better Answer the Phone!

As I look back on my life, I see that even though I had a rough start and not a whole lot of support from family in the traditional sense, I was always surrounded by an "entourage of angels," random people who went out of their way to show me kindness or help in some way. Angel Intervention at its finest.

It was like God said to my soul, "Alright kid, this lifetime is going to be a bitch. Are you ready for it?" "Yes," I said. And God replied, "Of course you are, because you are a brave and loving soul and willing to give of yourself to help others. You are going to forget who you are and you will be in search of real love for a big part of your life.

You are going to go down to some pretty dark places. It' s going to be so hard at times that you will even think about taking your own life from the miraculous physical vessel that your soul is in. But you are a strong soul, and you will always have a connection back to me and all the other souls cheering you on.

You must pay attention and listen though. We will always be by your side and we will send you nothing but angels. We will be whispering in your ear to get up and that we love you and have never left you.

And one day you will realize that your search is over because love is who you are. Then when you come to that brilliant and wonderful realization, you, the generous and loving soul will want to share that with everyone.

And know that in your innocent spirit, not everyone will be ready to hear your message. But don't give up, because there will be enough souls ready to hear what you have to share. And your light and your soul fire will ignite their light and their soul fire. And together you will bring peace and harmony back upon this beautiful planet earth."

***Authenticity

I've been consciously on the spiritual path for sixteen years now and I don't claim to be an expert on anything. The biggest room is the room for improvement, I believe. Yet I know within I have everything I need. That is the conundrum of being a spiritual being in a human form. We have everything we need within, yet we are always going to be a work in progress or rather, a masterpiece in progress.

I heard some good advice once, "Teach what you know." What do I know?

What I know for sure is that if I can transform my life from anger, pain, pity, poverty, abandonment, fear and worry into a life of fulfillment, inner peace, joy, gratitude, great health, surrounded by love, living my truth and divine purpose, that it is possible for you as well. It is possible for anyone because we are the same.

And while everyday is not perfect by far; I still go down into that dark place time and again, the time I spend there is minutes versus days, weeks, months and years. I spend more time happy and peaceful than stressed out and angry. Progress:)

Success is measured in not what you have, but what you have to overcome.

***Yellow Submarine

During a healing session/angel reading with my Reiki teacher, out of the blue her computer came on and started playing music. She turned around and said, "That's strange."

I was surprised that she would think something like that was strange. In our "woo-woo" world these things happen on a regular. I looked at her in confusion and she said, "It's strange because I don't have this song on my playlist."

Oh, that changes things. She tuned in to Spirit and said, "This song is for you." I knew that already though; it was a song I chanted during my long distance swims, which she had no knowledge of.

"Your angels want you to know that when you go down to that dark place of despair and you feel like you're alone and drowning, remember, just like a submarine rises back to the surface, you too will emerge and rise back to the top."

Another speechless teary eyed moment. And that is why I love God and my angels so much. I could not have been given a more perfect message. Every time after that when I felt like I was going down to that dark, scary place, I just started to hum "Yellow Submarine" (by the Beatles) and remembered I would rise back up.

*** We Are the Cage and We Are the Key

"We live in a world that worships limitations." ~ Tama Kieves, Author

During my St. Ignatius retreat, one of the insights I arrived at was why we continue to do things that cause us suffering. "Do you want to be in the passion or the resurrection?" asked my spiritual director. We are so used to the struggle and suffering that it becomes our comfort zone. When we are given an opportunity to escape we let it pass us by. Why? *It's what we're used to.*

It reminds me of the story of the elephants. They were trained to remain in place by having a shackle placed on one leg, which was then chained to a big tree. Neither the shackle, nor the tree, was going anywhere. After a period of time, the trainers would remove the chain from the tree, but leave the shackle on the elephant's foot. The elephant, technically free to roam about, stayed in place, having been conditioned to do so.

We are conditioned just like the elephant. One of the most important things we forget is that we are free. We are free to make our own choices, to think what thoughts we choose, to experience anything we would like to. It's the rote routine, conditioning and programming that keeps us shackled. We become bound by the mental and emotional shackles that we keep around our mind and our heart. Albert Einstein said the intuitive mind is a sacred gift and the rational mind is a faithful servant. We have created a society that honors the servant and has forgotten the gift.

> "Emancipate yourself from mental slavery. None but ourselves can free our minds." ~Bob Marley

The entire world is based on our own projection which stems from our beliefs and thoughts. That is why Yoga does not bother much about changing the outside world. There is a sanskrit saying, "Mana eva manushyanam karanam band mokshayoho." "As the mind, so the man; bondage or liberation are in your own mind."

Maybe that's how Nelson Mandela, one of my inspirations, managed to spend twenty seven years in a tiny prison cell, subjugated to physical, mental and emotional suffering, only to get out and become one of the greatest leaders of all time and president of South Africa. He was practicing yoga and probably didn't even know it. And we complain because we get caught in traffic on the Long Island Expressway.

This poem was Nelson Mandela's favorite... When he lost courage, when he felt like giving up, lying down and not get up again, he would recite it. The words would give him what he needed to keep going.

INVICTUS by William Ernest Henley (1849-1903)

Out of the night that covers me,
Black as the pit from sole to sole,
I thank whatever Gods may be
For my unconquerable soul.

In the fell clutch of circumstance
I have not winced nor cried aloud,
Under the bludgeoning of chance
My head is bloody, but unbowed.

Beyond the place of wrath and tears
Looms but the horror of the shade,
And yet the menace of the years
Finds, and shall find, me unafraid.

It matters not how strait the gate,
How charged with punishments the scroll,

I AM THE MASTER OF MY FATE:
I AM THE CAPTAIN OF MY SOUL.

***Walk your Talk, Fly your Vision

While we are on this earth plane in human form with an ego, the spiritual journey and the internal battle will never end. Most of the growth will be in relationship with others. That is the other thing I learned. There's only so much growth I can do sitting in my bedroom in lotus pose reading a good spiritual book.

The real growth comes when we take that spiritual knowledge and apply it in our relationships, then and only then can we really transform.

That's when we become as Emmet Fox says, the **"salt of the earth and the light of the world."**

The journey from your head to your heart or your mind to your soul is the longest journey you can make, even though it's the shortest distance. It's not just enough to know the path, it's about walking the path. But you have to know it first.

Kids today know it. They are born knowing it and walking it. As screwed up parents and adults we mess them up by allowing them to forget it. Then we spend our adult life having to unlearn what we learned and then re-learn what we already knew, (loosening and unraveling the threads, then weaving them back together again).

Hopefully we can get it right for the next generation, so they won't have to spend so much time in therapy to figure out that they are the love they are searching for and that they are perfect, whole and complete just as they are. Then maybe the next generation will be born flying and forgo walking all together!

Many children coming to the planet now are here not to "fit in" but to break out, break out of the invisible walls that we have created around our minds, our hearts, our lives, and to create a new way of being and living that is congruent with our soul. The are the truth showers, the light and the way.

I think it's our responsibility to honor children and their dreams, as well as to honor the child in each one of us and our dreams. Just as there is a purity and innocence within each child that we strive to nurture and protect, we must do the same with our own inner child. When we open our mind to the gift of imagination and curiosity of the child within, our lives become magical again, full of wonder and excitement. It is our soul, the purity of the divine that keeps our light shining.

"Logic will take you from A to B but imagination will take you all over the world." ~Wayne Dyer

***Dream Big Baby

"The true sign of intelligence is not knowledge but imagination." ~Einstein

At the end of one of one of my spiritual sessions my teacher told me my homework was to dream big and to journal it. She said not to let limitations in my mind stop me from dreaming my biggest, wildest dreams. You would think this would be a fun assignment, but for me it was torture. "Dream big," those two words drove me mad.

I went home that day and had a blank screen in my mind as I sat in front of a blank page of paper. Limitations were what I knew. I hadn't thought about my dreams since I was a child. Life just took such a beating on me that dreams were no where to be found.

I had been functioning in a limited way of thinking for so long that those treads in my brain were etched deep. Learning how to jump out of those grooves and create new ones was a slow process, like waking up a sleeping giant. Slowly, years later, my dreams started to re-emerge into my awareness. I am living one of them now, writing this book.

I also remembered when I was a child I used to imagine myself standing at a podium in front of thousands of people giving an inspirational speech that moved people to heal themselves and the world. This coincided with what Blanche told me in my first astrology reading, public speaking for the masses. Maybe we don't have dreams, maybe they have us?

However, along with the dormant parts of my mind that I hadn't used in years, something else started to awaken from the dark depths of muck: deep rooted doubt and insecurity. I heard them say, "That's pretty grandiose of you, saving the world. Who do you think you are?" That voice was always there! How could I make it stop?

I had this framed poem on my wall since I was twenty one. I didn't fully grasp the message, but something in me resonated with it. It was attributed to Nelson Mandela's 1994 inaugural speech. It wasn't until twenty years later when I discovered Marianne Williamson that I realized it was hers.

> "Our deepest fear is not that we are inadequate.
> Our deepest fear is that we are powerful beyond measure.
> It is our Light, not our darkness, that most frightens us.
> We ask ourselves, who am I to be brilliant, gorgeous, talented and fabulous?
> Actually, who are you not to be?
> You are a child of God. Your playing small doesn't serve the world.
> There's nothing enlightened about shrinking so that other people won't feel insecure around you.
> We were born to make manifest the Glory of God that is within us.
> It's not just in some of us; it's in everyone.
> And as we let our own Lights shine,
> we unconsciously give other people permission to do the same.
> As we are liberated from our own fear,
> our presence automatically liberates others."

I get it now. I was shrinking my whole life.

We live in a world where the scales have been off balance for a long time. We value information over revelation; fitting in over

dreams and passion; technology (machines) over Spirit (God); the love of power over the power of love.

PETAL 5

Yoga Philosophy

***The Three Gunas

EINSTEIN SAID IF you want to understand everything better, just look at nature. We have moved so far away from our true nature that we've forgotten how important it is to have time to enjoy the fruits of our labor. We are still acting as if we're living in survival mode from caveman times. Meanwhile we have all the abundance and resources to feed and shelter the entire population, but only a small percentage live at that level. Most of us are still acting and living in the rat race in survival mode because it is what we were born into or what we learned, to work hard and stay busy.

Guna in yoga (hindi) translates to quality. There are three qualities or state of being:

1. Rajas is the keeping busy, doing guna.
2. Tamas is the unconscious state of being where we "check out" by over drinking, sleeping, watching excess tv, shopping, eating, etc.
3. Sattwa is the happy guna where we are just being in our joy

When birds wake up in the morning the first thing they do is sing; they're in their sattwa guna. After their song, then they go to work, searching for worms or food: rajas guna. After work they sleep: tamas guna.

After Eugene committed suicide one of the first things I did was take a trip to the Roosevelt Field Mall, the largest mall on Long Island, and go on a shopping spree. I had no business going there and buying anything. I didn't have extra money, but what I did have were a lot of credit cards.

I sat in my car and waited for the mall to open. As soon as it did I went from store to store buying whatever I liked, even if I didn't need it. If was the first time I shopped without looking at the price tags. After my arms were full I walked out to my car, dropped the shopping bags in the trunk and went back in for more. I did this all day until the mall closed.

When I arrived back home my Jehovah's Witness neighbors downstairs helped bring my bags upstairs and I remember him mumbling under his breath, "This is not good, this is not good." I didn't care. I was numb and in shock and this day brought a little relief to the constant torture of my soul.

I was in *tamas gunas.* Retail therapy is how I checked out and thought I was finding happiness and relief, but at the end of the day all it brought me was anxiety. Ask me a year later what I bought that day at the mall and I wouldn't remember; but I remember the bills because I was still paying them off.

***Water your Spiritual Garden

Hans Selye, a Hungarian-Canadian scientist, coined the term "stress" and developed the idea of two "reservoirs" of stress resistance. The two reservoirs are our little tank and our big tank. We need to fill up our little tank every day so when major things happen like moving, divorce, death, having babies, marriage, etc., we won't have to dip into the reserves or our big tank. If we don't fill up our little tank daily and we are constantly dipping into the reserve tank, you know what happens? Illness, injury, disease and finally...DEATH.

We all have stress in our lives. As long as we are human living here on this earth in this century, expect stress. Stress can be healthy, if we have the right dosage. Stress can motivate us to take action and get things done. The danger lies when we are living in a state of ongoing, unrelieved stress.

We need to fill up our little tank and cultivate the Sattwa guna, the one we make our last priority or exclude all together. Watering our spiritual garden and nurturing our soul is something we cannot afford not to do. We have brainwashed ourselves into thinking that we don't have time, but when we participate in them, what it does is actually give us time.

I found this inspiring excerpt from the book: *Messages From Your Angels* by Doreen Virtue:

> "We have already talked with you about the importance of breath, exercise, and meditation, and we do not mean to nag you about this subject. That is why yoga is presented to you as a route to establish all of these conditions within a short timespan. When you engage in the practice of yoga, the rejuvenation establishes within you a great surge of energy. Establishing your yogic practices within a specific schedule makes the habit become second nature, which we highly recommend. We do urge you to consider some form of yoga practice, however that may come. For some, it will be on a casual basis, while others will consider it to be a necessary part of their lifeblood.
>
> Yogic practices were introduced long ago, and are only recently awakening in your lands. The practice now comes to you with an accumulation of prayers behind it-a force so great that by immersing yourself in its radiance, great transformation can take place. Those who originally practiced yoga sent prayers forward in time, asking that all who forever afterward conducted yoga, would receive those prayers. When you engage in the practice of yoga, you are immersed in the river flow of those ancient prayers.
>
> You who are intimidated by the extent of your flexibility, hear our call: The yogic practice is a silent path that enriches you from within. Use it as a measure to center yourself peacefully, and not as a route to establish your "inferiority" or "superiority" to another.

> You, who are scheduled so tightly that you cannot bear to add to your load of duties, this is a call to greater awareness through installing a yogic practice. It is a miraculous example of receiving more through giving, in that the greater your devotion to your yogic practice, the more you do receive."

The most *common* excuse is: "I don't have the time." We all have the same amount of time in a day, how we prioritize our activities is a different story. Doing what you love adds time to your life, because the quality of your life changes.

The most *accepted* excuse is work. No one will give you a hard time if you back out of things for work. But if you're are not careful, staying busy with working can be another form of not taking care of yourself and avoiding the REAL work, working on yourself and having healthy relationships. If you are unhealthy and unhappy but you work a lot, what's the point? Our culture has made work and being busy high ideals to strive for. Backwards.

Time (linear time), according to Albert Einstein, is "an illusion of consciousness." Time is malleable actually. Shallow thinking and being in the rat race literally speeds up our experience of time, while deep and peaceful thinking and enjoying life slows it down. When people say to me. "I can't believe how fast time is going by," I reply, "Not in my life." A day in my life feels like an eternity.

We need to make choices that support our souls growth as well as our bank account. Some people are good at sattwa guna, they have no problem relaxing and spending time doing what they love to do. Being programmed to be productive I had to re-train myself to relax. I have to tell myself it's ok to have a day off and do nothing and just be. It's still a challenge for me, although I have much more balance in my life. Happy people are productive people and vibrate at a higher frequency attracting good circumstances. Life flows better when you are happy. Making yourself happy is not selfish, it's the opposite actually. You are closer to God when you're happy. There would be no more wars if everyone was happy. What would there be to fight about? Make love, not war.

***AA for Yogis: Asana Addiction

When I first was introduced to yoga I learned all about the postures, or poses (asanas). Being a very physical person I was immediately hooked. I found it to be quite challenging yet freeing at the same time. Yoga felt so damn good! Most exercise didn't leave you with the feeling that I had after a yoga class. My teacher said Astanga yoga, the primary series, was like having sex. It was scientifically designed to lead you through series of poses that raised your kundalini (life force energy lying dormant at the base of your spine), so by the last pose, shivasana, you were floating in bliss.

Who doesn't want that? But just like anything else there can be a danger in getting hooked to the "feel good." Over the course of the last sixteen years of teaching I saw how students and teachers turned in one vice or addiction and replaced it with yoga asana or circus yoga, as I heard it called once-only focusing on the body. While it might be a better addiction, there is still an imbalance if you are not dealing with the "stuff in the basement." If you still don't know who you are, don't have inner peace and are unfulfilled, I would submit that yoga postures have become another substitute for dealing with your issues.

Nice asana! It's easy to get caught up in the asana. Our culture supports physical looks over substance and integrity, the body over the soul. If we remember that we are not our body, rather we have a body, we wouldn't spend all of our time focused on our body and our physical looks. While it's important to care and honor your body instrument, if it has become the source of your meaning and fulfillment you will suffer. No matter how much exercise and diet and grooming we do, we all age and the body changes. Focus on the beautiful light within and allow that to shine out.

Let your light be the source of your joy. I read that in one country, (Siberia maybe, don't remember which), the elders are greatly respected and honored. When someone says, "You are looking old today," it's a compliment. I don't think we've come that far yet, but it's worth striving toward!

When I first started studying yoga I took notes on every workshop I went to. What stuck with me the most was the teacher who first planted the seed, "Yoga is the path to self-realization," to your true self. I wasn't sure exactly what that meant, but it resonated with me. Now that I "get it" I can understand how yoga teachers that want to teach the authentic meaning of yoga can get frustrated in our Western world. The commercialized yoga world has veered so far from that basic truth. For most Americans yoga is more about health and the physical body than spirituality. It has become (for the most part) a superficial form of exercise in our country. The western world has painted a picture that a yogi is someone really bendy and flexible and skinny. That might be part of it, but there are many "yogis" who don't do asana, or the physical part. I've been asked, "Is yoga like Pilates?" almost as much as I have been asked, "Are you Chinese?" And that can get pretty annoying.

That's ok though. You have to start somewhere and that is where I started. However, if you want to find lasting peace and happiness and be a soul on fire, progressing past the asana and going deep into the meaning of yoga is the path to be on. When you are a serious committed spiritual yogi, you don't do yoga, you *are* yoga. Yoga is a path to self-realization, a way of becoming that which you already are- divine, whole and complete.

***Eight Limbs of Yoga

"Yoga practice would be ineffectual without the concepts on which Yoga is based. It combines the bodily and the spiritual in an extraordinarily complete way. In the East, where these ideas

> and practices have developed, and where for several thousand years an unbroken tradition had created the necessary spiritual foundations. Yoga is, as I can readily believe, the perfect and appropriate method for fusing body and mind together so that they form a unity which is scarcely to be questioned. This unity creates a psychological disposition which makes possible intuitions that transcend consciousness." ~Dr. C.G. Jung, Swiss psychologist

The word yoga literally means to yoke or to join or unite. What are we yoking? Individually, we are yoking the different aspects of our being together- the physical, mental, emotional, energetic, and spiritual; or you can say we are yoking our human selves with our God selves. As a collective we are uniting in our consciousness. Yoga is a systematic integrative approach to wholeness and wellness. When we are united within ourselves we find unity in the external world.

According to Patanjali, the great sage who wrote the famous *Yoga Sūtras of Patañjali,* 196 Indian sūtras (aphorisms) from 400 CE that constitute the foundational text of Ashtanga Yoga, also called Raja Yoga, there are eight limbs in yoga that if one follows with devotion and perseverance will reach enlightenment. In the*Yoga Sūtras* there is only mention of asana or poses *three* times and it is the seated easy pose for meditation.

1. **Yama : Universal morality**
2. **Niyama : Personal observances**
3. **Asanas : Body postures**
4. **Pranayama : Breathing exercises, and control of prana**
5. **Pratyahara : Control of the senses**
6. **Dharana : Concentration and cultivating inner perceptual awareness**
7. **Dhyana : Devotion, Meditation on the Divine**
8. **Samadhi : Union with the Divine**

When I started astanga yoga, which is what I studied in India, I knew in the back of my mind that no matter how challenging putting two feet behind my head and balancing on my hands would be, changing my mind and thoughts were going to be a million times tougher. That was the thought I had when it came to any physical challenge, and that is what helped transform my body and my yoga practice.

***Yamas and NIyamas

The first two limbs that Patanjali describes, called the yamas and the niyamas, can also be looked at as universal morality and personal observances. They are the suggestions given on how we should deal with people around us and our attitude toward ourselves. The attitude we have toward things and people outside ourselves is yama, how we relate to ourselves inwardly is niyama. Both are concerned with how we use our energy in relationship to others and to ourselves. Notice they come before the asana, postures!

They are as follows:

Yama: how we relate to the external world.

1. Ahimsa: nonviolence, inflicting no injury or harm to others or to one's own self, nonviolence in thought, word and deed. Deeper meaning: the Rishis (Hindu sage and saints) in their wisdom defined love as Ahimsa.
2. Satya: non-illusion; truth in thoughts, word and actions. Deeper meaning: we know who we are, we are truth itself, we connect to true Self versus little self-image
3. Asteya: non-covetousness, to the extent that one should not even desire something that is one's own; non-stealing. Deeper meaning: we need nothing outside of ourselves to feel complete
4. Brahmacharya: abstinence or moderation, particularly in the case of sexual activity. Deeper meaning: we use our sexual energy to

regenerate our connection to our spiritual self. It also means that we don't use this energy in any way that might harm others.

5. Aparigraha: non-possessiveness; non-hoarding. Deeper meaning: letting go of fear based attachments, including people. Having less differences.

Niyama: how we relate to ourselves, the inner world.

1. Shaucha: purity of body through proper diet, cleanliness and exercise and purity of mind through positive thinking, good company, prayer and meditation
2. Santosha: satisfaction; satisfied with what one has, contentment with everything as is, good and bad. Deeper meaning: living in the present here and now, ability to tolerate and find an equanimous mindset within the world of duality
3. Tapas: self-discipline, spiritual heat or fire that burns away the self-image and ego and allows us to live from our higher self and not from our emotional reactions
4. Svādhyāya: self study and study of spiritual scriptures, which leads to introspection on a greater awakening to the soul and God within. While doing every day activities tuning in to be the observer or witness
5. Ishvarapranidhana: selfless service, dedicating all of one's efforts to God or to the greatest good of All, surrender to God; love, truth and faith must arise in one's heart in order to live in complete freedom, unaffected by uncertainty and the unknown.

A wonderful book on yoga that explains the yamas and niyamas in further depth on a practical level: *The Yoga of Relationships, A Practical Guide For Loving Yourself and Others* by Yogi Amrit Desai. One of his quotes on love: "Addictive love is transactional. Unconditional love is transformational. When love exists, communication of the highest order flows spontaneously. Flowing from heart to heart rather than from head to head, communication then becomes communion."

***"Yoga is the rocket ship to enlightenment." ~ Mokshapriya

> "Yoga, through which divinity is found within, is doubtless the highest road." ~Paramahansa Yogananada "

There are many paths to healing and wholeness. Yoga was my prescription. It was the combination of the physical and the spiritual that was so effective and transformative. Yoga is not about flexibility, well actually it is, flexibility of the mind. Closed rigid mind- closed rigid body.

Yoga practice metaphorically speaking is like a clogged pipe. There are two ways to unclog a pipe, one is to bang on it from the outside and the other way is to go in and pull the muck out.

The asana/body postures and the pranayama/breathing exercise is the outside way of unclogging our pipes. Meditation, **changing our thoughts and beliefs**, and waking up to who we truly are by integrating the Niyamas and Yamas is the inside way of unclogging our pipes. Doing both together is the most effective.

No matter how many classes or workshops we attend, how many downward dogs and chaturangas we do, they are not a substitute for the real work. They might help us to uncover parts of ourself that are imbalanced, but the real work is discovering for ourselves who were really are. It is not enough to have someone explain it or lay it out to us. Daily practice and processing, investigation into our true selves, meditation, self-reflection, and the most important: experience are the keys.

My interpretation of yoga is that it's a way back from your head and your thinking to your heart and your soul. Yoga provides the map. First is understanding the knowledge, the next is applying it to your life. Without integration there is no change. The ultimate goal of yoga is liberation or freedom (moksha). Foremost, reconciliation with yourself, then reconciliation with everyone and everything else. Only then comes true peace and lasting freedom.

> "But what original commentary can you supply, from the uniqueness of your particular life? What holy text have you absorbed and made your own? In what ways have these timeless truths renovated your nature? Are you content to be a hollow victrola, mechanically repeating the words of other men?" ~*Autobiography of a Yogi*

From *The Untethered Soul* by Michael A Singer:

> "Yoga is not really about getting your body healthy, although it does that too. Yoga is about the knowledge that will help you out of your predicament, the knowledge that can free you. Once you've made this freedom the meaning of your life, there are spiritual practices that can help you. These practices are what you do with your time in order to free Yourself from yourself. You will eventually catch on that you will have to distance yourself from your psyche. You do this by setting the direction of your life when you are clear and not let the wavering mind deter you. Your will is stronger than the habit of listening to that voice. There is nothing you can't do. Your will is supreme over all of this. If you want to free yourself, you must first become conscious enough to understand your predicament. Then you must commit yourself to the inner work of freedom. You do this as though your life depended on it, because it does. As it is right now, your life is not your own; it belongs to your inner roommate, the psyche."

Experiment: Close your eyes and mentally say "hello." Say it a few times, even yell it. Start to notice who is saying hello and who is observing? You are the observer or the witness behind the word hello. You are not the thought, the sound or vibration or the word hello. As soon as you can notice the difference between the awareness of you as the observer and the thought you are having, you are one step closer to freedom. Even if you didn't notice right away, keep at it. This is your ticket out of the madness.

You are the eternal witness, the conscious observer, the clear blue sky, timeless beauty, everlasting peace, infinite presence, radiant remembrance, enduring love, God's shining light.

***My Unconventional Dream

> "There is only one success...to be able to spend your life in your own way."
> ~Christopher Morley

I have made the world a better place with my choice to follow my heart. I have helped hundreds of people heal through my work, I have also healed myself. To me there's no dollar amount you can put on that. **It was an easy choice,** but I had to live in debt for many years, sacrificing and working hard. I chose to live simply and was committed to making it work. I raised a daughter by myself and created a successful business out of nothing.

> There were many times I wanted to give up. Being alone for the most part I had to find some source of inspiration, that is why I have read so many books and have so many quotes. I hung on to the echoes of the inspiring people before me, "Nothing in the world is worth having or worth doing unless it means effort, pain, difficulty... I have never in my life envied a human being who led an easy life. I have envied a great many people who led difficult lives and led them well." ~Theodore Roosevelt

When I quit my job as a financial consultant to follow my heart, I know many of my close friends poo-pooed my decision, going from a job making a six figure income to a tenth of that. Being successful according to Long Islanders and the "American Dream" is having the big house, expensive cars and a good steady career with benefits. I could have had all that, but when I started waking up I realized my dream of the nuclear family with the white picket fence wasn't my dream after all.

I used to feel shame because I was a "renter." In our country there's a certain stigmatism if you don't own a home. But looking back I am very happy with my choice. Not that there's anything wrong with being a homeowner or with money. Zig Ziglar used to say, "Money is not everything but it ranks right up there with oxygen." Money is not evil, like the paradigm we were brought up with, it's the "love" of money that causes evil- worshiping and cherishing money over people. I like money. Money helps me live a comfortable life and it helps me to help others. And by the way, money does grow on trees. It comes from paper!

It's important to keep things in perspective though. Even if you buy a house, you don't really own your house, the bank does; and even if you pay off the loan, you are in actuality only temporary custodian. You never truly own anything- when you die it doesn't come with you, and neither does your money. The illusion is that we own things and sometimes we think we own people as well. It's not that I'm against material things, they can be fun, as long as we keep the main thing, the main thing. No person, place, or thing can give you happiness. They may give you cause for temporary happiness, but the joy of living comes from within. Everything we need to be happy is already within us. The outer material world, including our body, is just the icing on the cake. We come into this life with nothing and leave with nothing but the love in our soul.

***Your Love is Enough

As I continued to dismantle my walls around my heart it was painful to look at myself and my behavior. Many times I wished I could go back to "sleep." This "waking up" thing was not fun I discovered. All those monsters that were lying low were now in my face with their taunts and jeers. I felt like a horrible mother and all I ever wanted to be was a good mother and have a solid relationship with my daughter, something I never had. I felt like a complete failure in the one thing that mattered to me the most. During one of my sessions with Weston motherhood came up.

He acknowledged my feelings of what I considered failure, but said to me, "Your dedication to your daughter, your love... that is enough."

"Your love is enough" was just the silver lining I needed to hear.

"My love is enough." replaced my mantra, "I am a bad mother." I would hear this message again five years later from another angel in my life, Elizabeth, who made me write it down on paper to get into my thick head. I have come to learn that even if we screw up as a parent and think we've screwed them up, if we love them and we are dedicated to them, **love will prevail**. Our love will be enough to carry them through. It will be the one thing that will stay with them through out their entire lives.

And the cool thing is it doesn't matter to a child if you're not their real parent. As long as there is one adult or one person supporting and loving them and being a mirror for them in a healthy way, that child will grow up to be healthy and happy.

As much as I made outer changes in my life to accommodate having a child and being there for her as much as possible, and worked on believing that "my love was enough," I still had unresolved pain that kept me from being emotionally available for my daughter. If all of a sudden God gave me a chance to go back in time to do one thing differently, I would pick the time I had with my daughter.

I thought at the time I was being a good Mom. I did all the things a good mom does for her child, take care of her, bathe her, feed her, clothe her, buy her things, shelter her, school her, take her to dance practice, go to teacher meetings, drive her to playdates, have sleepovers, birthday parties, etc.

However there are two kinds of present. One is the physical part, mechanical if you may, and the other is the emotional part. I might have been there for her to do all those things physically, but emotionally I was not present. How could I be fully present if I was not present for myself? Doing and being are two different energies.

Either my mind was preoccupied or I was in so much pain that it prevented me from enjoying the present moment, just sitting and playing dolls with her, for example. I thought to myself numerous times, *I can't wait until she's older so it's easier on me.*

Now I would do anything to turn back the clock and have that time with her once more, even to play Barbies, the one thing I despised, or to drive her to high school one more time, even with the yelling. It's so fleeting and precious. I miss her so much. Being a parent is heartbreaking. It tests you in every way. But I wouldn't trade any of it for the world.

My daughter, my inspiration and my teacher gave me a run for my money. At my wit's end, I sent my thirteen year old to Georgia to live with my friend and her family for eighth grade. They had three children of their own and were a strict nuclear family. I thought having the family stability would help straighten her out. I didn't want her to feel like I was abandoning her, but I was scared that I was screwing her up. She was at a crossroads in her life and I thought she needed an exemplary family situation.

When she came home after a year in Georgia her immediate response was no longer, "No," but "Yes Ma'am." Quite taken aback with this new development, I thought maybe her oppositional defiant disorder was cured at last. It was music to my ears! Lasted about two weeks, then she reverted right back to her old ways. **As I look back now that was probably because I was still in my old ways.**

When she was seven years old she used to say, "When I'm eighteen I'm moving out and getting my own apartment." Strong and independent, right from the get go, there was no telling that child what to do. One day Aiyana's aunt gave me counsel, "She's a hard child to parent now but when she gets older she will be fine on her own. You won't have to worry about her." I used to say to myself again, *I can't wait.*

When she graduated from high school and turned eighteen she did exactly what she said she was going to do at seven years old, move out and get her own apartment. Since she was familiar with Georgia that's where she decided to move. We drove her small Toyota Corolla down packed to the brim. There was no where to put your feet in the passenger side, she had so much stuff. Whoever was sitting shot gun had to sit in lotus pose. When I drove, which was most of the way I actually put one foot out the window just to stretch my legs. Thankfully I'm flexible!

I moved her into her first apartment then flew back to New York thinking I would feel free and light now that she was gone. Instead, I felt the complete opposite. I felt like I lost a limb, completely empty and sad inside. I cried everyday for a month.

I could no longer shop at Target, where we bought her school supplies, and any store that we shopped in regularly together became a walk down memory lane. It was heartbreaking event each time I went. I already didn't like food shopping, now it was dreadful. Only shopping for one person was totally depressing. When I walked past anything that she liked to eat I would start to cry. Even the pickle aisle made me cry, as I gazed at the bottle of sweet gherkins. I totally get the empty nest syndrome. It's real and it's a bitch.

When I see parents with their children now I so want to stop and say, *I know life can be hard and can wear you down, especially if you are a single parent, but trust me, you are going to miss them when they are gone. You will miss when they are young and innocent and want to hold your hand. Even when they are awful alien teenagers, you will miss that too. Hold on to them and don't let the moments pass you by. You can never get them back.*

I am so proud of my daughter. Even though we had some rough patches and there were definitely times when I wasn't sure what the outcome would be, I guess my love was enough after all. She has followed in my foot steps, following her dreams no matter what the naysayers say. She is a light worker and healer. She used to eat a pint of Ben and Jerry's for dinner, now she eats healthier than I do! She practices yoga, meditates, takes risks and is going for dreams of becoming a singer on top of going back to college. My daughter is so much like me and I am so proud of her.

I sold everything to pay for her move to Georgia then downsized to a studio apartment. The only thing I couldn't part with were my books, containers and containers of books! I go back to them and read over and over again. I use them in my yoga classes and whenever I feel lost and confused or sad, I pick one up and open to the right page with just the right message.

I am definitely attached to my books. I never jumped on board with the kindle thing. I like the feel of a book in my hands, to turn the pages and write notes as I am reading. I feel like my books carry a certain energy and I love having them around. They are like my children. Nerdy by nature, I am.

***4:15 am

After the breakup with Soulmate #2 I was going through a period of time when I was waking up at 4:15am every morning. *Strange* I thought, as I turned to look at my alarm clock, then at my book shelf next to my bed, noticing a dark blue hard cover book with gold lettering in line with my eyesight.

After about a week of this daily strange phenomena I finally got up, took the book off the shelf, having no idea where it came from, and opened it to this: "Several years ago, I found myself waking up at four-fifteen each morning, my eyes popping open as if on cue. Later, I learned that in days of old four-fifteen was considered the witching hour. How perfect, that seemed to me. We would all awaken at the same time and join with one another, and worship, and know."

Oh my Goddess! Someone was definitely trying to get my attention. If this wasn't a sign from above, I don't know what was. I sat in the infra-red sauna that day after yoga class, devouring every page. I still didn't know who Marianne Williamson was, but this book, *A Woman's Worth,* was shouting to me. This became a book I gave to every woman in my life.

It turns out that Marianne Williamson has been the most influential spiritual teacher in my life. She became the big sister/mother figure I never had. I engulfed myself in her books, CD's, and *A Course in Miracles.* She has made a tremendous difference in my life by reminding me of who

I really am. When I start to lose it, I just say to myself, *I need Marianne.* What I love about her books is that I can pick up any one of them, open to any page and read something profound that will bring me back to my center of sanity- same thing with her CD's or videos.

I think because I have always been open to receiving guidance from above it comes through very clearly and loudly. Communication is a two way street. We have to remember to ask and then we have to be *open, clear and quiet* to hear. We have to be **"paying attention."** Simple but practical spiritual advice.

***License Plates

I get many messages through license plates daily, too many to include here. One of them came during the writing of this book as I was anxiously questioning the universe what I should and shouldn't include. No sooner than I asked for guidance that I saw the license plate: **WRITE4U.**

Divine validation once again. This message reminded me of what I heard Krishna Das say once… that when he chants, he chants for himself. I was surprised at first thinking that was selfish, then I realized the wisdom. When you are true to yourself and do what makes your heart happy for you and God and no one else, that is the only way to be assured of true lasting happiness and peace. Seeking validation from others and being invested in their opinion, judgments and beliefs will always leave you disappointed and deflated. As my angel friend Elizabeth says: "Life is like a tray of hors d'oeuvres, not everyone likes quiche, but that doesn't make quiche bad." What I have to offer is not for everyone, but that doesn't make my message wrong. This has been one of my challenges in life as I constantly sought out the approval and acceptance of others. The real reason for that is because I didn't know who I was yet and I didn't love myself.

Once again I am reminded to go within to seek my sustenance and source my joy. God sees me and knows the innocence and purity of my heart; that's all that matters. When we are true to ourself, that inspires others to do the same. "The mediocre teacher tells. The good teacher explains. The superior teacher demonstrates. The great teacher inspires." (William Arthur Ward) That's what it's all about! To thine own **divine** self be true.

Along with this much needed message from God, one of the most breath-taking validations I received from a license plate was during my divorce.

*** Guidance and Grace

Even though I knew we were going to be officially divorced, when I finally received the divorce papers in the mail, it was still a blow to my heart. I was sitting in my car in the Macy's parking lot after finishing some Christmas shopping, talking on the phone with my spiritual director and told her I had a little gift for her. For Christmas that year I took a poem that my husband gave me, made copies of it and gave it to my close friends. When I got off the phone I broke down and cried, the finality of the end sinking in. As I was pulling out of the parking lot in tears, a car cut in front of me. I almost had a heart attack as I read the license plate: GUIDANCE. This is the poem Soulmate #3 gave me that I gifted that year:

Dancing with God

When I meditated on the word GUIDANCE, I kept seeing "dance" at the end of the word.
I remember reading that doing God's will is a lot like dancing.
When two people try to lead, nothing feels right.
The movement doesn't flow with the music,
And everything is quite uncomfortable and jerky.
When one person realizes that, and lets the other lead,

Both bodies begin to flow with the music.
One gives gentle cues, perhaps with a nudge to the back,
Or by pressing lightly in one direction or another.
It's as if two become one body, moving beautifully.
The dance takes surrender, willingness, and attentiveness from one person and gentle guidance and skill from the other.
My eyes drew back to the word Guidance.
When I saw "G: I thought of God, followed by "u" and "I".
"God", "u" and "I" dance."
God, you, and I dance.
As I lowered my head, I became willing to trust that I would get guidance about my life.
Once again, I became willing to let God lead.
My prayer for you today is that God's blessings and mercies be upon you on this day and everyday.
May you abide in God as God abides in you.
Dance together with God, trusting God to lead and to guide you through each season of your life.

My tears of sorrow turned to tears of joy as I realized once again that I am not alone and that I am always being watched over. This is what I call GRACE...the feeling that God is holding you, embracing you, enveloping you, suspended in the very fabric of love. Time stands still, thinking stops, and knowing begins, knowing in your heart beyond a shadow of a doubt that you are loved and you matter, you matter, you matter. Amen.

*** Karma's Wings

"Your attitude determines your altitude."

Six months after my daughter moved to Georgia she asked to have Karma. I was pretty adamant that Karma was not going to live with her in Georgia. Aiyana's persistence won however, and I gave in. Concerned that my daughter was lonely living alone, I un-eagerly flew Karma down to Atlanta and said good-bye.

Since I no longer had the obligation and responsibility of a kid and now a dog, I thought I would be a free spirit party girl. However, the opposite was true. It was empty nest syndrome all over again, but worse. I was even more depressed I think, no child or puppy to care for. I was alone and it sucked. I didn't get off the couch, only to work and swim. I was driving my swim coach crazy. He encouraged me to get Karma back.

Finally, after five months I couldn't take it anymore. I wasn't sure if my daughter was giving her the attention Karma needed anyway and I was getting strong gut guidance to bring her home. My daughter reluctantly agreed. As usual she didn't want to see me sad. The day I flew home with Karma was an emotional day at the airport. My daughter and I were crying and if Karma could cry I'm sure she would have.

We had an issue with the plane, apparently Karma's carrier was too big to fit under the plane seat on the second flight. Already in an emotional state I fought to keep the tears back; I just wanted to get home. The airline clerk seeing my distress managed to get us on a flight that would accommodate Karma in her dog carrier non-stop to New York with another airline, no charge. I was so grateful for her kindness. She replied, "Anyone who rescues a dog is a good person in my book."

Relieved, I walked on the plane smiling and immediately received a look of disdain from the airline attendant. He scorned, "You know the dog has to stay in the carrier right?" "Yes, I know," I said, the pit in my stomach returning.

When he came over to take our drink orders he still had an attitude. I had the carrier unzipped so Karma could look out and breathe. He ordered me to zip it up. *He's obviously not a dog person*, I begrudged, starting to get a "tude" right back at him.

This was going to be a long flight. Ok, I have to take control of this situation. I could react with an attitude like the old me would have done or I could try to shift the scenario. I am the creator of my reality so let's put this metaphysical stuff into practice.

I closed my eyes, entered my inner sanctuary and thought, *he could be having a bad day, you have no idea what is going on in his life, people respond better to sweetness and kindness than rudeness and shortness.* I meditated on sending him love and positive vibes from my heart for the next few minutes.

He came back for another drink order and asked if Karma would like some water. Surprised, I said, "Yes please." Then he asked me her name. I couldn't believe it, a definite change in his attitude.

The next time he came around, I took a chance and had the carrier unzipped in the front again to give her some air and he said nothing. *Wow this stuff really works,* I excitedly thought.

When I arose to use the bathroom, the nice people next to me said they would watch her. As I was walking down the aisle I heard some murmurs and slight commotion behind me. I stopped, looked back and gasped. In the aisle was Karma, she had escaped out of her carrier and was following me to the bathroom.

I looked up and met the eyes of the flight attendant. Afraid that I would be reprimanded or something worse like arrested for misconduct, I stopped dead still in the aisle. He smiled and waved. Whew! I grabbed Karma, put her back in her carrier, went back to the bathroom and everybody was happy.

By the end of the flight this attendant was a completely new person... full of smiles, asking me personal questions, and seeming genuinely interested. He even asked for my business card. He offered more water to Karma and the final validation that we are powerful creators of our reality was when he said, "Here, these are for Karma," and handed me a Delta pin of angel wings.

I walked off the plane beaming and proud of myself. I turned the situation around with love and intention. The intellectual knowledge became physical manifestation through the integration of my thoughts, feelings and actions. Each one of these demonstrations builds our confidence in knowing the truth of who we are. We are the creators of our masterpiece. We are the Michelangelo's of our life and we are sculpting our life with our thoughts and the energy we are emitting.

PETAL 6

Beloved

My story interrupted...what do you do when you think you have arrived and found true love finally only to be blindsided...again?

My step-monster not only introduced me to the world of asking for what you want, but the song, *I Want to Know What Love Is,* by Foreigner. This song quickly became the anthem of my life which I have downloaded in every possible version by every possible artist over the years. In fact, when Krishna Das released his version in 2014, I decided to make it my wedding song. I should say "we," my Beloved and I decided.

Yes I met someone, my true love. It has been a beautiful and amazing journey filled with so much love and healing, and growth. When you ask God or the Universe to heal you, He/She will bring you just the right partner to do that with because there's only so much healing you can do by yourself, I have learned, again.

I didn't see this one coming, of course we never do. All of my intuitive friends told me this was a soulmate, "a monumental relationship," true love, that we had been together for many lifetimes and we chose to be together now in this lifetime, that he was someone who wanted to journey with me and create a life with me, and that is was rare to find a partner with the same intention and vision. Not only did we fall in love, we had confirmation from Spirit that this was truly a "binding relationship of the light." That was the icing on the cake for me. Looking back I made the assumption that since we were destined to be together *now*, it would last. I was convinced he was "The One."

I started my journey writing this book while we were together and I planned on spending the rest of my life with him, as I thought he was planning on the same. He was committed to me and to us, at least that's what he said. I just began to let my guard down and let love enter. It takes me a while to open my heart to someone, no surprise there with everything I've been through.

As I am sitting here writing my book about how I healed my abandonment issue, how I found my happy ending with my Beloved, which I read to him with tears streaming down his face, he LEAVES me. I can't believe this is really happening. It is so ironic I have to laugh, but I'm not, I'm crushed and I'm crying.

I am getting strong messages from my angels to write, to journal what I am going through, that this is happening for a reason. I trust in God and my intuition so I continue to write, but in the present tense as I am experiencing what I am going through.

I thought I was healed of my abandonment issue, but I guess not. How many f'in times do I have to go through this pain? I don't know if my heart can take this anymore.

We have been through so much in this last year and a half. We have had many ups and downs, mostly ups, from my perspective. We have grown so much. I have become a part of his family, staying at his house more than my apartment, gradually moving my stuff in. I even have a key to his house. I have grown close to his children and his mother and have grown to love them. I feel like I'm part of his family and belong somewhere, again. We started making plans for our future together, opened a joint bank account and visited Florida, his idea, to check out if it would be someplace we'd be interested in living after his kids went to college. I really thought this was it for me-security at last.

I have let go of so many of my fears and insecurities. He knows that as well. We used to joke with each other by saying, "we are on the fast track to enlightenment with our relationship," or "relationship on steroids," or "here we grow again!"

But I guess it's not enough for him. I am still allowing negativity into our relationship. I am still poisoning our love. I know his saying to me that he doesn't have time for a relationship is an excuse. I think he's just trying to spare my feelings. What he really wants to say is that he doesn't have time to put up with my selfish angry demanding attitude and that instead of bringing peace and harmony into our relationship, I am bringing stress and anxiety. Not a fun way to live.

I realized after I got quiet and went into my inner sanctuary, I was not practicing what I was preaching. I said I wanted a love that was unconditional, healthy and free. My Beloved showed that to me and I did not give that back to him. I wanted to, but I guess there was a part of me that still wasn't able. I still had walls.

This is not the person I want to be. This is not the woman I want to be to my Beloved. This person is an imposter. This is the little me, the scared and lonely little girl that grew up with a scarcity of love that only knows one thing: "All the people in your life will leave you, you are disposable, no one wants you."

I am done with this paradigm. Time for an upgrade for good.

While it's super easy to go to fear and panic I know I must stay focused on what I truly desire to create in my life. This is my battle now. I oscillate between thoughts of us not being together and thoughts of a happy ending.

I try to stay in gratitude for it all. I know that I am a creative being and every positive or negative thought I have is creating my future, paving my way. I must stay positive. I need to be the one who stays awake. I know my Beloved is in his head right now, "analysis paralysis." I am trusting and praying everyday that he shifts into his heart.

Day 1. Monday May 18th

My Beloved stops by on his lunch hour from work and tells me he wants to be alone, and that he doesn't have time for a relationship. He says I'm too demanding; I want what I want and there's no compromise. I can't really argue with him. I know there's some truth to his perspective, although it's not entirely right. I may initially throw up a wall but inside I'm a softie. He still doesn't realize this after a year and a half together. He's not strong enough to stand up for himself and say what he feels with me still.

I pushed him away. I don't know why, but I did. I told him five days ago that he is not really committed to us and doesn't want to be in relationship with me. He replied that maybe I was right and needed time to think about it. I was sure he was going to come back with, "I love you and want to be with you," not, "I want to be alone."

But this is really happening. Now he's saying he wants to continue on his journey without me. I know deep in his heart this is not what he wants. I know he's in his head. He loves me, I can see it in his eyes. After he tells me he doesn't have time for a relationship he says, "I just want to sit here and stare at you. You are so beautiful." I am torn. I feel his love, I see his love in his eyes, yet his words and behavior are doing something else.

I am sitting next to him as he is telling me this and all I feel for him is love. This is strange. I feel so much love radiating from my heart to his, *does he feel it?* I am so calm that I think it's not really me sitting here, someone has walked into my body and is being calm for me.

I begin to say we don't have to spend every weekend together, if you need a break you need to communicate it. I have no problem with it. He doesn't bite. He already has a foot out the door. I'm only half heartedly saying this anyway because I have this unusual feeling like this is suppose to be happening.

Instead of plummeting down into panic of being abandoned again, I am serene. Something is calling out to me from far away, faint, but I can still sense it, "stay calm," I hear. "You know the love you have between the two of you is real and profound. This is happening for a reason, just breathe."

This was at lunch time, by evening when my will power is weak I start to go into panic mode. I text him I am sorry and I miss him everyday we are not together and I love him. He texts me back, "I love you and I love your soul." That brings comfort to my scared heart.

I have to go to the supermarket, I literally have no food in my house. I am dreading it. My Beloved loved going to the supermarket with me and always held my hand and kissed me. We used to make it a fun adventure. I see an older couple, he leans over and kisses his wife. I start to lose it. I pray, *Angels, if you are here with me please do not let me start crying now in public.* I can't help it, the tears are coming. I hope no one is watching me. I am picking out sweet potatoes and crying as I have the thought that maybe I will never be shopping with my Beloved again.

I can't sleep well. I wake up in the middle of the night and I realize we are not together anymore. I feel an awful dread creep all over my body and makes it way into my heart. It's the worst feeling. My heart cannot bear this. *Please God, make the dread disappear.*

Day 2. I wake up and am overwhelmed by sadness. It's 5 am, this seems to be the time my angels have been getting me up in the morning now. There is work to be done. I light a candle, I sit, I meditate, I cry, I do distance Reiki healing on our picture, I cry some more, I pray, I send him an email, brief, but quoting my favorite book and an author he has come to love and respect as well, trying to jolt him out of his decision: *"It always blows me away when people say they 'don't have time' for a relationship. And what else is time for? For what other purpose are we living our lives? And can we really be passionate and creative in one area while we suppress our passion and creativity somewhere else?"* ~Marianne Williamson, *An Enchanted Love*, Page 185.

He doesn't bite. I told him I will give him all the time he needs. I am still in denial mode of this whole thing and am searching for a way to wake him back up to our love. I don't get a response. I work on my book on and off all day. I must keep my thoughts focused on the truth, the truth of our love. *I am the creator of my reality*, this is my mantra.

I go to yoga class, it helps, not the class itself, but the reading. I feel like it was for me. It was about loss. I go back to my yoga sutras. I find comfort in these teachings. I am the eternal witness.

Patanjali's Yoga Sutra 17, book two: The cause of that avoidable pain is the union of the Seer (Purusha) and seen (Prakriti, or Nature).

"Pain is caused by the union of the Seer and the Seen. Yoga philosophy speaks of two important things: one is the Purusha, the other is the Prakriti.

The Purusha is the true Self. It is the Purusha who sees. The Prakriti is everything else. The identification with other things is the cause of all our pain. Instead, if we are just ourselves always, things may change or stay as they are, but they will never cause us pain because the changes will be in the things we possess and not in us. Stay in your true Self. You are the knower. You know everything. You are the conscious observer. Nature is here to give you experience and ultimately to liberate you from its bondage. Even if people do not want to be liberated, it educates them gradually so that one day they will come to feel, 'I'm tired of this whole thing. I don't want it anymore. I've had enough.' When will we feel this way? Only after we've gotten enough kicks and burns. The purpose of Prakrit is to give you those knocks. So, we should never condemn nature." (Nature is matter or anything that changes including the intellect, mind, body, senses, everything but your Purusha. Nature can also be referred to as the Illusion or Maya).

This yoga sutra in my opinion is the most important and most practical one to learn and to take as one's truth because it brings much relief from suffering. I have to keep reminding myself, *I am not this pain, I am not this pain, I am not this pain. I am the witness, observing this pain.*

Day 3. I do the same thing in the morning. This time I have a clear picture of the stress I caused my Beloved. I see that I was acting selfishly and only thinking about myself. He said he needed down time on the weekends and I pushed him to do what I wanted. What's wrong with me? I totally stressed him out. I realize how stressful his job has become and how draining it is and the weekends are his only downtime which he wanted to relax and enjoy with me. I was acting like an emotionally unbalanced lunatic. What the heck is my problem? Type A in full force. I feel so bad. I behaved so badly.

I email him again. This time with my confession, but it's not fully there yet, I am still not seeing the big picture. I told him I am sorry and please do not give up on our love, I get no response.

I need Marianne. I go to *A Return to Love* and open it at the most perfect page. *Holy shit, Marianne wrote this about me!* page 146 chapter 12, "If anger isn't brought up into conscious awareness, it has no place to go. It either turns into an attack on self or an inappropriate unconscious attack on others."

She continues, "The healing, in fact, was bound to come ultimately from men who would not-because no one can, really-tolerate my neediness, or the guilt I would try to project onto them in order to get my needs met. By defending myself from being abandoned, I continued to recreate the conditions in which it was bound to occur."

"Why can't men commit? Men haven't committed because the women have been armored against it. Our armor is our darkness-the dark of the heart, the dark of the pain the dark of the moment when we make that wicked comment or that unfair request."

I know I've read this chapter a million times before but now it is REALLY SPEAKING TO ME! I see my dysfunctional behavior, my wicked comments, unfair requests, the guilt and manipulation I was projecting on to him to cover up my neediness and insecurity...the negativity that slowly eroded our love. I brought it, I brought negativity to our sacred love. Please forgive me Beloved, give us a second chance.

Hysterics and panic are not the way. Inner stillness and calmness is. Here is where I will find my inner peace and guidance. I decide to leave him alone, no texts, no calls, no emails, I am giving him his space.

I go to another yoga class. I dedicate the class to my Beloved, maybe he will feel my love from afar. I am going back and forth between anger in his decision to walk out on me and sadness; between giving up and shutting down, to going deeper still and sitting with this pain.

Day 4. Everyday I do the same thing, up at 5am or earlier, light a candle, sit and meditate, or just sit and be, do long distance Reiki on our picture, cry my eyes out, pray for our reconciliation, write my story.

Today I see the whole picture. I cringe in regret, I was awful to him. Even though I moved through a lot of my fears and insecurities with him, I reverted back. I still gave him a hard time about every thing! No wonder he wants to be alone. I can't even stand myself looking back at how I behaved. All he ever did was be unconditional love and support to me. All I ever did was act like an insecure immature selfish pain in the butt. Well, not all the time but enough to send him running the other direction.

I am crying in regret. I messed up, I was trying though. I am trying to be compassionate to myself, but it's hard. I want to beat myself up. How could you mess this one up? I see my errors. I see everything. My anger, my bitterness, my impatience, and even more clearly I see how patient he was with me, how he tried to love me. I just didn't let him. I see the emotional pain and disturbance I must have caused him. That man really must have loved me to stick it out like that.

I don't blame him anymore for leaving me. I chant, *I am sorry, so sorry please forgive me.* I feel like I can communicate with him through my thoughts and feelings. I can't give up. I go from anger to compassion toward him.

My friend tells me if it doesn't work out with my Beloved he has someone he wants to set me up with. I don't know if he's kidding, in that moment though, it brings me relief. I guess it's knowing that there still exists the possibility that I won't be alone after all. I thought about it for a split second then all my spiritual teachings and Marianne Williamson books came rushing back to me at once: "That's the ego's trap into making sure you never find real love, because that is the death of the ego. The ego wants you to believe that the grass is greener on the other side. The problem is not you, it's the combination of the two of you that doesn't work, maybe you just need to move on and find someone new."

New, sounds alluring right? New and no drama. But my higher self kicks in and says *if you don't fix this relationship and heal your wounds once and for all, it will follow you to poison the next relationship. This is your opportunity to face your deepest darkest fears.* Besides this is your Beloved, your true love. I do love him.

Day 5. Same morning routine. Today I go down. I have the thought that I am damaged goods and I am beyond repair. I will always be damaged and I will never be able to be in a healthy relationship with a man. *I belong on the island of misfits.* I am in full pity mode. These thoughts bring such horror to my heart, I can hear my higher self saying to me, "Stop, stop this now. This is dangerous, do not go down this road, this will lead you nowhere good." I choose to stop, it's so tempting to go on and feel sorry for myself. After all I screwed up the best thing and the best man I ever had. Something in me is telling me this is not going to help though. I realize what a truly amazing man this person is. Yes he has his faults as well, he is not perfect, I am not putting him on a pedestal. But I see him, I see his light, his soul, how in every way he is perfect for me.

The thing that breaks my heart is that I could not receive his love, there were still walls. And his love is oh so sweet, meant for me. I am so sad at this realization. I need help to get me out of this drowning despair. I go to my yoga sutras again, book 2 sutra 18. I have to remember I am the Purusha, I am the soul that is seeing. I am not this pain, I am not this pain. This helps me to distance my emotions and brings me temporary relief.

My days are so long. What the F****! One day feels like a week to me. I wake up at 5 am everyday, now it's starting to be 4:30am. No alarm, I am just woken up. Wide awake. How early can I go to bed? Is 8pm too early to go to sleep? I need some reprieve from this misery and fear. I have to get away from myself. I shouldn't nap so I can fall asleep early, the night time is the worst time for me. It seems to be first thing in the morning and before bed I am plagued with sadness and fear of losing my Beloved. All I do is write, pray, meditate, read, cry, talk to my angels. walk my dog, This is so hard. I wish I can make time speed up. Torture. Everyday I do an angel reading and everyday I get Gabriel, creative writing. Ok I get it, I have to write.

Day 6. Same morning routine. Still haven't heard a peep from him. This is the worst feeling. I have to let go and trust, trust, trust. I am busy today and it brings relief. I have clients and made plans to meet up with a girlfriend. I have been trying to have dinner each night with one of my friends. It helps to ease the pain and helps me to eat. I'm back on the heartbreak diet and am losing weight fast. I confess to my friends what I did to my Beloved to drive him away. They comfort me by saying it's only temporary. I believe them in the moment. It brings relief to my heart but by the time I go to bed I am in panic mode again. I pray before I fall asleep to visit my love in my dreams.

I plead, *Please God give me some sign of hope, something, a sign, something that I know he is still in it and hasn't checked out completely yet,* I get nothing.

> "Most men have no idea of the lengths to which a woman will go for love or the depths of despair when we feel it cut off. This is not to say that men don't fly hight or crash tragically. Of course they do. But their love doesn't fuel the world the way ours does. Their love is the car; ours is the gas." ~ *A Woman's Worth,* Marianne Williamson

Day 7, Sunday. I feel a sense of peace come from within me, it's amazing, it feels so good, I don't know where its coming from, but I'll take it. I hope it's a good sign. "Nurture yourself," the angels are telling me. Ok, today I am going to nurture myself and it feels good.

The sense of peace comes and goes but mostly is gone now. I am back into fear. It's amazing how time is going so slow in my life. Also amazing how the Universe cleared my schedule so I don't have much work. All I do is meditate, write, cry, pray, talk to my angels, walk Karma. I spend most of the day outside with Karma writing. The weather has been beautiful and I find it very healing to be in nature. I go from writing at the picnic table in my backyard to lying down and reading on a blanket under my favorite tree.

I am dog sitting as well. I am with three dogs and one of the dogs, Sylvie, senses my sadness. She comes over and snuggles next to me, puts her head on my lap. I am grateful for this unconditional love.

My neighbors are having a party and bbq in their back yard which is connected to mine. Should I go over? Should I make plans with friends? Go to Fire Island? It's Memorial Day weekend after all. No, my higher self is telling me to sit still, be with this, don't run away, you are healing and finally reconciling your past. Sit and bear it out.

Ok, but my butt is starting to hurt bad from all this sitting. My left sitz bones is so sore, I'm going to have a flat pancake butt soon. I should be exercising all day long. I have the time now and beach season is right around the corner. No, this is more important, this relationship takes precedent. I have to fix this. I have to fix me. I'll fix my butt later.

The longer we are apart and not communicating, the harder it's getting. The easier it is to give up and just say fuck it. I will just slowly disappear into the night and never see him again. But something is calling me, it's not letting me give up. It's the hope of a miracle of love and a happy ending.

Day 8, Memorial Day. Today is a bad day, a very bad day. Today I am not nurturing myself, I am punishing myself. I refuse to eat. I will starve myself I am thinking. I don't deserve to eat. I go down to a dark place, a place I haven't visited in a very long time. I get on my indoor bike to release this negative energy and it makes me even angrier. I get off and go into the shower, maybe it will clear this enraged energy I am feeling. It doesn't work. I lose it in the shower and start bawling. I'm angry, really angry as I pound my fist on the shower wall. I tell God and the Universe that I give up. I am done. I am in complete temper tantrum mode and not holding back any of my rage.

I yell, "My whole life has been an uphill battle and I'm tired. I'm tired of being alone, tired of the fucking struggle and maybe it wasn't meant for me to be here. I am no use. I want out of this body. Yes I know it's a gift, but I don't care anymore. My daughter will be fine without me, so will Karma." I feel this darkness envelope me, it's scary. It feels like a dark entity is taking over my body and my mind. I am having a hard time breathing.

I get out of the shower and collapse on the floor gasping for air. I think of the best way I can end my life. Pills? No I don't want those chemicals in my body (thinking organic and healthy even with my suicide) *How,* I think? The way I want to die is by drowning, I come to the conclusion. I will return to the sea, the water is my home. I think I will go to the ocean today. I picture myself walking into the water, drifting away and never coming out, drowning peacefully in the ocean.

I'm on the floor on my back sobbing uncontrollably, my whole body is shaking. I can't seem to rid myself of this dark negative energy that feels like it's taking over me. Now it's pushing down on me. I feel like I'm being suffocated.

I am pleading for help, no one is answering me. I am alone and I am mad at God and the angels for not being with me when I need them most. All I hear is foreboding silence. *Where are you? Why can't you send me a sign? Please help me,* I cry; *please help me,* I beg. *Please take this from me God, I surrender. Please,* I beg, *take this from me, I can't do it anymore.*

There's a voice, so very faint, I can barely hear it. It says, "Get up, go outside in the sun." I don't know if it's *me* making it up, but I don't know what else to do. Taking all my strength, I pry myself up off the floor, go outside with my blanket, put it under my favorite tree and lie down. The sun feels so good. I fall fast asleep.

I wake up, not sure how long I've been sleeping, I don't think I've been sleeping for that long. Wow, I feel different, completely different. That dark energy is gone. Not only that but I feel refreshed, like a new person. Wow. Ok I'm back I guess. That was intense and scary. The earth healed me. Thank you Mother Earth. This was a **miracle.** Back to writing.

I light a candle and a make an alter for my Beloved and our love with sweet prayers of compassion, forgiveness, healing, friendship, and reconciliation. I lay crystals around our picture. I put clear quartz by his head, hoping he will come out of his analytical ego thoughts; I put rose quartz on his heart, hoping he will return to his heart soon and I put rose quartz with an OM symbol on it between us reminding me that there are three of us in this relationship, Me, my Beloved and God. I pray to God for healing of our relationship.

Day 9. I wake up at 4:30 from a beautiful dream with my Beloved, We are in bed in front of a fire place and he is holding me, so strong, the way he holds me. I feel so safe, so loved in his arms. This dream gives me hope. I lie in bed half asleep as I chant *I am sorry, I love you, I am sorry, I love you, I am sorry, I love you,* hoping he hears me somehow in this in between state of sleep and awake, that his soul can still hear me. I fall back to sleep.

I get up my body hurts, I have to do yoga asanas today. I haven't been exercising. I do my morning routine with an angel reading and am getting strong signs to rewrite my book verbatim, like a journal. I write all morning then I roll out my mat.

I dedicate my first sun salutation to my Beloved. Then I stop, I have a brilliant idea, why don't I dedicate my yoga practice to the little me, the little baby and girl that didn't get any love and affection. I decide I'm doing 46, one for each year I have been alive. I count one, inhale and raise my arms up, the tears come gushing out as I imagine me as a baby. How can I do sun salutations and cry for 46 years? Ok well I'm committed.

I cry really hard at specific ages of 4, 9, 11, 26, 31, 40, not sure why. I just go with it. The tears are subsiding and I'm going to do the last three dedicated to my Beloved. I met him when I was 44. I'm changing the sun salutation to Surya Namaskar B, adding Warrior One and Chair pose because I feel strong now, and I am sending him my strength.

I feel free and light. It is amazing. I feel like I just let go of a huge burden that I've been carrying around my whole life. I smile, wow it's been days since I've smiled I realize. It's so freeing, my heart feels free and light. To think I can be happy even if we are not together. This is good, this is really good.

I am starting to feel happy again being alone. Maybe I am supposed to be alone? Maybe we weren't destined to be together. I was happy alone before I met him and I can be happy again alone.

Stop, this is another ploy of the ego. I know we were not meant to be alone. I don't want to be alone anymore. I want to be with him, I love being with him. I feel so good when we are together, like two peas in a pod. I remember the time we took nap and fell asleep with our foreheads connected, woke up with two giant red circles on each of our foreheads. That is how I want to be with him: connected.

But what if he doesn't want to be with me anymore? He was also happy alone. He is used to being alone. The thought ruins my light mood and brings fear back into my heart.

Whatever happens, he will always be my Beloved.

Day 10. Something shifted yesterday, big time. I feel completely different inside. I feel calm, strong, a sense of peace, it's unusual, I'm not used to feeling this way. The best way to describe how I feel is light. I feel so light.

In my head I am thinking I'm not with my Beloved, I should be feeling upset still. It's no longer there though. It's gone, there are no more ill feelings. I am free. Yes, I am free.

Thank you Beloved for giving me this gift. You are a brave soul. I love you.

I confess that I am scared, even if we got back together what if I revert back to my old ways? What if he wants to leave me again? I don't think my heart can take this on and off roller coaster ride with him anymore. It's been our pattern from day one. I want something secure and solid so I can feel secure and rooted. I want to grow more. I start to cry because imagining being without him is sad to my soul. I miss him so much now it hurts so bad. A day without my Beloved is like a day without the sun. We have been apart now it feels like for an eternity. I miss you.

Day 11. Today is the day I decide I am giving my Beloved the beginning of my book. I am scared beyond. This is me, my story transparent. I am trying not to have expectations but deep down I am hoping this will wake him up and come back to me. I'm hoping he will see that I have changed and am truly sorry. I am so scared to give this to him, but I know I must. Trust, trust, trust. I have written and rewritten my story so many times. Each time I wanted to print it out and give it to him, my laptop wouldn't send it through my email. It just stayed in the outbox. Now, I just emailed it to myself and it went immediately. This is a good sign. I know it.

Abandon: "letting loose, surrender to natural impulses"

I use a thesaurus a lot when I am writing. So I looked up the word freedom and I couldn't believe what I found. Abandon is a synonym for freedom. Yes, it makes sense. Other synonyms were wildness, spontaneity, uninhibitedness, power, flexibility, unrestraint. Depending on your context of the word abandon could mean something negative or something positive. It's all up to you. Such is our life. Our meaning is what we give it.

OPPORTUNITY IS NOWHERE. How do you read this statement? Opportunity is no where, or opportunity is now here.

I can choose to keep replaying the past trauma and dramas of my life and say I was abandoned or I can change the script and say I abandon any thoughts of being shackled, I am free in abandon, I am free. I am the light and I am free.

The pain, suffering, and love are all real but the only thing that will last is the love.

I am the phoenix bird. I have died and I have risen from the ashes, again. I am reborn and made anew. **I am the light and I am free, eternally free.**

(I have about another 75 pages of journal entries until October, but to spare my readers of my sad story because I did go back into the suffering, I did not include them. I only included what I feel is most relevant and helpful for others in similar situations).

PETAL 7

Integration

***Feeling with the Mind

I BELIEVE THIS was the final, final healing I needed to do-something I avoided five years ago as part of the St. Ignatius retreat I participated in. It included writing about your personal history and praying over it. I only pretended I did it. I didn't know how I could face my entire life of pain and suffering all at once. It seemed overwhelming to me at the time. I wasn't ready, I guess.

I was acting like I healed that part of me but I was only rationalizing it. And that type of pain and heartache is not something you can intellectualize or rationalize through your head. I was fooling myself into thinking I was healed. The residual pain and anguish within me never had been fully felt. I was feeling these anguishes of unworthiness and despair with my mind; and therefore, never processed the emotions in order to release them. I didn't feel into the trauma through my heart and actually feel compassion for the little hurt girl within me.

Feeling with the mind DOESN'T HEAL. We are programmed to be living in our head and not our heart. We are not aware that processing emotions through our head never get resolved or integrated. They just keep regurgitating over and over again, rearing their ugly heads in our most intimate relationships and causing tremendous pain to both parties involved. That's why most talking therapies don't work. Talking about issues can be helpful to bring awareness to them. But that's only the first step.

"The key to healing lies in going into our pain and wounds from the past, not running away from them. It's only by confronting our obstacles and facing our fears do we transcend them. We have to feel what we want to heal. We have to clearly see and understand our past and our part in creating it before we can become fully conscious of how we want to move forward and onward in life without repeating the past." ~Archangel Metatron through Earth-keeper.com

***Don't Set Up Camp

It's important to be cautious that we don't get stuck in the feeling from the past though and stay there. That's the scary part about traveling back into the past, we must feel the feeling in order to process it, then let it go and move on. I think that's why many people, myself included, never face our past because the thought itself is too scary and we are afraid to go there. But go there we must if we expect to move forward with a clean slate and a free heart.

I never heard from my Beloved after I gave him my book with my confession. I continued to reach out to him, not pressuring him to talk but just with little reminders that I am here for him, I love him, have faith in our relationship and will wait. I also wrote him another letter about a month and a half later, pouring out my heart with unconditional acceptance, patience and love. I made him a DVD slideshow of all of our beautiful memories together. I stayed faithful and true, praying every day for our reconciliation for months.

I wrote beautiful heartfelt letters to his children since I never got to say good-bye. I never heard from them either, or his mother. One of the things I learned from Bob Cooke was that having a "moon in Scorpio" as a woman means you are the *mother to all.* I got that. I felt like a lost an entire family. I really grew to love his children and I think that was one of the most painful parts of our separation, not being able to say good bye- it broke my heart. Every day was torture for me as my hopeful heart held on.

***God Sends Nothing but Angels

This is the hardest part but I know it's the truth, on another level My Beloved's soul chose to be the one to help me move through my issues and finally heal the last unresolved part of me that was hanging around. And I chose it as well. ***How could I have healed my abandonment issue if I had no one that I truly loved abandon me?***

I loved him so much that his walking away from me was exactly what my soul needed. There was darkness in me that I was still harboring. Even though I had done so much introspection and work on myself over the last fourteen years, I had ignored one last piece.

*** Final Integration

When I was little I loved putting puzzles together. My brothers and I had jigsaw puzzle contests that I usually won. It was one of the things I was good at. I picture myself as a jigsaw puzzle. I was almost 100% put together except for one piece that wasn't quite securely fit in yet.

This was the abandonment piece, it was still a loose piece of the puzzle. Every time I was in an intimate relationship it would get triggered, even though whatever situation was coming up had nothing to do with what was going on presently. I would then react from the past trauma, a place of fear and insecurity and not from love. It wasn't pretty or healthy for anyone.

Now thanks to my Beloved, I got the opportunity to finally face, heal, integrate and secure the final piece of my jigsaw puzzle. The only way through the pain was the pain itself. My puzzle is complete. So now the piece has transformed into **PEACE.**

When I first met my Beloved, I learned from Spirit that our relationship was of the highest divine light, that he was "an aspect of me, here to birth a newness and creation within my being." After he left I learned that my soul chose to experience this abandonment so I can be free, once and for all, of the darkness I was harboring. This was the "newness and creation" they were talking about. I had no idea it was going to happen in this excruciating painful way. I keep reminding myself, **I chose this**. *Note to soul: next lifetime, take the easy path.*

***Being Accountable

I couldn't heal this part of me alone. That is why we need each other. And that is why ***with each sorrow or pain always comes bearing a gift*** if you can seize the opportunity to sit with it and look within to find the healing. Some of our greatest lessons and gains on the "earth-school" are made when we are in states of seeming crisis.

But we need to put our ego and pride aside and that is not something that is easy to do all the time. We need to be meditating or at least finding time and space for solitude, quiet reflection or contemplation. We need to be awake and aware, smarter than the ego. The ego is very cunning and will keep us shackled and under it's control by doing the blame game and the denial game.

> "Time heals all wounds," is another socially-programmed lie we tell ourselves. All time is is a buffer, hiding your wounds in the background ready to jump out on to the next person who triggers them. It doesn't heal anything, really. "The only cure for the pain is the pain." ~Rumi

If I wasn't taking the time to do the spiritual practice and the work on myself, I wouldn't have been ready for this. I would have done what I always did in the past. My old self would have gotten angry and defensive spouting out, "Fine, your loss," and gotten rid of all our pictures, deleted him from my phone and laptop and trashed all the things he gave me so I wouldn't have any reminders of him. Then I would have made a list of all the negative traits I see in him and how he was not really a good partner anyway and moved on. I am good at that. I would have focused on his transgressions and blamed him, then moved on unhealed to do more damage.

***Muscle Memory

It seemed like his life was conveniently set up just for me- to trigger all of my wounds. Looking back now I can find humor in it, although at the time it was nothing but conflict, turmoil and distress. Only God and Spirit could have orchestrated such a perfect match!

To give you an example: My Beloved would tell me he wanted to do something that was different from what we had planned, without me. A reasonable request right? Why then did my immediate reaction be a sick feeling in my gut?

It was like the Universe said, here you go, you have abandonment issues, let's amplify it 100 times and give you a partner who also has the same issues, plus poor communications skills and his way of dealing with it is walking away and shutting down and then ultimately abandoning you. *Perfect.*

I wondered, *did I do something wrong?* Was he about to leave me? It had nothing to do with the present moment of course. Let's call it, **"muscle memory."** As soon as I got the sick feeling in my gut, it was my old wounds being triggered.

My mind began to wander down a road of imagination of what was really happening or what his ulterior motives were, making up stories in my head, when all he wanted to do was just do something different. A simple change in plans triggered the A bomb. I know it sounds crazy, but that's how it felt. **Hysterical-historical**. Before I was aware of what was happening I would go into fear and panic and start to manipulate him to make him feel guilty for doing something without me or changing plans. I became the actor, the director and the producer of our movie, leaving him without a role.

Sometimes it would work and I would get my way, but really I was sabotaging the relationship. He would give in to me because I can be pretty stubborn at times. On top of the guilt and manipulation, I unleashed an emotional tsunami on him. He would then shut down, retreat and abandon me, the thing I was trying to avoid in the first place.

This was how I became his jailor, not his lover. Love and freedom are synonymous. I was doing the exact opposite. I was acting out of fear, not love. It soothed my abandonment issues, but only temporary. It was just a bandaid. All it did was wear away at our relationship. Being this needy and insecure is a sure way to drive any man away, which I did. My daughter's therapist gave me a mantra when I was 28 years old, "Loose lips sink ships." I had no idea at the time how true that statement was. Boy did I sink many ships.

*** Coming Out of the Crazy, Re-writing the Script

In order for me to change this destructive pattern I had to re-learn new patterns and rewire my sub-conscious programming in the moment it was happening. The first step was becoming aware when it was my past muscle memory being triggered and not let it take over; the second step was not reacting with my old sabotaging ways, and finally re-writing the script- reacting in a new healthy way. I could say something like: "Ok that's great, have a good time," and mean it or whatever. The point is taking different action with a better reaction.

The only way to do that is by staying awake and aware in the present moment because it happens so fast. I was starting to get better at it even though it was challenging. There were times when I overcame them, and times when I did not. Sometimes the best I could do was say," Ok," take a deep breath, walk away and talk to him later when I was more rational. Sometimes I'd let him walk away and call later when I was more sane and apologize.

When I was in a more calm state we would talk for hours and I would feel a shift inside, returning my power back to me. It was very healing to have a witness to this event. It felt so good and I began to trust him that he understood what I was going through.

The breath is what gives us the space to make a healthy positive reaction, and not respond with anger and insecurity from past fear. The breath awakens our energy and helps release the old patterns.

***Changing the Subconscious Patterns

"If you want to change your life, *change* your life."

Einstein's definition of insanity, "Doing the same thing and expecting different results," is seen on a micro and macro level. Change will not stick if it's not changed in the physical realm. Talking about changing doesn't change anything. I know people who talk and talk about what they want different in their lives but never take any steps to make it happen. Yoga philosophy reminds us that all our knowledge comes through experience, therefore there must be an altered action taken.

Remember when recycling bags first started coming out at the supermarket? I bought a couple which were left in the car every time I went into the supermarket. I'm sure many of you can relate. Without fail, every time I got up to the register I realized I left my bags in the car. After I rushed through the store trying to escape as fast as possible since I'm not a big fan of shopping and get anxiety if I'm in the supermarket too long, there was no way I was going to lose my place on line to get my bags. So I would just settle and take the plastic bags and say to myself *next time you have to remember them.*

Then one day I was frustrated enough and had had it. I left my full shopping cart with the cashier, didn't care if I lost my turn in line and walked out to my car to get my bags. I mean it's really no big deal if you think about it, but at the time it felt like it. I thought it would stress me out more, but it actually felt good. Since that day I never forget my bags.

For a change to happen in the physical realm it can't just remain a thought in your head, in the mental realm. It has to be brought down into our physical body, we have to take action and do something different to create that change. It may make us uncomfortable temporarily, but that is the only we can grow. We don't grow if we stay in our comfort zone.

Change first has to start with awareness. Easy when it's plastic bags at the supermarket, harder when it's your old wounds lashing out on your sweetie.

1. Recognize the pattern (awareness)
2. Make amends if you need to (atonement)
3. Take different action (action)

With intimate relationship we have all the emotions that go along with it, plus the dynamics of another person. But if we want to truly walk our walk, not just talk our talk, we need to apply our spiritual knowledge to every area of our life, especially in relationships. Unless you are a hermit, there's no getting around being in relationships on this earth-plane. It's why we're here.

***The Hypocrite

The final piece I had to learn to do was take that self motivation from my teachings and apply it to my relationships. Something I was still not doing. One of my students, who became a friend and spiritual guide, had the courage to say something as I was sharing a struggle I was having in my relationship with my Beloved. He said, "How could you be all spiritual and teach yoga and not apply that to your relationship with your boyfriend?" Touche. Sometimes we forget that.

My Beloved called me a hypocrite during one of our arguments which caused us to spend one night apart on our romantic vacation in Aruba. Even if we are on one of the most beautiful beaches in the world, if we still have a pissy mind, we will be unhappy. Looking back now I see that he was right and that's why I reacted so defensively.

> It is these relationships that trigger us and push our buttons. They are doing that to give us an opportunity to look deeper and heal those broken parts of us. "The wound is the place where the Light enters you." ~Rumi

> Peace in your heart.
> Peace in your family.
> *Peace with your Beloved.*
> Peace with your neighbors.
> Peace with your community.
> Peace with your country.
> Peace with the world.

If we skip some of those parts, we are not completely peaceful. We see it often in society. Strangers being cordial to you in the store then go to their car and yell at their kids. I used to do that with my daughter and I was doing that to my Beloved. It is our closest relationships that tempt us to take out the daggers, but this is where we must practice what we preach.

***Fruit Loops of the Mind

I tried to stay in my resurrection, in that free and light place that I had journeyed to after integrating my pain through my writing, crying, feeling and the yoga sun salutations. I didn't do such a good job. Part of the reason was because he never responded to my book. I mean I wrote a whole book and dedicated a huge chunk of it to him for crying out loud!!! I got nothing! How could he not respond? Is he that numb and shut down? I obsessed day and night. The silence hurt. I was definitely attached to a response and had expectations. How could I not? I honestly thought I was gong to end this book with our reconciliation.

Even though I transformed the pain and released the darkness harboring within me, I traveled back into the mind loops of the past. I spent moments, days, weeks, months, reliving everything over and over in my mind. It was mental and emotional self-torture. *The Vrittis are coming! The vrittis are coming!* I chanted to myself. Vrittis mean thoughts in Sanskrit. When I get stuck in these mind loops I try to use humor to let them go. If that doesn't work I bang my head against the wall. No, I don't, but I imagine doing it, that's how obsessed my mind gets.

***Heal Me of My Fear-Based Thoughts

"Fear is just love distorted." ~Me

Instead of banging my head against the wall, I called upon my angels. Since my fears ran deep and were etched into my subconscious from birth and subsequently every chapter of my life, I definitely needed extra help. Because of the trauma I experienced in my child hood and in my adult life, my mind liked to focus and obsess on something, even if it wasn't positive. It's a way of control. There came a point in my journey that I had done the work, I was healed. Now I just needed to maintain that state of being, staying in my free heart and not journey back into the darkness with my thoughts.

The angel that is always with me and helps me get out of my fearful thinking patterns is Archangel Michael. Everyday I would call out in frustration and despair, "Archangel Michael, please help me release my fearful thoughts and regain my emotional footing back again. Thank you." Even though they don't need it, angels love to be thanked and feel appreciated.

I would take a deep breath because that is how divine thought gets in and old negative thoughts get out, and in a minute or so I would feel a shift from within and feel centered and grounded again. It worked just like that. The mantra, "**Please heal me of my fear based thoughts,**" from *A Course in Miracles* was the only thing I needed at this point.

***Bleeding Heart

I even heard my angel Michael in a meditation say, "He no longer serves you," after I asked for guidance. I have come to learn we have many soulmates. Some are meant for a lifetime and some are meant for a time in our life.

Ecclesiastes, chapter 3, verses 1-8:

> "For everything there is a season, and
> a time for every matter under heaven:
> a time to be born, and a time to die;
> a time to plant, and a time to pluck up
> what is planted;

a time to kill, and a time to heal;
a time to break down, and a time to
build up;
a time to weep, and a time to laugh;
a time to mourn, and a time to dance;
a time to throw away stones, and a
time to gather stones together;
a time to embrace, and a time to
refrain from embracing;
a time to seek, and a time to lose;
a time to keep, and a time to
throw away;
a time to tear, and a time to sew;
a time to keep silence, and a time to
speak;
a time to love, and a time to hate;
a time for war, and a time for peace."

I had to accept that all the growth that I could achieve with this soul was achieved. Now it was time to let go and move on. I didn't accept it though. I wasn't ready to let go yet. I really thought this was going to be a temporary breakup and we would get a second chance, that I would conclude my book with a happy ending between us. I kept visualizing our reunion, jumping into his arms and giving him my love, free and unhindered. A new woman, happy and healed.

Because I had to find peace and closure on my own without getting the opportunity to talk with him face to face and heart to heart, it created more unrest and unsettledness.

Coming to grips with the fact that he is not choosing to come back and give us a second chance was another loss I had to sit with and brought me back into the questioning and despair. We were soulmates and when you reunite with one it's a special and blessed occurrence. However, free will, the gift we were given on the earth plane, is always at play with the power to make conscious or unconscious choices. One soul can choose to say "no." Not everybody is ready for love.

I waited in hope for months, then decided I had to let go and move on. This mental and emotional torture was draining me and toxic to my soul. It's not easy to let him go. When I give my heart to someone, I give it 110%, loyal and faithful to the end. As time goes on the ole saying, "What doesn't kill you makes you stronger," soothes me, but how much stronger do I have to be? I am tired of being so strong. I just want to be loved. Sigh.

Even though I brought many wounds into the relationship, I also brought so much positive energy, love and beauty to his life and his family. I gave so much of me. I'm starting to feel stronger, as I realize I can't take all the blame for this. I forgive myself as I move forward.

***There are Always Two People in Relationship

One thing I learned from my relationship with Soulmate #3 (my former husband) from Bob, the astrologer, was that when men (I'm saying men because it's more their pattern) shut down and walk away, they leave you holding their emotional baggage. So in addition to your feelings and emotions that you are trying to process, you have theirs as well. Men often complain that women are crazy. Sometimes the reason women act so crazy is because of just this, we are left with the unresolved emotional energy of two. Then men wonder why we have a breakdown and act irrational. That was a huge A-HA moment for me. I used to think I was f'in crazy, but now I understand why I become so intense.

I realize that Soulmate #4 (my Beloved's new identity) had just as much to contribute to the demise of the relationship. He said he loved me and had the choice to come back and work things out, but he chose to shut down and walk away. That part I cannot control. He chose to focus on my weaknesses and not on my strengths, my openness and willingness to grow and change. I remember him looking me in the eye one night sitting in his kitchen asserting that I must have faith in our relationship. In the end it was he that lacked the faith.

Now the roles have been reversed. He is now my jailor if I choose to allow that. But I know in my heart that I have to move on. I cannot be shackled by anyone. I have seen the light, I have healed my heart and I will never go through that pain again because I faced it once and for all. If he chooses to keep seeing me in the past with all my wounds and traumas and not whole and healed as I am now, then he isn't the Beloved for me.

One of my wise spiritual friends said once that relationships are like a game of catch. You throw the ball to someone, they catch it and throw it back. You catch it and and throw it back to them and so on. There is a balance and equal give and take. What I realized was happening with my dilemma, I was throwing the ball to Soulmate #4 and he was just letting it drop. Forget about catching it or throwing it back, he just let it fall to the way side. The ball was my love and that's not the ball game I want to play anymore.

***Stuck Again

After five months of dreadful silence, he texts me, saying he has been thinking about me for last few days and asked if I wanted to spend the day and night on his boat on Fire Island to watch the lunar eclipse. I was shocked. I had been waiting for this moment for months. I felt like a weight was released from me as I thought maybe he still cares, maybe he's still in it, and maybe he still loves me. Maybe the miracle I was praying for had finally come true? For me, there is nothing that could be more perfect in my heart than to be at my favorite place in the world on the ocean watching the moon. He knows me so well. I was so excited!

But immediately my higher self kicked in and said, "Don't get too excited, don't set yourself up to be hurt again." That voice within was warning me. Thank Goddess for my higher self, because that is exactly what happened.

Even though at this point I wasn't sure if I wanted to get back with him, being a peacemaker at heart, I was longing to see if we could come to a place of healing and harmony between us. I still loved him and was desperate to speak my peace and to understand what happened…how we spiraled from this beautiful awesome connection and relationship to nothing.

I cleared my work calendar for the next two days, including the fund raiser I was supposed to participate in and rescheduled my clients. The last thing I heard from him was a text that the weather was looking "iffy" and he would let me know. Well, he never let me know, he left me hanging. It wasn't about me or us after all, it was about the weather and the stinkin' moon.

I was crushed. My Spirit sank back down. *How could he do this to me? I obsessed, day and night. Doesn't he realize how he just crushed my heart, again? How could he not?* Yet, I knew it happened for a reason.

It was like God and my higher self knew in my optimistic mushy heart I was still holding on to a shred of hope that we could reconcile. After this there was no chance. This was not the relationship for me anymore and I needed to be banged over the head to see it clearly for what it was. Still, I felt like I had to work on forgiving him all over again and letting go. I went right back down into the mental and emotional self-torture. I was back in the questioning, back in the contemplative mind, back in the darkness.

***Retreat

Listening to the guidance of my angels, I booked a rest and relaxation weekend retreat upstate at the Omega Institute. It would be my first road trip vacation alone, to someplace new. I was excited at first but the day I was leaving I started to rethink my trip. It's amazing how fear and doubt love to come into your mind and try to hold you back from things you want to do. I was thinking how I could just stay home and relax, (stay in my comfort zone), but no, I knew I had to do this for myself. I made myself go.

Road trip it was! The entire drive upstate I obsessed and replayed what happened over and over again in my mind. I was still so upset that he could do that to me. I felt awful and had such a heavy heart. I tried to make it stop by listening to Yogananda's CDs on faith and God. I chanted and sang with Krishna Das, who always lifts my mood, but even that didn't work. I was in so much mental and emotional pain and wasn't sure what to expect when I got to Omega. It turned out this was exactly what I needed for my soul.

Before I took this trip, one of my intuitive friends during a reading asked me if I was groggy in the morning when I woke up and having a hard time getting out of bed? I was indeed, which was unusual for me, being a morning person. He told me that I was getting downloads, information from Spirit when I awoke in the morning but was too busy thinking about Starbucks.

Busted! They really know you, those angels, because that was exactly what I was doing. So I brought my journal with me and the first night before I went to sleep I wrote the question, "How can I let go of this?" then left my journal beside my bed.

When I awoke in the morning I stayed in bed in the alpha state, half asleep and half awake, thinking *I am not getting out of bed until I hear something!*

Then I heard, **"Blaming him keeps you stuck."**

Holy holy holy! Thank you God and Goddess. I got up, wrote it down in my journal and felt a shift within me already happening. Sometimes we just need one little sentence to cut through the uncertainty and disillusionment and bring us back to our inner truth and clarity.

This was perfect advice to help me let go. I got it. I had already done the healing, now I needed to stay in that space and not resort back to the old mind loops. Challenging however, when someone does something that warrants blame. But the blame is a drain. It keeps the negative attachment and negative energy alive with that person.

I spent the weekend enjoying myself and doing things alone. I had many firsts- first time hiking alone, kayaking alone, running through the mountains alone. It was the perfect setting because I could choose to be alone or choose to socialize, yet I never *felt* alone. Each time I went into the main dining hall I sat with new people and shared a meal and authentic conversation. It was refreshing to meet other like minded souls that were there seeking healing and peace. This showed me once again that while we need our alone time to process, heal and grow, we also need the bond of brotherhood. This was the perfect setting for solidarity and unity.

This road trip was the best thing for my spirit. Feeling empowered and centered again and grateful for my free heart, I was practically in tears the day I left.

***"Do you want to be right or do you want to be happy?"

When I first read this line from Marianne Williamson's book, *A Return to Love*, something shifted within me. It was one of those thoughts that went right into my intellect and my heart at the same time. Being right is a function of the mind, being happy is a function of the heart.

Being right comes with a price. In my case, being right and still focusing on his transgressions over and over in my mind kept me in mental and emotional anguish. I was still struggling over something he did, or rather did not do and he probably had no clue. He went on living his life without even giving it a second thought, while I was stuck reeling and blaming and hurting for weeks! It kept me attached to him and I wasn't even in a relationship with him anymore!

Even in times when we have the "right" to be angry and someone has done something so hurtful, there's always a lesson and room to grow. There's a popular phrase, "someone is either a lesson or a blessing." I believe they can be both. When you forgive someone and let them go, it doesn't make you weak, dumb or a doormat, just peaceful and free and who doesn't want that?

***Rejection is God's Protection

> "The primary cause of unhappiness is never the situation but your thoughts about it." ~Eckhart Tolle

Rejection is God's protection, is a mantra I have recited many times in my life and this was one of those times. God was protecting me. When we re-contextualize our pain, the negativity dissolves and returns us back to the love in our heart. This soulmate was no longer the man for me and since I was having such a hard time letting go, this was Spirit's way of showing me. After this happened, whatever tiny shred of hope I had left lingering in my loving heart was gone. God knows me better than anyone. Divine intervention needed to happen here. Even so, my heart is a little slow catching up to my intellect. I honor myself where I am and tell myself it's ok to feel the way I do. I practice kindness and compassion toward myself as I allow myself to feel everything, and know that this too shall pass.

I remind myself that we are energetically connected. Negative thoughts not expressed out loud are still harmful. If we have ill thoughts about someone over and over again, they will receive them on some level. Ahimsa in yoga, which in the practice of non-violence, pertains to our thoughts just as much as our actions.

Science has proven that thoughts are energy and can be measure outside of our head. That's why we feel so peaceful in the mountains or at the beach-there are less thought forms hanging around. In the city it's mayhem because of the condensed population. Imagine if each person had 60,000 thoughts a day and there are 8 million people living in New York City! That's a lot of thought forms floating around and I bet most of them are not positive.

Each time I had a negative thought about Soulmate #4, I would *try* to catch myself and redirect by saying, "I bless you and let you go." I wasn't successful often but I did put the intention out there. This way I am not adding to the conflict and negativity of the unhealed relationship or to the world and am giving it space for Spirit to work its magic.

I like this Hawaiian prayer called Ho'oponopono. It's simple and straight to the point. It purifies whatever unresolved unharmonious karma is still between you:

> I am sorry.
> Please forgive me.
> I love you.
> And I thank you.

If you're not in the place yet of blessing them, that's ok, at least stay positive in your own thoughts. Sometimes we have to fake it till we make it. When I was going through that two year depression over the break-up of my marriage, intellectually I knew that I had to stay positive in my thoughts, but my heart still hurt so much. So whenever my mind became still, before the negative thoughts crept in, I would say "**I am blessed, all is well.**"

I call it neutralizing the negative. While I didn't believe it completely and it didn't make me jump for joy, it kept me from spiraling down into the pit of despair. That became my mantra for about a year. And you know what? Eventually I did feel that I was truly blessed and all was well, It just took some time.

***Life is a Mirror

> "Everything is a reflection of the condition of your own heart."
> ~Geshe Michael Roach, *How Yoga Works*

When I first heard this concept I didn't get it. *How could I be a mirror for someone who is abusing me* I thought? *I'm not abusing myself.* Yet I was, but in a different way. The men were reflecting back to me all the areas in which I was abandoning myself and not loving myself. As long as we hold beliefs of unworthiness, which I was covertly because I was feeling them with my mind, we will inadvertently create a reaction of subconscious rejection and denial in another. It is a double edge of the law of attraction. Until I learned how to show up for myself, how could I expect anyone else to show up for me?

About three years ago before I met my last Beloved, Soulmate #4, I heard another divine message from Archangel Michael. He said, **"Saying you love yourself is not the same as being it."**

He continued, "**There is a disconnect between what you say and what you feel. You cannot say you love yourself and still feel unworthy inside"** Busted again! *How does he know that?* I muse, *Oh yea they know everything.*

I was at a point in my spiritual awareness and intellectual knowledge that I knew loving myself and having an open heart was the single most important aspect in my transformation. So I walked around saying I loved myself. I wrote about it in my blogs and newsletters, I emphasized it in my woman's groups and book clubs. I thought I had the love myself thing down.

Apparently not.

It was my ego and intellect that wanted to be proud and show everyone that I loved myself, but I was still living in my head. I was dealing with the abandonment issue from an intellectual perspective and healing cannot happen that way. It wasn't until this final darkness that left me from my last relationship that I could fully live up to loving myself.

I know one day I will get my happy ending and will be with a partner who will be more patient, understanding, open, compassionate, empathetic and supportive. When the going gets tough, he won't get going.

How do I know this? Because we are all mirrors for each other. I am not reflecting a fractured incomplete picture anymore, harboring darkness and unresolved pain. I will never have to go through that experience again because I faced my demons at last, I went into my pain, felt it, released it and have risen from the ashes once more. I gave myself an upgrade for good. Of course, the only way to truly find out if my transformation will stick is with another Beloved, and I'm looking forward to experiencing that.

My challenge on the next time around will be to keep my independence while maintaining a healthy loving relationship, and not lose myself in the man. Easier said than done, but I have confidence in myself for the first time and most importantly: **self-love.**

Relationships give us feedback on what is working and what is not...nothing of great value is obtained without effort. Don't I know it and then some!

What I learned from all of my relationships is to be aware of wearing my rose colored glasses and projecting how I wanted my partners to be versus how they were actually showing up. **Actions speak louder than words.** That's not to say that people can't change, but as Marianne says, "The right person at the wrong time is still the wrong person." Being an natural optimist and seeing the best in people is a wonderful trait, I just need to balance that out with what's happening in the present moment through their actions.

People run from relationships thinking they will be free. But running away is not freedom, it's just running away. It doesn't heal you on any level. It only represses your issues and hides them ready to spring forth in the next relationship. Sometimes people think that changing houses, lovers or moving to new state or country will solve their problems. The problem with that is wherever your body goes, your consciousness goes, and the problem *is* your consciousness. It may be a temporary fix, but if you are not doing the work, looking at yourself honestly and taking action steps to resolve any unresolved wounds, they will come out sooner or later.

That is why when people come to my yoga teacher, Mokshapriya, asking about divorce she advises them to work things out first, then talk about divorce. (Of course I am not talking about abuse or when you fear for your life or well being).

***My Yoga Angel

Speaking of Mokshapriya...this wise woman is one of those people who can nail it with one sentence, bringing you back to your center of clarity and peace with her authoritative tone and confident advice.

Bemoaning when my former husband, Soulmate #3, left me, "I trusted him, he was the first person I ever trusted," I said to her.

She replied walking by me without missing a step, "We aren't meant to trust people. We are meant to trust God."

That one sentence shifted something inside of me and I got it. It's not that people are bad, they are wounded and have their own set of baggage, like we all do. God, you can rely on.

With Soulmate #4 I lamented, "I need closure, I don't understand what happened."

She replied, "You don't need closure. He gave you closure by walking away. He did you a favor, that's your closure."

Man, she's good! A living breathing walking paradigm shifter!

She reassured me one day by reframing my abandonment, "At least the men you are choosing to walk away from you are good sweet soulmates." Indeed they are. Always look for the silver lining.

***The God Squad

One of the positive things that came out of this latest experience of abandonment was it deepened my connection to the spirit ensemble that is always with me. I feel like I have my own personal cheerleading squad. I have come to know I have four guardian angels: Victor and Carmen, Archangels Rafael and Michael and my spirit guide, Omi. I call them the "Fab Five." I am in constant communication with them, and receive validation when I'm on the right path and when I have strayed.

We all have angels assigned to us whether we are aware or not. I'm always amazed how disconnected people are from their angels. If you knew you had help from above wouldn't you want it? I couldn't live a day without them.

The only thing I can do is let go and trust that hopefully my relationship with Soulmate #4 will be brought to the heavens for healing. I have done all I *humanly* can, now I let go and let God. Surrender to what is. Let go of what was. Have faith in what will be. All is well.

People disappoint, God doesn't. THANK GOD FOR GOD. God will never leave me. *"The only beloved who can always be counted on is God."* ~ Marianne Williamson

***The Bigger Picture, The Divine Picture

"The most important decision we make is whether we believe we live in a friendly or hostile universe," said Einstein, "God does not play dice with the universe."

I believe there's a benevolence in the universe that is looking out for me. I can feel it. It whispers, "It's going to be ok, hold on, a little more patience SoulFire. All is in perfect order, trust, my love trust."

Even with all the madness, hostility and turmoil that exists on the planet, there is still an inherent movement towards goodness, toward creation, toward love. The Universe is self correcting and self organizing, just like GPS. We just have to make sure our GPS is set to the right destination. What state are we headed toward? The state of suffering or the state of freedom?

There is another Reality beyond and above our current events, for our individual lives as well as universally. Each time I get lost re-living the past, I redirect myself to the bigger picture reminding myself that it is fruitless to judge this situation until I have an understanding of it in the context of the complete narrative of my life. How can I do that when I have a limited perspective from a keyhole view? If I take a bird's eye view of the hawk, everything changes.

We must go within and connect to our higher consciousness and our divine intelligence. Our human self only sees the drama, uncertainty, confusion, fear, doubt, despair, and limitations. Our spiritual self only sees the clarity, perfection, divine order, harmony, peace, love and endless possibilities.

Which one we choose to focus on is our choice. And our choice will either bring us heaven or will bring us living hell. I choose to focus on heaven. Focus equals freedom.

The Two Wolves

One evening an old Cherokee told his grandson about a battle that was going on inside himself. He said, "My son, it is between two wolves."

One is filled with fear, resentment, anger, envy, sorrow, regret, greed, self-pity, guilt, frustration, conceit, jealousy, inferiority, lies, false pride, superiority and ego.

The other is filled with joy, peace, play, gratitude, passion, enthusiasm, wonder, curiosity, hope, contentment, love, humility, kindness, trust, focus, generosity, truth, compassion, and faith.

The grandson thought about this for a moment and then asked, "Grandfather, which wolf wins?"

The old Cherokee simply replied, "The one I feed."

***Detachment from Attachment

When we detach from the human drama, we are able to look at things from a higher perspective, our purusha, our soul, our higher self. We get a bird's eye view when we detach and look down and within.

When I first started studying Buddhism and yoga, I couldn't fully grasp the concept of detachment. I was befuddled about how I could be detached without being cold and uncaring. And how the heck can I not be attached? We as humans attach to everything; but we as *spiritual beings* do not.

Attachment is human energy, detachment is divine energy. Attachment keeps us stuck in the problem or conflict. Detachment allows us to be free from the pull and push of human drama and emotions and helps us to connect to the well spring of peace, love, guidance and wisdom that's within us.

Detachment doesn't mean we are apathetic and it's not checking out. It's actually checking in. That's the difference between sympathy and empathy. When someone has fallen into a dark hole, sympathy would jump in with them, which would cause you both to be stuck with no way out. Empathy, on the other hand, would stand at the top and lower a rope down to pull you out. When you have sympathy for a person, you descend to their level of suffering. You become that suffering with them.

When you have empathy, you can relate and feel for them, but you hold the space of truth and strength for them. Sympathy is reactive, empathy is proactive.

I've learned the best way to help someone when they are in pain, is just to be there for them. There's something very sacred and healing about sitting with someone in *silence*, being a witness to their pain, without trying to change it, fix it or judge it.

***How Do You Love Yourself???

I was at a drum circle recently and noticed a soul sister struggling. When she confided in me she told me a man she had slept with was there with another girl and he was completely ignoring her. She was beside herself to say the least. She didn't feel comfortable being there and definitely not dancing. I think this scenario is one most of us can relate to, hoping the sex was something more than just sex, when in actuality it was just sex. I heard this once: "Women use sex to get love, and men use love to get sex." And after sex, not knowing how to be honest mature adults we ignore the other person, hoping they will just go away or dissolve so we don't have to deal with our own uncomfortable feelings.

She continued on with details of the story. I listened and heard so much of my old self in her. *Been there, done that; felt that, did that, yup I know exactly how you feel,* I was thinking. She asked me what she should do.

With understanding and empathy, I told her she was selling herself short and while it was ok that she slept with him, if that is what she wanted to do, it wasn't ok that she was beating herself up now over it. She was allowing him to take her power and make her feel small and less than. She agreed with me.

I continued, "The bottom line is that you are not loving yourself."

She then asked me as innocently as a child asks their parent, why is the sky blue, "***How*** do you love yourself?"

Now that's the million dollar question!

I paused, feeling her rawness and vulnerability in the moment. First thought I had was, I wish my book was done already because I have been in this same situation so many times, I might as well been talking to myself. How do you explain to someone a journey that took my entire life to figure out? I was aware that this was an opening and I didn't want to blow it.

Silence can be more powerful than words and this was one of those times. I didn't say anything but took off my jingly coin hip scarf, tied it around her waist, brought her out to the middle of the circle and danced with her. As I twirled her around and around, I watched her light begin to shine again. She looked like a new woman, smiling with delight and aglow with self confidence. She thanked me profusely for getting her out there and dancing with her. In that moment she was free, and in that moment she was love. And that is how you love your self.

We forgot how to love ourselves because women have been oppressed and objectified for thousands of years. We have been programmed to be seen, not heard. There is still a double standard when it comes to sex and expressing our sexuality as a women versus a man. The more sex men have, the more they are looked up to and held in high esteem. Women, on the other hand, are labeled sluts and whores. In addition, we carry the shame of our sisters from lifetimes ago. We are taught to not have an opinion, especially one that goes against the status quo, or we are labeled a bitch. If we are emotional we are labeled irrational or "too much." How many times have I heard that about myself. Of course we are emotional, every month our bodies prepare for a baby and creating life and most months those eggs die and we shed our uterine lining. You don't think that has an element of sadness to it? As women it is our right to be emotional and for it not to make sense or be rational! Most of the time *we* don't even understand where our feelings are coming from.

My advice to men: just accept a woman's feelings without trying to rationalize them. And never, never make her feel bad or crazy because she has intense feelings that you don't understand. You will never succeed at that!!! Just hold her, tell her you love her and be the rock.

Loving ourselves means accepting ourselves, irrational feelings and all. The Goddess is back, and she is beautiful and powerful and sensual and not afraid to express herself. The old way of thinking and living keeps us locked in the cage, and we are birds that need to soar. Our wings cannot be contained inside a box.

***God Is In the Gut...COLLECTING DATA

Our connection to our higher self, or our internal compass, is felt through the gut. When we shift from living in our head to living from our heart or our gut, we can feel and filter everything through the heart/gut center. And trust me, it's a much better way to live.

If something or someone brings you discomfort and you get that intuitive warning pang in your gut, it is something to look at and pay more attention to, not ignore. These are red flags or our higher self communicating with us. If we ignore these signals, we are in essence betraying ourselves.

I got those pangs in my gut with Soulmate #4 as well as all my other soulmates, but ignored them because I was headstrong that he was "the one." After watching me suffer for months, one of my angel friends suggested it's time I write the negative and positive list, something I had been avoiding. I was still sporting the rose colored glasses. She gently coaxed me to see the big picture and take him off the pedestal. Even though I didn't think I had him there, I did. There's nothing wrong with believing in love, we just have to believe it with someone who believes it back.

There are many ways in which we betray ourselves and not listen to our gut. It doesn't have to be a grandiose event either. Usually they are what seem to be insignificant things, but in reality are not. Every time we don't want to do something and we do it anyway, we are betraying ourselves. And I'm not talking about exercising or doing things that are positive for your well being that you are just being lazy about. I'm talking about saying yes when you really want to say no, that's negativity in disguise. You give your power away and part of your self.

It's not healthy for us or our relationship partner when we are not true to ourself and give in to their requests, demands or manipulative behavior. We only resent them in the end. I've done that too many times in my life to count. One of the most significant times was after the breakup with Soulmate #2.

***Integrity

A few months after Soulmate #2 walked out on us, he came back to me to reconcile. I had already done the work, processed my feelings, shifted to a place of forgiveness and had moved on. But because I was still attached to the idea of love and didn't want to be alone, I decided to try again, even though my heart and my gut were saying no. Our get togethers turned into "booty calls" which went on for about a year or so. I knew deep down this is not what I wanted but was attached and stuck in the pattern.

Then one day during my studies of *The Science of Getting Rich* with Bob Proctor (enlightenment comes from all sources), Bob said something that made me stop and think:

> **"Honesty with another person is fairly easy, while honesty with yourself is much more difficult."**

I always thought of myself as an honest person. For example, if I found a wallet with money I would return the wallet complete with the money, even if I was in need or gave the cashier money back if they made a mistake. I prided myself on being impeccable with my word as well, "Say what you mean and mean what you say."

But being honest with ourself is a lot harder to notice. It means that our thoughts, feelings and actions are all in alignment, which is a definition of integrity. I had an A-HA moment after I heard that. I was thinking and feeling one thing about my ex-fiancee and then doing something else. I was not being honest with myself, I was not in integrity. The "booty calls" stopped after that. I realized I was giving away my power because my heart wasn't in it. That lesson has stuck with me to this day.

Integrity is what you do when no one is looking. It is being honest with yourself and that translates into self-love. Loving yourself means saying, 'no thank you' at times. However, just because we say 'no' doesn't mean we close our hearts. We are simply honoring our healthy boundaries by loving ourself. <u>We can say no and stay open</u>.

One valuable lesson Soulmate #3 taught me was that it was not necessary to answer everyone right then and there when they ask you a question. Seems like common sense, but when you are a people pleaser it could get tricky. His response was, "I'll bring it to prayer." I love that come back because instead of over committing and saying *yes* when you want to say *no,* it puts the power back in your court and gives you time to make a decision based on self-love. It doesn't have to be a spiritual reply, you can say, "Let me think about it and I'll get back to you."

***My Housemate

"Love is blind," is true statement but it's not really love, it's temporary hormones that are taking over our brain. It's not a bad thing to take it slow and learn about a person first before we get intimate and physical. Once we cross that line, something shifts and we are not as objective as we would have been if we remained just friends for a while. I believe it's different for women, although energetically when we have sex with someone we are still connected to them even if the sex ends.

I've learned that if I'm goo goo gaga over a man, if I take the time to get to know him before jumping in the sack, more than likely I will feel differently about him and the intense emotions that go along with sex will be more manageable. After my former husband, Soulmate#3 moved out, the Universe, probably feeling sorry for me listening to my wailing sobs, bestowed me with a gift.

A few months had passed, I was in the basement doing laundry when the door to the downstairs apartment opened and out came this perfect specimen of a man, my new housemate. Trying to act like he didn't just rattle my world, I introduced myself while thanking God silently. He was a former Navy Seal with the face of a GQ model, beautiful blue eyes and a killer smile. Every friend that came over who I introduced to him would respond the same way, "*That* is what lives downstairs?" "Are you kidding?"

For the first time in my life I didn't let my hormones take over and did the "get to know him first." Not that there would have been anything wrong if I didn't, but I was being true to myself, finally. While he was and is a great guy and we had many things in common, at the core, not so much. We were at different times in our lives with a different vision for our future. Although his dog, Joey, fell in love with Karma, we remained friends and still are to this day. During that vulnerable time my heart was in recovery he was a Godsend to me. We developed a beautiful friendship and spent a lot of time together. Not only was he there for me, he helped my heart to heal. He was another angel in my life, and I will always cherish the time we spent together.

***Living Your Truth, Being the Light

I use to think my daughter's anger was caused by my dishonesty or hiding the truth about her father. Since she was still angry after I told her the truth, I got the feeling she was angry because she watched me betray myself and give my power away, in so many ways, over and over again.

I don't think our daughters necessarily know why they are angry at us, it's more subconscious. Our daughters are angry and mad because we are letting them down by not living our truth. When we become empowered women, goddesses and co-creators of our heaven on earth, then they will shift. They will feel it, they will know we are back in our light and in our glory. Until then, they will remain with chip on their shoulder.

Our kids are wise beings of light and truth. They know. They know. They know.

***Thinking With the Heart

> "Don't think. Feel. It is like a finger pointing away to the moon, don't concentrate on the finger or you will miss all that heavenly glory." ~Bruce Lee

Most of the time the pain we are experiencing is not coming from the heart. I submit that our heart is perfect, whole and complete as is. It is our mind that screws us up. We have to stop listening to the *thoughts* in our mind that take us away from the *knowing* in our heart.

We are so used to living in our heads that we aren't aware we even have a heart. And I don't mean the heart organ that pumps blood through our bodies and keeps us alive- the heart center that is the gateway and key to unlocking our full potential as spiritual-human beings.

> "In your heart is where wisdom lies, and where truth dwells. Do not confuse what is in your mind with what is in your heart. What

is in your mind has been put there by others. What is in your heart is what you carry with me- is where God resides in most intimate communion with you." ~Neale Donald Walsch, *Home with God, in a Life That Never Ends.*

In order to reconnect with the divinity of our hearts, where we will find guidance and all we need to be fulfilled and happy, we need to silence the mind. Our minds have become the enemy because it has become so fierce. Fierce thoughts are the pre-programming and the signal however. It is YOU battling you. They are becoming fiercer now because they are telling you they are no longer serving you. It is divine You signaling to human you to wake up. They are signals of your divine heart because there must be compatibility of the mind with the Spirit.

Don't be afraid of them, welcome them and say thank you. *Thank you for showing me that it's time for me to wake up and let go of these limiting thoughts that no longer serve my soul. I am bigger than these thoughts, in fact, I am not these thoughts.* Then release them and ask they be transmuted back to the light.

And...the dark nights of the soul are actually You (divine you) waking up you (human you). The dark nights of the soul serve a purpose, a grave and grand and inviting purpose. It is your higher self calling out to your human self, trying to get its attention, "Hey buddy, wake up! There's more to you than meets the eye and if you realized all that you have and all that you are, you would not be able to contain your joy!"

When we live from our soul we don't fall prey to other people's opinions and beliefs. When we live from our soul we become the most powerful presence upon the earth.

***A Broken Heart is an Open Heart

For those of you reading this right now who are suffering from a broken heart, I know there's nothing more painful, but take advantage of staying open. By shutting down your heart and blocking out your feelings, you may think you are playing is safe, but you are just hurting yourself.

We close our hearts down and numb ourselves as a survival mechanism of the ego, but all we're really doing is creating a game of self-deception and self-denial. We walk around with so many walls around our hearts, not even aware we have them. We defend, reflect, argue, blame, defend some more, protect, shield, hide, fight, battle, resist, thinking by doing so we are preserving and safeguarding our heart. We are not, though. The walls keep us in conflict, keep us prisoner and shut down our joy and the flow of life. They are where we have not yet learned how to be unconditional love to ourselves. Just like the protective Berlin Wall came down, we must do the same. As Rumi says, "Your task is not to seek for love, but merely to seek and find all the barriers within yourself that you have built."

***One of my favorite yoga poems by Swami Kripalvanandji:

My beloved child, break your heart no longer.
Each time you judge yourself, you break your own heart.
You stop feeding on the love, which is the wellspring of your vitality.

The time has come. Your time to live, to celebrate and see the goodness that you are.

You, my child, are divine. You are pure. You are sublimely free. You are God in disguise and you are always perfectly safe.

Do not fight the dark, just turn on the light. Let go and breathe into the goodness that you are.

***Emergency Contact

"Happiness is having someone to write in the emergency contact space." ~Me

A lot of people have hang-ups when it comes to going to the doctor, as well as myself, but filling out the emergency contact form is probably not one of them. For most there isn't a second thought. For me, I stare at the blank space considering who can I put down, which can rouse feelings of loneliness and if I'm not careful bring me down into the "nobody loves me mode." Sometimes I would just leave it blank, which sparked the question from the medical admin, "Are you sure there is no one?" Feeling worse.

Before I met Soulmate #4, I was content with being alone and growing old alone. I thought I would be like the Golden Girls. But now I know that was just another lie I was telling myself. No one wants to be alone, maybe temporary, but not forever. Bonding is on our biology. It is innate. Human beings are not meant to be alone. I realized I want to grow old with someone who will stick by my side through thick and thin. I don't know what that is like, I had a wart on my hand that stuck around longer than any of my relationships. My heart is calling for someone that will stand the tests of time, the trials and tribulations, the up and downs, the good, the bad and the ugly. My heart is calling for that unbreakable love.

> "Women need to be in love: with themselves, with a man, with a child, with a project, with a job, with their country, with the planet, and-most importantly-with life itself. Women in love are closer to enlightenment. For angels and lovers, everything sparkles."
> ~*A Woman's Worth,* Marianne Williamson

I just want to sparkle.

I think those of us who are alone crave company and those who are in relationship, especially if it's challenging, wish they were alone. But there are many ways you can have relationships that are healthy and rewarding. I think it's important that we don't define a relationship so much as to the *form* of it, but rather the *content*.

*** Love Never Dies

> "When you lose someone you love, you gain an angel you know."
> ~Oprah

During my separation from Soulmate#4, my father passed away. It wasn't a big surprise because he had been sick and disabled from a stroke years ago and never recovered. I hadn't seen my dad in over ten years and the amount of conversations we had I could count on one hand. Even so, the finality of death, especially a parent is a major loss.

It was Saturday, September 5th, and I was on my way to Fire Island to do massages. I opened my email in the morning and deleted the usual gazillion emails from my Dad, most of them silly forwards. Since the stroke, the computer and technology became his best friend.

There was one however that caught my attention: *"And God shall wipe away all tears from their eyes; and there shall be no more death, neither sorrow, nor crying, neither shall there be any more pain: for the former things are passed away."* (Revelation 21:4)

Sadness took me by surprise. This was the scripture I chose for Eugene's mass card. All day long, even in my most favorite place in the world, I couldn't shake this sadness. I had a new client that day with back pain and her seven year old daughter, who was extremely intuitive, insisted on staying next to me while I worked on her mother. Her mother said that was unusual for her. This little angel wouldn't leave my side, even hugged me as I was massaging her mother and told me she loved me. I welcomed this pure love even though I thought it was a little odd. I had to fight back the emotions. She hugged me about ten more times before I left their house.

As I was riding my bike back to my car I passed by a church with a mass happening which I thought strange since it was the middle of the day. I never knew there was a church on that street even though I had walked by a thousand times. I stopped my bike and sat outside on the front steps and listened to the mass. I thought about my father and couldn't help feeling this terrible ache in my heart. I couldn't sit there any longer.

Still feeling this haunting sadness, as I was driving home across the Robert Moses Bridge I put out a call to my angels to send me a friend. I didn't want to be alone that night. When I got home I got a text from my brother, "Dad just died." I knew it. My Dad knew it too, he knew he was going to die that day.

I always wondered how I was going to feel when my Dad died since we never had a close relationship. It still felt like a loss, actually a double loss. I felt sad because I never had a relationship with him, sad because I wasn't there for him and I cried because I lost a father that I never really had.

But then I had an epiphany. At that moment I began talking to my Dad like he was right next to me. It felt like he was, so I said to him, "Dad if you are here, can you be a father to me now and be there for me? I need help. I am struggling and I am hurting, please help me." I was still feeling the loss over Soulmate #4 and now this was too much to bear.

I was walking Karma crying and praying to my father and within a few minutes I felt the sadness dissipate and the pain in my heart dissolve. It was a miracle. I could breathe deeply again. *Thank you Dad,* I whispered as I walked home.

The angels had a call in to my wonderful friend Lisa, who arrived at the perfect time with my two favorite foods: sushi and chocolate. She was an angel, stayed till midnight talking with me. I am so blessed to have such wonderful friends in my life. I don't know what I'd do without them.

> "You road will be made smooth for you by good friends." ~Fortune cookie I saved from 15 years old

Since my Dad has passed I have a better relationship with him now than I had when he was alive. He couldn't help me when he was stuck in his disabled human body in Florida, but now that he is free, in his spiritual essence, he is with me and helping me everyday to heal my heart. My Dad can be with me now just as quickly as I think about him. I find peanut shells, (his nickname for me was peanup), and I see his initials FJZ on license plates almost every single day, sometimes twice a day when I really need him.

> In India when someone leaves their body they say they are now in their "big form," meaning they are now everywhere, connected to

us all. It makes sense. Our true essence is soul, light, infinite and eternal energy. When we are in a limited human body there is only so much we can do. When we are free of the body, or the "suit," we are truly free and our spirit can be everywhere. "Don't grieve. Anything you lose comes round in another form." ~Rumi

I am amazed at this miracle and grateful to have my Dad in my life now when I need him the most. It's the *content*, not the *form* that matters.

I pray that if you have lost a loved one and your heart is broken, that you find comfort in knowing they are still with you in spirit and always will be just a thought away. Know that they are truly free and at peace, home with God, surrounded by unconditional love and acceptance. The only thing that lasts is love.

When there are no words, know that the whispering of the winds carry the love of those you hold dear. Peace be with you.

***Love as Content

A couple of months later I met someone, not someone I would want to be in a committed relationship with as he was going through his own healing crisis, but someone who turned out to be very special to me none the less. I only realized this after he moved away and I felt a loss. Even though I only knew him for five months, my soul felt like I knew him forever.

Being with him was so easy, and talking with him was like continuing a conversation from another lifetime. We became instant friends. There was no drama, no expectations, no conflict- much different than anything I have experienced before. The universe was making up for the lack of communication from Soulmate #4 apparently as we would talk for hours upon end about things that really mattered.

Our bond came from our unmasked conversation which led to real communion. In each other's presence we healed simply by being a witness to each others' pain and a reminder to each others' light. He was a gift to my soul. He showed me there are men in the world that show up and are in touch with their feelings and their heart. The form was different but the content was *pure love*.

Then there's the opposite, when the content is gone but the form is still there. I know many people in loveless marriages and relationships that they choose to stay in for many different reasons. The most common is the children.

> "It is better to be alone than to be living at half throttle." ~ Marianne Williamson

There are only so many hours left in your life, actually there are 8,448 hours in a year. If you live forty more years that's 337,920 hours left. How do you want to spend them? There will never be growth without coming out of your comfort zone. Staying together for the children is a noble idea, but what are you teaching your children? Sometimes we need to stay and work things out and sometimes it's time to go. Only your heart will know what is right for you. Like Mary Oliver says: "Tell me, what is it you plan to do with your one wild and precious life?"

THE INVITATION by Oriah Mountain Dreamer

It doesn't interest me what you do for a living. I want to know what you ache for, and if you dare to dream of meeting your hearts longing.

It doesn't interest me how old you are. I want to know if you will risk looking like a fool for love, for your dreams, for the adventure of being alive.

It doesn't interest me what planets are squaring your moon I want to know if you have touched the center of your own sorrow, if you have been open by life's betrayals or have you become shriveled and closed from fear of further pain.

I want to know if you can sit with pain, mine or your own, without moving to hide it or fade it or fix it.

I want to know if you can be with joy, mine or you own, if you can dance with wildness and let the ecstasy fill you to the tips of your fingers and toes without cautioning us to be careful, to be realistic, or to remember the limitations of being human.

It doesn't interest me if the story you're telling me is true. I want to know if you can disappoint another to be rue to yourself, it you can bear the accusation of betrayal and not betray your own soul.

I want to know if you can be faithful and therefore be trustworthy. I want to know if you can see beauty even when it's not pretty every day, and if you can source you life from God's presence.

I want to know if you can live with failure, yours and mine, and still stand on the edge of a lake and shout to the silver of the moon, YES!

It doesn't interest me to know where you live or how much money you have. I want to know if you can get up after the night of grief and despair, weary and bruised to the bond, and do what need to be done for the children.

It doesn't interest me where or with whom you have studied. I want to know what sustains you from the inside when all else falls away.

I want to know if you can be alone with yourself, and if you truly like the company you keep in the empty moments.

***Unexpected Help from an Unexpected Soul

During one of my intuitive healing sessions, (before my father passed), the guide asked me about my daughter's grandfather, she said he was coming through to communicate. I told her my daughter's grandfather was still alive in Florida. She said "No, it's her grandfather and he's definitely not alive." Then I thought maybe he was from Eugene's side of the family. She said, "No, he's connected to you."

All of a sudden it dawned on me that it could be my biological father. I normally don't think about him since he was never a part of my life. She concurred that it was my biological father. I didn't know how to react. Here was my father, sort of, in spirit form, coming to me for the first time in my life.

She asked me if I had any questions for him, as long as she was still in the space of communication-you never know how long these connections last. Of course I wanted to ask him questions! I had so many but his appearance was so sudden and unexpected. The only thing that popped into mind which I had wondered from time to time was the most important question of all, and I was afraid to ask. I did anyway, since I thought this might be my only chance to know the answer. Bravely and reluctantly I asked...

"Did he know about me?"

This question brings up so much emotion in me as I am writing this part, I realize that no matter how awakened or enlightened we become, there will always be a part of us that hurts, that yearns for that fatherly or motherly love.

I waited for what seemed like an eternity, my heart hanging on a limb...

She responded, "No, he did not know about you."

Phew, my heart saved.

She continued, "He wants you to know that he wishes he did know about you and was a part of your life. He sees how you have grown into a beautiful woman, and regrets not being there for you. His karma is to watch over Aiyana now. She will never be alone, he is at her side. He kisses her on her forehead and is always with her."

I was at a loss for words. I didn't know what to say or how to feel to be honest. I wanted to ask him more questions but the connection was gone. I knew it would take time for me to process what just happened.

On the practical side since family support is not something I ever had, it was comforting to know that my biological father is watching over my twenty year old daughter who is living across the country.

A few days later, I shared this with my daughter as she listened quietly. When I got to the part that he kisses her on her forehead, she replied, "That's pretty creepy, Mom." Laughing at her response, she, on the other hand, was not so convinced.

Now when I pray for my daughter I say, "All three fathers in heaven, please help Aiyana- there's three of you now! Someone's gotta be able to do something!" Even though my daughter and I grew up without a father we each have one now, actually three! Grateful. Amen.

PETAL 8

Whoooooooo Are You?

***The Jeannie in the Bottle

> "We are energy. Energy cannot be created or destroyed, it just changes form. Einstein realized that. When seen out of context, a cloud in the sky could just as easily be a wave in the sand. Perceptual experience is choice. Can you open your mind to the infinite possibilities?" ~D. L. Robinson

THE SUN IS 93 million miles away from us. It is so far that the light from the sun, traveling at 186,000 miles per second takes about 8 minutes to reach us. Astoundingly, we can still see and feel the sun beams. That is incredible if you think about it. Just like a sunbeam can never be separate from the sun, we can never be separate from God and each other.

Next time you are in the sun, squint your eyes and notice the golden light coming from the sun right to your heart center. No matter where you move, that light follows you. That is how we are connected to our higher selves, to God, and to each other. With normal eye sight we cannot notice it, but if we change the lens, we see with new eyes.

> The Japanese mourn when babies are born and celebrate when people die. The Japanese along with other eastern cultures understand that taking human form is a tough job with a lot of heartache and pain. Death is a freeing of the soul. Our eternal expansive soul is freed like a genie in the bottle. "Life is LOVE which

> is a gift from God and parents, and DEATH is gratitude for going to a new dimension." ~ Masaru Emoto, scientist, pioneer, author

How we view life is up to us. There is no reason that we have to follow along with what we were brought up with, what the majority thinks, what society thinks, or what our family thinks. Think for yourself. Make your own rituals and follow what is true in your own heart.

I decided a long time ago that when I die (or leave this body to be more precise) I want to have a life celebration party, not a funeral. I want my ashes to be scattered in the ocean, my home. No need for my body to be rotting in the earth when I'm not in my body anymore. I will be free, in my big form!

A wonderful true story about a NDE, near death experience, by Anita Moorjani, *Dying to be Me, My Journey from Cancer, to Near Death, To True Healing* is one I recommend highly. One of the things that stuck with me from her story and many of the other NDE accounts I have read about was the discovery that the "other side" was much more real than this world. There is more to us than meets the eye and there is another Reality that is slowly manifesting on our planet. The invisible is becoming visible again.

> "You are different from God, but you are not divided from God. The fact that you are not divided from God is why you can never die. The wave lands on the beach, but it does not cease to be. It merely changes form, receding back into the ocean." ~Neale Donald Walsch, *Home with God, In A Life That Never Ends.*

If change is the only constant, what doesn't change? We go back to our yoga sutras, the Purusha, or the Seer, the true self is the only thing that remains indestructible. It would make sense then to hold on to what is changeless is a changing world, otherwise we are bound to suffer. It all comes back to the same fundamental question I have been asking throughout my book, who are you?

Abiding ageless timeless perpetual constant steadfast immovable unwavering eternal boundless everlasting imperishable unfading enduring unfailing continual light and love.

***Unchain Your Brain

Did you ever wonder why we use only 10 percent of the brain? I have my entire life. The brain is the biological computer that only allows in what we have been programmed with. Most social programming teaches you to accept a very limited view of human existence and human ability. Our limited thinking programs also come from what we experience with the five senses: sight, hearing, taste, smell and touch...and not the whole reality. Although the brain is capable of receiving higher information and frequencies, it only receives what we allow and what we allow comes from our narrow viewpoints and programming. Any thought that doesn't fit into the limited thinking programs of our brain is deflected and that's why the Law of Attraction does not work.

> "We can only see what our brain's filter allows through. The brain-in particular its left-side linguistic/logical part, that which generates our sense of rationality and the feeling of being a sharply defined ego or self-is a barrier to our higher knowledge and experience." ~ Proof of Heaven, Dr. Eben Alexander

***The Law of Belief

In the beginning of my awakening I became a Law of Attraction practitioner. In my recent awakenings, I have come to learn that there is more to the the Law of Attraction and that's why it never stuck. I learned how to manifest money and material needs but it was temporary. The Law of Attraction is the *cosmetic* of real creation.

We cannot manifest what we do not believe. Ultimately it's our beliefs that become our reality, not our thoughts. If we have positive thoughts but underneath (in our sub-conscious) we don't really believe them, we will not manifest anything. If we harbor doubt that will automatically block the creation. Doubt stems from fear which stems from forgetting who you are. That is why people say affirmations and write them down on sticky notes and nothing happens. The **Law of Belief** is the ultimate law of creation.

We need to reprogram our brains and our thinking in order to re-open our sacred minds to not just the five senses but higher dimensions. When we live our life sourcing our joy from our senses and the material world, we are bound to suffer. That all changes; our divine essence remains.

The moment we realize who we are we no longer have to manifest anything. It goes from a mechanical exercise to an automatic response from the universe in reverberation of our vibration. Then praying for something outside of us turns into praying for something inside of us when we realize we cannot manifest what we don't have. When we want or desire something that implies we don't have it and that presumes lack. Lack is the illusion. There is an abundance of everything we need on this planet to survive and thrive. All we need to do is believe and become it. A deep and concrete inner knowing of who you are is the key to manifesting. Your prayer then becomes- help me step into the vibration of the God/Goddess that I truly am.

***Got Love?

Asking this question is a silly one. It's like asking if the ocean has water. Of course it does, it *is* water. You have love, of course, because you *are* love. "Enlightenment, for a wave in the ocean, is the moment the wave realizes that it is water." (Thich Nhat Hanh) Enlightenment, for a human on the earth, is the moment the human realizes that it is God.

That's when DO, HAVE, BE turns into BE, DO, HAVE. When you have allowed love to be the backdrop of your life, you no longer have to say it. You just are it. And that is how mantras become you. At first we say mantras, write them down, chant them over and over, write them on sticky notes and put them up everywhere around the house and in the car. Then one day, if you are doing the work and you wake up to the truth and corrected perception, you realize you no longer need that sticky note or the mantra. You no longer need to say the words because you are it and your life is a reflection of it. The conscious mind merges with the subconscious mind; the thinking and believing stops and you exude it through your presence. Integration.

For me there has been no greater feeling of relief and happiness than when people notice and say that I exude love, openness and light. It is complete 180 degrees from where I was- exuding dirty looks, rolling eyeballs and angry yells.

***Holy Shift!

That's when spirituality isn't 5 minutes of meditation in the morning or the one hour yoga class. You've stop trying to cram it in to your busy schedule, there is no need once you've transformed into a more evolved being with a different perspective. This is what spiritual integration means. Everything you do comes from a knowing of who you really are. You are God choosing. You see everything as spiritual, you see God in everyone, everywhere. You are still in the world but you know you are not from the world. You have a greater awareness and see with different eyes. This is what the Ascension, the Fifth Dimension, the New Earth, the Shift that we moved into on December 21-22, 2012 is all about.

Jesus proclaimed, "But seek ye first the kingdom of God and His righteousness," he declared, "and all these things shall be added unto you" (Matthew 6:33). With these words, Jesus gave voice to a teaching that is universal and timeless. Seek God first. Seek You first-the true You. All else but this is the illusion, the maya, the temporary world. This is the foundation for true inner peace and happiness.

The Kingdom of God is within you is a universal teaching in all the great religions. When you wake up and realize who you are, that there is no thing that is not you, you are all encompassing, a hologram, a part of All That Is, you are God expressing itself through the lens of your chosen human form, your whole life will change. It's not because you are *not* worthy that you should receive, it's because you *are* worthy that you should receive.

From The Starseed Transmissions, by Ken Carey:

> "Your entry into the eternal awesomeness of the present moment, into the Presence of God, will be through what we call a 'psychological process.' This process is a process of identity shift, a process through which balance is restored in your awareness of the two realities. Through it, you begin to realize that you are not the form you animate, but the force of animation itself. Through it, you will reawaken to an awareness of all that you are in Spirit and in wholeness. It is a process that will return you to a state of grace, a state of health, a state of intimate association with all that is. This state already exists. It always has. Yet most human beings are blinded to it by the incessant machinations of the rational thought process that they worship instead of God and His simple truth."

***The Isness Business

That's when we exist in the state of Isness. Isness is a pure state of beingness. It's allowance, there is no will, no thought. There is no more turmoil, no more entanglements. You can say Isness is like surrender; accepting all that is in the moment without trying to change it. Most people think of surrender as defeat, hoisting the white flag. Surrender on the New Earth is actually very active and courageous way of being because it takes faith in the unknown for some that are just waking up. But for others that are conscious, faith takes a backseat because it is has become a *knowing*. Being in a state of Isness doesn't mean we deny our human self. Actually we acknowledge that our human self has imperfections and we accept that part of us. But we also connect to our God self and acknowledge the perfection and wholeness of who we truly are in our deepest core essence.

Dr. David Hawkins describes it as "A thought free state of knowingness, that's complete and all inclusive, with neither need nor want, and beyond the limitation of experiencing the merely individualized personal self."

Inspiring and comforting words from *Home With God, In A Life That Never Ends:*

> "There is no way to get into the Kingdom of God. It is not a place you get into or out of. It is a place where you always ARE. It is the only place that you can ever be.
>
> The great misunderstanding of all those who have forgotten Ultimate Truth the great illusion of all those who live in temporary amnesia, is that there is somewhere they have to "go," somewhere they have to journey, in order to "get to heaven," or "unite with God," and experience eternal bliss.
>
> There is nowhere you have to go, nothing you have to do, and nothing you have to be expect exactly what you are being right now, in order to experience the bliss of the divine.
>
> You ARE the bliss of the Divine, and you simply do not know it."
> ~Neale Donald Walsch

***Essence of Love

During my time of solitude from Soulmate#4 I looked to my angel cards for solace and comfort. The divine inspirational messages are just what my soul needed to be pulled back from the inescapable pain coming from the unending mind-loops. They are beautiful reminders of timeless truths. The one card I pulled more than any other was this one:

> "The Angel of the Essence of Love helps us to strip off the mask of illusion and see that love is the essence of all life. This angel works to help us unfold from the limited cocoon of our ego and be the magnificent creatures of light we are. When we have penetrated the illusions of personality and the destructive nature of negativity we realize that what we are, at our core, is a fountain of love.
>
> This love lives at the centre of every living cell in our bodies, and in the heart of all living things. The consciousness of which we are made permeates all other living substance too. Our own sweet essence is the same as the universal essence of love which unites us and bonds us intimately with the Source.
>
> We can offer prayers to The Angel of the Essence of Love to help us recognize the essence which lies at the heart of our being. When we choose to identify with this essence we are coming from our Higher Self, which is an aspect of the Divine, rather than from that other self of the small, individual ego. We seek assistance to help us detach ourselves from the illusions of our being and to find the underlying reality that we are one with the Source and with all life. We pray to be able to connect with that oneness and remember the eternal and unconditional nature of that love.
>
> As we open our hearts to the love within us, we find that the essence of love is the basic and fundamental substance of life.

Without it nothing could grow or flourish, and life would cease to exist. The Angel of Essence of Love carefully guards this substance within each of us. When we choose to live from this space we are given untold treasures in the shape of experiences which acknowledge to us that love is who we are." ~*The Angel Oracle,* Ambika Wauters

***Finding Peace

"Live each present moment completely and the future will take care of itself. Fully enjoy the wonder and beauty of each instant. Practice the presence of peace. The more you do that, the more you will feel the presence of that power in your life." ~Paramahansa Yogananda

Peace is only possible in the present moment. I can't tell you how many times I have read this statement or heard this concept expressed in different ways, but never took it seriously until I began to seriously wake up. Eckhart Tolle, a world renowned philosopher, devoted an entire book to the present moment, *The Power of Now.* There had to be something to this. It wasn't until this last episode of complete heartbreak and abandonment that I finally got it. I finally realized how precious the present moment is.

Zig Ziglar, who was one of the first motivational speakers I listened to on cassette tape in my car, had an interesting definition of a genius. He said a genius was someone who was able to stay in the present moment. I love this definition because it's not dependent on IQ and it's available to everyone.

Nevertheless, how many of us actually put this practice into action? Meaning, when you are at work, you are at work, and not

> thinking about family matters; when you are at home relaxing, you are home relaxing and not thinking about work; when you are in the shower, you are in the shower, and not thinking about your to do list, etc. Your mind is where your body is. As simple as this concept is, this is one of the most challenging things to do. "Your mind, with all its preset misconstrued neural pathways, is the root of all your problems." ~Pam Grout, *E-Squared*

One of the things that transforms when you practice the art of being present is the amount of energy and vitality you have. One experience that made me stop and realize the power of the now moment occurred a few years ago during the time I was fund raising, training to swim across the Great South Bay, teaching yoga, personal training, doing massage and decided to get another part time job waitressing on top of that. I tend to be on the lazy side, I know. What was I thinking?

I had just finished walking Karma and didn't realize I had to be at the restaurant at 3:30 for my evening shift. I was enjoying the moment when I got the call, "Where are you?" If I had known I had to work that day I would have not enjoyed my time with Karma, or any of my day for that matter. I would have been thinking about work with apprehension; it had been twenty years since I had waitressed and found it quite challenging and anxiety provoking. Not knowing I had to work was a gift because it allowed me to see the difference in the quality of my time spent when I wasn't fretting about work.

What takes us out of the present moment? I found the most practical insight about staying in the present moment from Dr. Richard Moss's book, *The Mandala of Being, Discovering the Power of Awareness:*

> "How can we take the heightened state of consciousness achieved during the retreat and maintain it at home? My answer is simple: Past, Future, Me, You. Energy, as I am using the term here, is really

our power of awareness, and this is always a product of our proximity to the Now-moment. At the beginning of ourselves, we are united with the Source, the further we move away, the faster we leak that energy and diminish our capacity for awareness. Our past, future, me, you stories are little black holes that continually suck away our energy by creating their own vortices of unreality. This unreality, like a dream, seems real to us at the time, but from within it there is no way to be replenished by the Source. We seem to always be at the edge of exhaustion, wondering why are we so tired, why is there so little (or so much) time. Why can't we seem to pull ourselves together? The answer is simple: we are paddling without putting our paddle in the water. We don't grasp that we are replenished only by the Source, and that for this to happen we must return to the Now, to our beginning. We have to take the risk of staying in the present. Therefore, one of the most important things we can learn is to see clearly the four places we go when we leave ourselves. Then we can wake up from these stories and "re-source" ourselves, moment by moment."

The eternal now moment is all we really have. Everything else we are just making up.

Our emotional body is usually stuck in the re-playing of the past drama, re-living experiences of pain or failure and our mental body is projecting into the future with fear and uncertainty. When I start to feel cruddy I pause and examine the thoughts I was just having. Yup, it's my mind out of control. When I heard the message from God, "No the preoccupies mujer," (Don't worry woman), I didn't fully get it until now. By the way when we re-live the past by obsessing over it in our minds, it produces the same chemical effects as it was actually happening. If you want a cocktail of cortisol, norepinephrine, cytokines and histamine, think fearful thoughts; if you want a cocktail of dopamine, oxytocin, vasopressin and growth hormone, think loving thoughts.

What is worry anyway? I love Patanjai's definition of worry: "Worry is a thought that hasn't happened yet." Joyce Meyers says, "Worry is like rocking in a rocking chair, keeps you busy, but get you nowhere," and Mark Twain, "I've had a lot of worries in my life, most of which never happened."

Worry is faith inverted. Worry is getting lost in the world of illusion and forgetting who you are, temporarily. You can always get back.

> "Harnessing the power of your mind can be more effective than the drugs you have been programmed to believe you need."
> ~Bruce Lipton PhD, Cell Biologist

Over 40 million people suffer from anxiety. Medication is not the answer. Meditation is.Truth is. Charles Spurgeon (Author and England's best known minister,1834-1892) said it best: "Anxiety does not empty tomorrow of its sorrow, but only empties today of its strength."

***Empowered Meditation

In the beginning of my journey I would attend all these inspiring motivating workshops doing the ole "woot woot," then after a couple of days being home the pep in my step was gone and I was back to the same ole negative thoughts and boring routine. Over coffee with a friend one day, who also was experiencing the same phenomena, we questioned how do we maintain that good feeling of bliss? The reason for the temporary high was because I hadn't learned yet how to stay in the present moment, so when I wasn't thinking or being present I defaulted back to my distorted subconscious programming. What I was learning did not yet sink into my subconscious, it had yet to become a habit.

The subconscious mind is like a sponge, it doesn't judge or differentiate with the information that is being supplied. It just takes it all in, no questions asked.

We can all relate to learning how to drive. At first it was all very mechanical- concentrating and focusing on putting our foot on the brake and gas and so on. Over time with practice driving became something we did without consciously thinking about it, it was now engrained into our subconscious mind. That's how we can get in our car, drive somewhere and not remember one detail about how we got there? That's because we are driving on autopilot from our subconscious mind. This is how we live most of our life, including how we relate in our relationships as well.

One of the most helpful insights I found was in the book, *The HoneyMoon Effect,* by Dr. Bruce Lipton. He says there are really *four minds* in a relationship. Your conscious mind, your sub conscious mind, your partner's conscious mind and their sub-conscious mind. If we are not paying attention, the sub-conscious mind is running the show and it's not a pleasurable one. We react from our wounds, lash out from our wounds, relate from our wounds and next thing you know you and your wounds are moving on, like me.

Now I understand why Osho, a wise spiritual teacher, said that the only way for a relationship to work is if both people were meditating. What he meant by that is not sitting cross legged with eyes closed off somewhere in la la land; rather, meditation meant actually bringing your awareness into your interactions and daily life. I call it meditation in action which might seem like an oxymoron but it is not. Personally I don't think it's such a great feat to sit alone in quietude somewhere peaceful and clear your mind. Big whoops! Try having a peaceful mind in the midst of a turbulent relationship or in the midst of your children having temper tantrums while you are trying to pay the rent and put food on the table. I think it's a great feat when you can be in the crazy and still be steady and centered.

Meditation is not the goal of yoga as some people think. Meditation is a tool that can help you reach the goal. The goal of yoga is freedom, liberation, or self-realization. You might be born, like most children now with the realization of who you truly are already and never lose it; therefore, you don't need to meditate. Of course, meditation comes in handy in our modern busy world as a means to re-center yourself and enrich your being from within. However, being a spiritual vagabond or vague mystic doesn't serve anyone. Combining the introspective, inward focus of Eastern philosophies with the creative outward focus of the West is the best way to serve the world. We came here to be human, not to transcend it. Divinity in action.

***Our stifling stories...blah, blah, blah

Not only do we leave the present moment with past-future thoughts, we pile on more negative self-sabotaging thoughts that support our subconscious programming and old stories. Mine was, "Everyone always leaves me. I even have back up evidence to prove it."

Or it can be as simple as your mother gave you fresh squeezed orange juice in your bottle when you were a toddler and you swallowed a pit from the juice that made you gag. Fifty years later you still don't eat oranges. When someone asks you if you want an orange, you reply, "I don't eat oranges," and then proceed to tell them your story. When all you need to do is just eat an orange! This is how your "story" keeps you stuck in the past and becomes your reality. Where is there time for joy in all that muck?

The present moment is where we create our lives, where we become the artists of our masterpiece. The problem is we are always creating whether we subscribe to it or not, and most of the time we are creating unconsciously and unintentionally. When we live in the present we are God choosing, master creators of our world. The present moment holds infinite possibilities, it's a gift, that's why they call it the PRESENT. It's a restart of coming back to what really matters. It is the only time where the pain and suffering can dissipate because we've dropped our false identifications and our limiting stories we tell ourself.

> "Everything that you need exists in this present moment, and this moment is all that exists. In its brief flicker you will find all the time in the world. Through it you will contact the Living Information that will guide you with infallible direction. This present moment is the stargate through which you will leave the prison of human definition and expand into awareness of divine perception. It is the crack between the worlds, not only the worlds of past and future, but worlds of time and space, spirit and matter, form and being. It is a timeless zone, the gateway through which you will again begin to participate in the adventure of creation." ~ Ken Carey, *The Starseed Transmissions*

*** The Spiritual Practice of Catching Ourselves

> "Live in the now, for when you live in the consciousness of the now You are light taking the lead whilst human." ~The Arcturians

How do we do that? We go back to our yoga sutra #17, book 2...You are the observer behind the thought, the witness, the light. You are not the pain, the emotions, the thoughts, the mind, you are just the watcher. At one point in my journey recently I was wondering how do I *stay* in the witness perspective, in the present moment and maintain my freedom? I can get there but it doesn't last too long.

Of course my questions and prayers are always answered. During a group meditation, paramount divine messages came through the channel. When you are in deep contemplation in the past or future you are not living in the NOW moment. Ceasing the thoughts is a conscious choice.

As soon as you have the awareness that you lost yourself in the thought, in the illusion of the ego mind, the mind loops, you are already back in the conscious observer -back in the light. Thank you, that's encouraging and doable.

So basically waking up and becoming an empowered self master is all about catching ourselves over and over again, bringing us back from the confusion and turmoil of the contemplative mind and returning to the Now moment...to the peace and clarity of the knowing heart...remembering that we are the light. Again, we must know who we are. Knowing who we are is the foundation. Catching ourselves is the practice.

If you still think you are junk, it's not going to do you any good. You have to know who you are. Once you know who you truly are there's no more finding peace, you are peace. The questioning and searching stops because you are everything you are looking for. Why is this such a hard concept for us to get? It's because we've been asleep in the dark ages for lifetimes upon lifetimes. This is not something we are taught in school. Socrates said, "Know thyself." Which self is that? This two word imperative is found throughout all the great teachings (including my book) from all over the world. It's one of the Niyamas in yoga: Svādhyāya, self-study. This is a priority on the path to awakening and the most fundamental and important question one we can discover, "Who are you?"

God Games

> The gods and goddesses of ancient Greece, I am told, once gathered on Mount Olympus to play one of their favorite games: Hide the Truth from Humankind.
> "Let's hide it at the bottom of the ocean," cried one.
> "No, he'll eventually build submarines and find it."

> "How about up on the moon?" suggested another.
> "No, he is too ingenious for that. He'll eventually get there, too."
> Finally, the most mischievous of the gods, the one represented in humorous drawings as the little angel whose halo is always somewhat askance, spoke up.
> "I've got a great idea. Let's hide it deep inside of him. He'll never think to look there."

When you know who you are, consciousness or light, which are synonymous, it's easier to catch yourself and bring yourself back from the outer drama and craziness to your center. It's not that you won't have all those crazy thoughts anymore, they will still come, trust me, but you can bring yourself back faster. Less suffering, more joy. When I'm in it, I catch myself and say, "I'm not these crazy obsessive thoughts. **I am the light** having these crazy obsessive thoughts." Then I breathe, re-center and sigh with relief.

> "The only thing that ultimately matters is this: Can I sense my essential Beingness, the I Am, in the background of my life at all times? To be more accurate, can I sense the I Am that I Am at this moment? Can I sense my essential identity as consciousness itself? Or am I losing myself in what happens, losing myself in the mind, in the world?"
> ~*A New Earth,* Eckhart Tolle

***Namaste

When we come to know ourself as the word, *Namaste*, our whole world will transform. The word, Namaste, has many different interpretations which ultimately mean the same thing:

The Divine light in me acknowledges the Divine light in you.
The God in me greets and meets the God in you.

I honor the spirit in you that is also in me.
I bow to the godly/goodly qualities in you.
I see you, Te veo (Spanish)

My namaste: The soul fire in me, I give to you!

My favorite: "I honor the place in you in which the entire Universe dwells. I honor the place in you which is of love, of light, of truth, and of peace. When you are in that place in you, I am in that place in me. We are One."

The first part of the word Namaste is recognizing that we much more than the changing garment of our body, we are a changeless soul; a spiritual being having a human experience. The second part means that deep within us, our truest essence is nothing but pure goodness, light and love. We are not the body, mind, thoughts, feelings, ego, or personality. The third part means that all beings everywhere have this essence or soul or light, no matter how obtuse or disconnected they might be. Fourth part is that we are all One, we are connected in consciousness, our spiritual essence; therefore, what I do affects you and what you do affects me.

It's easy to say or read over this word and let it go in one ear and out the other. But the truth is this one little word is so profound; if we all abided by it, it has the power to heal and change the world. It has so much meaning and depth to it, all packed into one little word that you could study for a lifetime and still wonder.

> "Men go abroad to wonder at the height of mountains, at the huge waves of the sea, at the long courses of the rivers, at the vast compass of the ocean, at the circular motion of the stars, and they pass by themselves without wondering." ~St. Augustine

***A God Glimpse

"Be kind for everyone you meet is fighting a hard battle." ~Plato

I struggled with being "so spiritual" teaching yoga and changing my life, yet I was still judging people. And it wasn't on purpose, it would happen automatically. Judgment was my first thought when I saw someone. I was programmed deeply and it really bothered me. *How can I change this destructive, harmful habit?* I pondered. Since I had been praying to be less judgmental, and our prayers are always answered, I had a prophetic vision during the writing of this book.

It began with a literal dream I had where Spirit was showing me the *new yin/yang* for the New Earth, which I incorporated into my logo and explain at the end of the book.

A couple of days later I had a direct revelation and experience-challenging to put into words, but I will try. I was walking Karma when suddenly I was out of my body. I'm not sure where, but I was so high that I could look down and see all of humanity and the earth at once-my awareness was everywhere at the same time. It was like a sun roof opened, I peered down and saw the reason for all the suffering in the world-everyone was walking around in a fog of forgetfulness. Humanity was asleep to who they truly were- suffering from spiritual amnesia. Then I felt this enormous emotional wave of the pain of the world, perhaps, go through me. I gasped, then it was gone as quickly as it came in. The sun roof closed and I was back in my body. Intuitively, I knew this was not mine to carry as it would only bring me down to the depths of despair, and I've had my share of that already.

I stood there for a few minutes like a statue, taking in what I just experienced. I was speechless. It was a profound experience and I didn't need mushrooms or ayahuasca to have it. Words don't do it justice. You had to be there-probably what God says every day. Everything I have been studying, re-learning and writing about was now a direct experience. I got it. People are asleep to who they really are and they don't know what they don't know. How can I judge them or be angry? This was just what I needed to shift from judgment to compassion and to honor everyone in their journey with a gentle heart. Compassionate Heart, I AM.

You don't need to have this insightful vision to become less judging. Before I experienced the "God Glimpse" and only understood intellectually the reason for people's behavior, I would have an inner dialogue with myself.

I noticed my judging thoughts first, then I would download a new thought stream like, *"You can't blame anyone for being the way they are, from being so far from their true essence. We live in a dysfunctional world that is 180 degrees from who we are and what the truth is. Don't judge anyone until you've walked a day in their shoes."*

That shift in thoughts would then make the space for compassion to rise up in me. After all, if we want to be a powerful presence for peace, people will not respond to judgment or criticism. They will feel it even if you don't say it with words. When we come from true compassion and understanding, people will listen because they will sense our sincerity. They will see it in our eyes and they will feel our heart. It's love, acceptance and kindness that will change the world, not judgment and holier- than-thou attitude.

In Buddhism they say to look at everyone as your mother; since we've had so many lifetimes, you never know. That was one I latched on to being adopted and never knowing who my mother was. Also, what I have found works for me when I have a wall up, I say to myself, *They could be my student."* As soon as I have that thought, my "looking lens" or perspective shifts and I'm released from the shackles of judgment and returned to my pure intention of serving the world through acceptance and compassion.

***God Sees You, God Loves You

During the writing of this book I had a misunderstanding with two different people I was close to that was blown out of proportion- you know how those go. I watched how the old me wanted to continue the drama by defending my position that I was right and they were wrong. I was dealing with all different emotions, especially anger toward them and had to battle with my thoughts...*How could they say that, how could they think that, how could they do that?*

This is the practice and I was being given an opportunity to walk my talk in the most important area of our life: our relationships. If I continued with the internal battle in my mind I would be adding to the conflict of our already conflicting world. Having negative thoughts about them, even if they are not expressed is still adding to the violence of the world. It wasn't easy but I held the space of love and detached from the drama, let go and blessed them. I have grown wise enough to know when it's a futile waste of time and energy to explain myself to unconscious people that are shut down mentally and emotionally anyway. Sometimes it's "your stuff" and sometimes it's a projection of others unresolved wounds. You didn't cause it, you can't fix it, let it go.

Although I felt good about staying in my center of calm resolve while I was being attacked and misunderstood, I am still human and it still hurts. One of my angel intuitive friends gave me a message at the time this was all going down. She said, "God see you, God loves you." I cried when she told me this. God knows my heart and knows my pure intention and that's all that matters. It's easy to forget when we are caught up in our human mess. It reminded me of the touching passage from *Home With God, In A Life That Never Ends,* by Neale Donald Walsch:

> "If you call out to me in hopelessness, I will be there, but your despair may blind you, and block you from seeing me. I say... Nothing you have done is so horrible, nothing you have had happen to you is so beyond repair, that it cannot be healed. I can and shall make you whole again.
>
> Yet you must stop judging yourself. The one making the strongest judgment is you. Others may judge you from the outside looking in, but they do not know you, they do not see you, and so their judgments are not valid. Do not make them valid by taking them on as your own. They have no meaning.
>
> Do not wait for others to see you as you really are, for they see you through the eyes of their own pain. Know, instead that I see you now, in wonder and in truth, and that what I see of you is Perfect. As I look upon you I have but one thought: This is my beloved, in whom I am well pleased."

That was all I needed to hear to ease my heart. No matter how much "enlightenment" we may have, we are still human and will mess up, fall down, miscommunicate and continue to make mistakes and others will too. We must remember to see ourselves through the eyes of the almighty Father/Mother God/Goddess. God will always forgive us, love us and accept us, flaws and all.

Neale Donald Walsch said something in an interview I watched that made a lasting impression on me. He was asked the question about friendship, how do you keep it alive? I loved his response. He said the key was **tolerance**. We are all going to fall short and make mistakes, is that a reason to shut your friends and family out of your life? That not only hurt them but hurts you as well. It shuts your heart which is the most detrimental spiritual pitfall one can make. Why not extend tolerance, generosity and compassion and let them down off the cross. Isn't that what we all want? To be pardoned.

If you cannot pardon or forgive it's because you haven't pardoned and forgiven yourself. You cannot give what you don't have.

Prayer of St. Francis

"Lord, make me an instrument of thy peace.
Where there is hatred, let me sow love;
Where there is injury, pardon;
Where there is doubt, faith;
Where there is despair, hope;
Where there is darkness, light;
Where there is sadness, joy.

O divine Master, grant that I may not so much seek
To be consoled as to console,
To be understood as to understand,
To be loved as to love;
For it is in giving that we receive;

It is in pardoning that we are pardoned;
It is in dying that we are born to eternal life."

***The "F" Word

"To err is human, to forgive is divine." ~ Alexander Pope

Just because we forgive doesn't make us a doormat. Soulmate #4 came back after nine months of silence, reaching out to me via text messages, and sending a picture of us on our anniversary. I was shocked to be honest. After a few more friendly inviting text messages, I asked him if he was finally ready to talk. He said yes.

I was really nervous- going back and forth on whether I wanted to see him. I wasn't sure if I wanted to open this can of worms since I had worked so hard on letting him go. But I knew I needed to be brave and see him face to face to get final closure or even just an indication of what happened. My prior vision of jumping into his arms, happy to be reunited quickly dissolved as I realized my heart was closed to him as he was hugging me, to be expected. After talking and spending a couple of hours in his presence, I realized he was still in the same place. He might have shed a few pounds from his body, but his mind and his heart were the same.

Since I had done so much introspection, healing and growth over the last nine months I didn't think it wise to get involved with him again on any level. After a few more conversations, *because I had a lot to say,* I decided that the emotional roller coaster ride was not an option for my heart anymore. I am no longer that insecure wounded girl, I have self-love that I didn't have before. I want to be with someone who is willing to grow and change with me and be that steady rock in my life. Still, he is a part of me and was the catalyst in my "rebirthing." I am grateful to his soul for being the one to play the role of abandoning me. The love we shared was real and will always be.

The word "forgiveness" is such a loaded word. It's heavy. Replacing it with the word, acceptance, feels lighter, taking Alexander Pope's quote to another level, "To forgive is human, to accept is divine." God doesn't forgive, He/She doesn't need to because there is nothing to forgive.

The highest truth is that only love is real, everything else is an illusion. I chose my relationship with Soulmate #4 and chose to be abandoned so I could heal the lingering darkness I was harboring once and for all. If I remember that, there is no need to forgive him for anything. I should be thanking him instead. Having this understanding changes everything.

We chose our parents, our family and those we would interact with during this lifetime for the same reason - those who would project or mirror to us the positive as well as the negative attributes we needed to integrate and overcome. All of the precious souls in our life are a part of the great drama we have chosen to experience. After we play out our roles, even if our bodies are harmed, (our bodies are not who we are); our souls are never harmed, we leave the physical vessel and our soul goes on to other experiences. The problem or where we get stuck is that we have all forgotten this basic understanding.

From *A Course in Miracles:*

"When a brother acts insanely, he is offering you an opportunity to bless him. His need is yours. You need the blessing you can offer him. There is no way for you to have it except by giving it. This is the law of God, and it has no exceptions. What you deny, you lack, not because it is lacking, but because you have denied it in another and are therefore not aware of it in yourself. Every response you make is determined by what you think you are, and what you want to be is what you think you are. What you want to be, then, must determine every response you make.

PETAL 9

True Healing

*** Miracles Happen

EINSTEIN SAID "THERE are only two ways to live your life. One is as though nothing is a miracle. The other is as though everything is a miracle."

What is a miracle anyway? A miracle is really just a change in perception. If we were living "awake" and aware of who we really were, the word *miracle* wouldn't even exist. Miracles would then be just the way of life. It would be called a *normal.* It would sound strange if we said, "why don't you ask for a normal?"

I experience miracles on a daily basis. Most people that are asleep just roll their eyes at me and tell me it's just a coincidence. Well, I don't believe in coincidences, just like they might not believe in miracles. My version of Einstein's quote is, "There are only two ways to live your life. One is as though everything is a coincidence. The other is as though nothing is a coincidence." I read once that coincidence is God's way of remaining anonymous.

Jesus walked the earth with that knowing, he was a master of miracles, the greatest mental scientist, yogi and quantum physicist the world has ever known. Jesus was "in" the world, but not "of" of the world. He was a master of "normals" because he was awakened from the dream-state, saw through the illusion and walked the earth with the knowing of who he truly was. There have been many other enlightened being who were able to play with the time-space continuum and create miracles.

Marianne Williamson first introduced me to the concept of miracles, that they are available to everyone, we just forgot that fact. We also forgot to ask, since free will reigns supreme on the earth-plane, if we don't ask for what we want, Spirit will not intercede.

One memorable demonstration of a miracle, or shall I say a normal, was during my challenging times with my daughter. She was always defiant, which is kind of cute when you are five, but when you are fifteen and defiant, it's a whole other story. One scary time she threatened to kill herself with a knife she had in her hand then proceeded to lock herself in her bedroom. I couldn't help but think about Eugene's suicide. I was calmly freaking out inside. I remember Marianne saying to ask for a miracle, which I did and miraculously she did 180 degree turn around. She came out of her room, put the knife back and was rational again. This happened many times with my daughter. She would start to go to that unruly place and I would start to lose it, but then catch myself and pray for a miracle. Next thing I knew she was smiling and sweet again. Sometimes it was hard to believe because of the drastic change in behavior, but I was a witness. Thank you God, angels, and thank you Marianne for reminding me.

Just as in our individual lives, we can also ask and pray for a miracle for the whole of humanity. Why don't we? Simply because we were not taught. Right now if there is a situation in your life that is causing you distress, conflict, and pain... pause, close you eyes, take a deep breath, enter into your sacred temple within your precious heart and talk to God, Spirit, your angels or the Universe and ask for a miracle. WITH EVERY PROBLEM LIES THE SOLUTION; WITH EVERY SICKNESS OR DISEASE LIES THE CURE. We just need to keep our mind and heart open to **believe and receive**. And so it is.

My prayer for you is that you receive all that you need, but most importantly that you realize that: **You are the miracle**. Amen.

***You are Healed in God's Eyes ~Archangel Rafael

What is healing? Healing then is simply awakening...awakening to the truth of who you are, to your authentic spiritual self. You are the light. Everything else is what you are choosing to experience. We chose to come to the earth-plane to experience duality so we can intermingle with it and experience who we are from another perspective. *A Course In Miracles* defines healing as *the recognition of truth and corrected perception.* It also defines health as the result of relinquishing all attempts to use the body lovelessly.

When we are sick, it is a wake up call. It is our higher selves rising to the desire to be free of the illusion of sickness. It is our soul wanting to remember that our natural essence is perfect health and wholeness.

In her book, *Hands of Light,* Barbara Brennan, one of the most influential spiritual energy healers of the twentieth and twenty first century says: "Illness is the result of imbalance. Imbalance is the result of forgetting who you are. Forgetting who you are creates thought and actions that lead to an unhealthy life-style and eventually to illness. The illness itself is a signal that you are imbalanced because you have forgotten who you are. Illness can thus be understood as a lesson you have given yourself to help you remember who you are."

Again, the importance of knowing who we really are. Emmet Fox from *The Sermon on the Mount* says: "As man becomes spiritually awakened he recognizes that any external disharmony is the correspondence of mental disharmony. A person might receive instantaneous healing through the realization of his body being a perfect idea in Divine Mind, and therefore, whole and perfect, but if he continues his destructive thinking, hoarding, hating, fearing, condemning, the disease or pain will return."

In the beginning of my "awakening" through one of Dan Millman's books, I learned that I gave myself the injuries and imbalances in my body so I could re-remember how to heal myself. When I read that I had a huge A-HA moment. Although intellectually I didn't one hundred percent understand what that meant at the time, in my deeper instinctual awareness, I knew it to be true. Many of us have created illnesses to wake us up to the truth of who we really are.

Once you know who you are, illness, disease and sickness cannot exist in your temple. The best way to avoid colds and viruses: raise your vibration. Germs cannot exist in a frequency of love. My affirmation is: "My love is stronger than any sickness, disease or illness manifesting itself in the 3D world of illusion. My love is far more real. I have the power to heal." Truth is, we all have the power to heal ourselves.

***The Devoted Wart

I've been practicing healing myself for years now since I discovered Louise Hay. I have even come to know that I astral travel in my sleep and heal myself and others. Even so, it's still a surprise when you witness alchemy right before your very eyes. I will admit I was slightly attached to the wart on my hand since I had it longer than any man, but it was time for it to go. I had gone the eastern route, western route, doctor and dermatologist many times with no success. I decided I would put the truth into practice. After all, I am a healer and I am the creator of my reality.

I began saying to my biology, "My wart is gone, my finger is healed (I had sprained it on my water bottle), and I threw in a vain bonus... my eyelashes are getting thicker." I was trying to avoid the $100 mascara that supposedly thickened your eye lashes. I figured I would do it with my thoughts and beliefs. I'm still a girl.

Within a couple of days my wart started going away, my finger was pain free and yes, my eyelashes started getting thicker, even my friends noticed. Fast forward two weeks later, **my wart was completely gone**!!! I couldn't believe it, yet I could! It was a miracle! No, it was a normal. I had that wart on my hand for two years and within two weeks it was gone.

This tangible demonstration of the power of my healing abilities was part of the best year I have lived so far. There are no prizes or awards for these things but to me there's nothing better. It felt amazing to take everything I had been reading and studying and witness it actually manifest in form-in my body. If there was any doubt lingering around, no more. I skipped around chanting, "My wart is gone! My wart is gone! I *am* a healer." Through the fire I went, now it's time for joy!

PETAL 10

The Year of My Confident Heart 2016

AT THE END of 2015 my angels said 2016 was going to be the "year of my confident heart," and I will have to agree with them. Along with the tangible demonstration of my powerful healing abilities, 2016 was the year for me to fly. It was the fourth year in a row of making my yearly inspirational calendar I sell. 2016's theme was, "Finding Your Wings." It was my best calendar so far and I had so much fun in the creative process of making it with wings for each month.

YOU CAN SAY 2016 was like, "show and tell" for SoulFire. I had so many wonderful experiences by stepping out of my comfort zone and being in the public eye, but not only that, for the first time in my life I felt peaceful and happy for no reason. I just wake up like that! The "feel good" is not dependent on anything or anyone. I just feel content. I have so much energy and enthusiasm that when I walk Karma I feel like skipping, which I do sometimes. It's a very different way of being that I'm used to. I learned that when we achieve a certain level of harmony within, we gradually incorporate more and more of our Light body. (Our Light body is another term for a level of our Higher Self or our I AM Presence that exists on a higher dimension. It is our divine blueprint- underlying our physical body. Part of the shift in the evolution of consciousness that we are undergoing now involves incorporating higher frequencies of light into our physical beingness. More about this in book two.)

***Living Liberation

My year started with setting healthy boundaries for myself with Soulmate#4 and continued with my trip to Costa Rica the following month. While there were so many things about this trip that were unforgettable and magical, what stood out for me the most at first was that I didn't think about Soulmate #4 at all. I was free of the mental and emotional torture for the first time in ten months. It was such a relief to my heart. I don't remember the last time I had so much fun and smiled so much. I was unhindered, uninhibited, and abandoned in my highest joy thinking *this is what it's like to be in the present moment.* I learned the ancient healing art of Qigong from one of the most talented and humble teachers, Robert Peng, fell in love with Qigong, with Costa Rica, and with myself.

One of the highlights of my trip occurred after the soul sister-friend I went with and I had got done horse back riding for two hours along the beach that morning: two of my favorite things in one, the beach and horses. We lied our towels down at the waters edge to relax. I said a little prayer to God and the Universe, thanking in advance for a delightful surprise which I felt coming. I got up to stroll along the beach, when something in the sand moving very slowly disguised as the same color of the sand caught my eye. I knelt down to get a closer look, then gasped! I started to yell for my friend but had lost my voice, so started jumping up and down screeching.

It was a LIVING sand dollar! When I was a little girl one was given to me that I cherished dearly. It was the legend behind the magical creature that captivated me. I was told there were five doves of peace inside the sand dollar which you can hear if you shake it. That fascinated me so I kept it in my treasure box until one day it broke open and out really came five little doves. I revered the doves wearing them around my neck in a small plastic container on a string. Ever since then I would find sand dollars randomly on beaches all over the country. This winter I had the fortune of finding hundreds on Fire Island due to the dredging, but never found a living one, until now.

Sand dollar story: Galleta del Mar (Cookie of the Sea)

There are many interpretations of the sand dollar. According to some legends and poems, the sand dollar represents the birth, death and resurrection of Jesus Christ. Sand dollars are also symbols of peace. The five doves inside the shells are said to bring goodwill to the world when the sand dollar is broken.

In numerology, five is the number of growth, progress, transformation and change. Without change, there is stagnation. The sand dollar is a powerful reminder of Earth's Beginning as well. Our Beloved Mother Earth is going through a massive transformation as we are too, and the sand dollar like other fossils, i.e. the Nautilus holds wisdom and information regarding the necessary changes we have to make in order to move with grace into a new dimension.

If you ever held a sand dollar in your hand you probably noticed how fragile it is, yet it holds strong vibrations. The sand dollar is designed to survive storms. It teaches us to be gentle in our approach in life, regardless of environmental conditions. It teaches us to go with the flow and be flexible in our thinking and work on changing the belief systems that are detrimental, replacing them by new healthy belief systems. It is the slowest moving being on the planet. Sand dollars represent strength intertwined with steadiness and patience… the perfect talisman for me. I was over joyed to find a living one and video taped it as it made its way back into the sand. If God could give me the perfect present, this would be it.

Every day in Costa Rica I was in my highest glory, making new friends, experiencing new adventures, learning new skills (re-learning I should say), and making memories that I will never forget. I don't need much to make me happy, just swimming in the ocean, walking on the beach collecting beautiful shells and dancing at night under the stars- my perfect dream life. I don't even need to eat!

The last night a group of us were at the beach for one more glorious view of the heavenly night sky that seem to hang lower in Nosara. I made a request to the Universe to see a shooting star, the one thing I didn't encounter. Within a couple of minutes a small star shot across the sky, but it was nothing compared to the one we saw a few minutes later. A brilliant star as bright as a comet with a white blazing tail of light behind it, streaked across the celestial sky. Everybody gasped in unison. I chuckled to myself, *you can thank me for that.*

I felt in synchronicity with everything and everyone. I was at peace at last and I believe part of it was that I was in the present moment almost all the time. I came home with the knowledge of an ancient practice called Xi Jin Jing which Robert said if you do this practice every day for three months your life will transform. Being the good student I am, of course I did it, and something definitely shifted within me. I feel good for no reason-just content and happy to be. Qigong has definitely changed my life, like yoga did when I re-discovered it. I have been sharing and teaching it since I've been home.

I received a short letter from my dear soul sister who is another brave soul who walks her talk, shortly after we came home. I cherish her words for this is all I ever wanted to be. She saw me in my true light, and I am so grateful she was a witness.

> Dearest SoulFire,
> I just want to say to you THANK YOU. Thank you for being you! The you I got to know a little better on this trip. Your open heart and free spirit truly inspired me and I am grateful for the energy you shared with me on this trip. Not only did I witness your open and loving heart, but a women who truly wants to be inspired by life and is not afraid to embrace inspiration and then by doing that she becomes the inspiration for others! You teach others how to take off their shell and be who they are, have fun like a child and be free as a butterfly. Thank you for being patient with me

on this trip as my issues and shadows I know are not easy to deal with and you dealt with all my stuff gracefully. I'm glad we had this time together and I know that there will be much more to come.

Let your soul shine!

***Spirit Weaver

The year of my confident heart continued as I began performing with a new type of musical group creating a new style of dance and yoga. The performances moved me to get over my stage fright, fears and insecurities and be an open and spontaneous channel for love and joy. Each time I performed I gained more and more self confidence. We actually performed on stage in a theater once which totally freaked me out at first. Considering we didn't have rehearsal I went out there and danced my heart out in front of an audience and had a great time. HHMMMM... this seems like a pattern in my life...I am getting the feeling I will be doing it again.

The feed back I received was enormous for my self-esteem, again reflecting back to me exactly what I want to be. People told me when I dance I exude an energy that is tangible and infectious because they can see and feel my passion and joy. Since I didn't have formal dance training this was a huge compliment for me. It validated the power to uplift people by simply being in your highest joy and doing what you love to do. Spirit Weaver, I learned, was a name I was called in another lifetime as a Shaman I danced around the fire bringing joy to people's hearts and smiles to their faces.

I also was a guest on a cable TV show with one of my dear friends and clients. She interviewed me for half an hour without any preparation. The same thing happened to me as I was sitting in the chair waiting for the cameras to roll- my legs were shaking uncontrollably. This time there was no where to hide them, so I had to get control. I took a deep breath and remembered that this wasn't about me and someone listening might benefit from my experience. That always seems to work. The interview went great and I received a lot of positive feed back. Sheesh! Why do I have to keep doing this?

***Surfing

"You can't stop the waves, but you can learn to surf." ~John Kabat-Zin

Another fear I overcame this year was my fear of surfing. I had a block around surfing. I felt pressured that I should be this amazing surfer since I'm athletic, love the water, swim, do yoga, even look Hawaiian. All I ever heard was... "why don't you surf, you should be surfing, I can't believe you don't surf." Along with this block, I had limiting thoughts that I was too old to start at forty seven, scared to get hurt.

So one day when my dear surfer friend *casually* suggested I try to surf since the conditions were perfect for learning I immediately said ok, even though I was silently freaking out inside. I knew I had to overcome this fear as Bob Marley's quote went ringing through my head: "My fear is my only courage." My surf lesson was not what I expected. My friend put the board down in the sand, demonstrated how to pop up, I did it once then he said ok and put me right in the water. I was like, "Ummm that's it?"

After a few times of him helping me get up and me falling a lot, he told me the next wave to get up on my own as he pushed me forward on the board. Shaking, I called out to him, "How do I know when to get up?" He called back, "You will feel it." I took a deep breathe, centered myself and said *I can do this, don't think, just feel.* The wave came and viola, I popped up at the perfect time and rode it in. I couldn't believe I did it. My friend said when I turned around and looked at him my face was beaming with a smile from ear to ear. I have so many good friends that are surfers. I get it now. It was one of the best feelings in the world. I was hooked and really proud of myself.

***Bloody Noses

Along with my confident heart, there was more healing to do. Like I said in the beginning of my story, healing doesn't quite come in organized steps, and apparently I had another layer to peel back.

When I was a little girl I used to get bloody noses like it was nobody's business. They were so bad I thought I was dying. Not just blood, but clots of gooey red and black matter would come pouring out of my nose and my mouth as well. It was scary and usually I was alone when they happened.

As I got older, they stopped coming as frequently and weren't as intense but they still visited me from time to time. It would bring me back to that worried feeling I had as a child. A few years back I looked up bloody noses in my bible, *You Can Heal Your Life.*

It wasn't really a surprise that the psychosomatic-emotional bloody noses were coming from "feeling unrecognized and unnoticed, crying for love," which made me cry even more.

The new thought pattern or affirmation that replaces it: "I love and approve of myself. I recognize my own true worth. I am wonderful."

Mama Hay was right once again. The bloody noses eventually stopped. I haven't had one in years, until just recently as I was writing my book.

Am I ever going to believe that I am truly loved ? Memorial Day Weekend, one year later...

I woke up on May 30 and couldn't move my neck. I didn't do anything to hurt it, came out of the blue. I haven't felt that much pain in my neck ever, even with all the neck issues I have experienced. I had to wear a neck brace the pain was so bad. If I moved my head slightly the wrong way a searing pain caused me to stop dead in my tracks. The pain was paralyzing and I was steeped in fear.

Immediately, I called my healer friends and one by one they came over. (I'm getting used to asking for help now). The first two days nothing really worked, I received acupuncture, MFR massage, Reiki, chakra clearings, chiropractic, more Reiki, yoga therapy, Phoenix rising, more Reiki, more massage. Finally after three days I could move it without searing, paralyzing pain. By day six it was 50% better, and each day after that it got progressively better.

On the second day my friend said he would do a distance healing and for me to lie in bed, it would take about 20 minutes. My body started shaking and a huge sob of sadness came up. It hurt my neck to cry so I tried to hold it in but my body wouldn't let me. *I think you need to cry,* I said to myself. So I started to let the tears flow and the thought and feeling of "nobody loves me, nobody wants me," came up...**again**.

At first I resisted it, being hard on myself as usual: *Not you again. I thought I was done with you already. How much more pain do I have to feel? How much longer do I have to have this annoying belief?* The emotional pain building on top of the physical pain.

Finally, I decided to just let go and just cry. As I was crying and feeling those feelings of anguish of not being loved and wanted, my higher self kicked in. The Goddess said, "You know this is not true. You know you are loved. Look at how many people came over to help you." Still not convinced though, my Goddess self continued, "Ok well it doesn't really matter if no one loves you because the truth is, you are love itself. You are the light."

As soon as I affirmed that statement to myself I felt the emotional pain and sadness dissolve. I took a deep breathe to let the truth sink in. It was an amazing shift and transformation. Once again I was offered the opportunity to travel into the darkness and transform it.

After the pain in my heart went away, I still had the pain in my neck. I took time to reflect and understand why this was coming up again, then it dawned on me. I had legally changed my name in November of 2015 to SoulFire, and in April 2016 had a name-changing ceremony, guided by my angels to celebrate this blessed event.

Over the last five years I gradually received information about myself and my divine life purpose through an intuitive medium/channel. My spiritual name, SoulFire, is how I am referred to in the divine realms. It is my God given name that I received through Archangel Michael. My name represents what my whole life's work is about. I'm still in the process of re-remembering some of it because there are many different facets to my divine purpose-writing this book is one of them. I also know energy healing is in my DNA. I not only heal with my hands but I have a signature energy transmission called the Dragon's Breath performed at the feet. It is a cleansing of the sacral chakra. It assists people in releasing and cleansing residual karma, wounds and darkness held in the sacral chakra that is blocking the transmission of the flow of life force energy. In essence I use my "fire" to ignite another's "soul" through this sacred process. I (my God self) activated it on myself (my human self) through Dana, the channel, on December 21, 2015 and was told it was the final part of the series of synchronized movement that I am suppose to remember that will help people heal as they awaken to the truth of who they are. Still with me?

I decided I wanted to legally step into the vibration of this name and become SoulFire on every level. It was time to own my truth and my light! It was a unique celebration. I don't know of anyone else having an event like this. Pioneering pathways for others, the event was another deposit in my spiritual bank account and my confident heart. I received so much support and love from everyone, except my mother.

I woke up a few days later only to find on Facebook, nonetheless, a not so flattering letter my mother wrote to me and made public. I only knew about it because my sister chimed in and added her negative two cents to the comment thread and tagged me. While social media can be a wonderful tool to connect and share in the positive love, it can also be a source of drama, which I choose not to participate in.

There's no need to include the letter and the comments. I'd much rather forget about them. Still, I was so shocked I couldn't read it all. I closed out Facebook and said to myself *I can't deal with this now, I'm in a great place and I don't have time for this negativity.* I was on such a high still from my name changing ceremony that I was not that upset. Plus, I knew not to take it personally, that my Mom was projecting her unresolved abandonment issues on to me, as she was also adopted.

I guess I didn't really deal with it, so it found it's way into my neck. The bloody noses started again too. It was a site, me in a neck brace trying to tilt my head back with blood squirting out of my nose. I realized once again that "What you don't address, you repress." Not feeling understood and supported by my family was a constant theme in my life. But now I love and support myself unconditionally; so while it would be nice to have theirs, I don't need it to be happy.

When I hear someone say my name it brings such joy to my heart. It's my soul song. It uplifts me every single time and reminds me who I really am. As St. Catherine of Siena says, "If you are what you should be you will set the whole world on fire!

***Masterpiece in Progress

You know you are making progress when you can look back or better yet, *during*, and be grateful for everything that happens, even the things you don't like and bless them- that's true self-mastery. I'm still working on that one, but getting better. We must continue to remind ourselves that our journeys are perfect. There's nothing to stress or worry about. It's all perfection.

It's important to remember that in our core, our true spiritual essence of light, we are perfect. Our imperfections are only the result of our forgetfulness of who we really are. Our imperfections stem from our human ego personality and imperfect conditioning and programming. The highest reality is that we are perfect, whole and complete as is.

***A Second Chance for My Confident Heart

What I wanted more than anything after Soulmate#4 walked out on me was a second chance. I never got that, from him at least. I met someone about fifteen months later who ironically or not, was Soulmate#4 all over again. When he started telling me about his life I thought, *Really? YOU'RE KIDDING GOD!* I knew we were meant to meet.

They had the same family and living situation with even more triggers than Soulmate #4! It was uncanny. I was torn between embracing him and running. Plus, we came from two different worlds. He was meat and potatoes type of guy and I'm... well, you know. I try not to define myself. I was in my head thinking and analyzing how this wouldn't work and by our third date my fear won. I invited him over for dinner to part ways amiably, since he was such a sweet man.

When he showed up he had the biggest bouquet of sunflowers that I have ever seen. Sunflowers, if you hadn't noticed from my logo and my book have a major significance in my spiritual journey, of which he had no idea. If that wasn't a sign from above I don't know what was. "Ok," I said to God, "I will let him in. I will get out of my analyzing head and stop judging this and go with the flow. I will not run away and I will stay in the moment and not worry about what could happen in the future."

I'm so glad I did. It turns out this is my second chance, the one I had been praying for. For the first time in my life I get to be an adult in a relationship. I get to be rational, supportive, understanding and trusting of a man, which surprisingly, is coming pretty easy. I don't have all those crazy, insecure feelings I had with Soulmate#4, and every other relationship. I've never had this before. My insides feel different. I feel secure and confident and it FEELS GOOD!!!

It's been a couple of months and once I get out of my head, I truly enjoy his company. Although every other day I battle with myself. It really is a trip to watch me battling me. Then I think *why don't you just give it up already? Take your own advice. Surrender SoulFire, let it happen.*

Deciding to be vulnerable one night I asked him how he saw me. He paused and then said, "I think you are selfless." My heart melted. I was not expecting that response since his personality is fun and light, I thought he would respond with a joke. If he saw that in me in only two months, I'm on the right path. When he said that an old memory came flooding back into my awareness. I was around seven years old, standing on the stairs in my home, my mother screaming at me over and over again that I was selfish. It was the worst thing you could have said to my sensitive altruistic soul. I felt so hurt but mostly misunderstood and frustrated that my own mother didn't know me or see my heart.

I realize this man is a mechanic for a reason, he fixes things and he has fixed and restored my heart with this one little word, selfless. Although it didn't work out between us as a long term relationship, we remain friends. He was a gift to my soul as he reminded me that there are good men of integrity in the world that "show up." His beautiful soul and our divine connection opened my heart back to love again.

***I Want To Know What Love Is, I Want You To Show Me.

We're all in search of love, of real love, the true enduring love, not the here today, gone tomorrow love. What I've come to know is that the everlasting unconditional love we all yearn for is within us. And until we can access it, feel it, be it, live it, we will always be in search outside of ourselves trying to find it with another person. The only real way someone can truly show us love that we can receive is if we *are* love; then, we can see and feel it from others, because it is a **reflection** of us. And the reflection is not dependent on anyone else. The reflection is **us** being LOVE.

***I'm Screwed

If I took to heart the research that confirms that the first five years of a child's life are fundamentally important, that they are the foundation that shapes children's future health, happiness, growth, development and learning achievement at school, in the family and community, and in life in general, we would not be here now- there would be no book.

When I first read that children learn more quickly during their early years than at any other time in life and that they need love and nurturing to develop a sense of trust and security that turns into confidence as they grow, I thought, *Well, I'm screwed.* It gets worse, from *The Biology of Belief*, "A new field of study know as fetal origins asserts that prenatal development constitutes the most consequential period of our lives, permanently influencing the writing of our brain and shaping our intelligence and temperament. A pregnant woman's mental state can shape her offspring's psyche."

Great again, my mother was in prison, selling her body for drugs, addicted to heroin on methadone. How good a mental state could she have been in? On top of the gloomy research that I'm destined to be a half-wit socially undeveloped psychotic hermit, one of my first private clients, who became a dear friend, asserted to me one day at lunch, "No one ever really changes."

That could have been the final nail in the coffin, if I took that as *my* truth. I would have had at the perfect scapegoat along with back up research to substantiate the reason I was an angry wounded victim. And I guarantee I would have had people on my side, agreeing with me all the way, like my friend. But after reflecting on that information I said, "Screw that. I'm breaking the mold. I'm making my own research."

Maybe I needed to hear those statements to light the fire under my butt to prove him and everyone else wrong. Rebel at heart, while visiting my brother at college, he said to me, "Whatever you do, stay away from Justin M." Guess who became my boyfriend? If you tell me I can't do something, I am going to do it. That's how I'm wired.

It doesn't matter if you didn't have a happy beginning. That doesn't define who you are. **Who you are is who you choose to be now in this moment.** We don't have to let the past define us, stay stuck in what Mommy and Daddy did or did not do. We don't have to let research, programming and conditioning rule us. We can break free and start over with the next breath. We are free to reinvent ourselves and recreate ourselves anew the moment we so choose. Life is always changing and so are we. No matter what anyone says: your family, your friends, your boss, your astrological chart, your negative voice within, **you are the creator, you are in charge. If you don't like what you see in the mirror, choose something different. This is your life. It is a gift, one to be cherished, not wasted. You have the power.**

***A Part of Me

When I received the letter from the adoption agency besides the confirmation about my mother, I also received some information about myself as a baby. Since I had no pictures or knowledge of any of my life from birth until four and a half years old, this one paragraph helped fill in the blanks and gave me something positive to hold on to.

"In 4/69 you were able to turn from your back to your side and you could move up in the crib or to the side using your feet. You were said to 'love your bath.' A developmental exam, on 5/6/69, revealed you to be 'way above average in development.' You were said to be very alert and a very good sleeper. On 6/19/69 you were beginning to teeth. You would 'smile very easily.' You would 'coo immediately upon someone looking at you.' You 'noticed everything that was happening around you.' You were able to 'sit remarkably well.' You could 'stand extremely strong and you were able to turn from your back to your stomach.' On 8/11/69 you were able to say 'dada.' On 9/18/69 you were described as being 'very bright' and that you had a 'charming personality with a winning smile.' At this time you were able to stand and hold on and vocalize back. On 10/7/69 you were able to take one or two steps without assistance. You could 'move quite adeptly in the walker.' It was noted that your 'back and legs were very firm and straight when standing.' In 9/70 you were described as being 'very alert.' You were walking well with no help at all. You were 'trying to imitate words that were spoken.' You were said to be able to 'communicate your needs very well.' A developmental exam, on 10/17/72, revealed you to be a 'normally well adjusted child of above average general development and intelligence.' You were described as being 'generous and lovable.'"

I cried so much when I read this. It was a gift to know who I was as a baby. **I make sense now.** This was me and still is! Perhaps who we become gets shaped by our environment, but who we are, I would have to say- that remains changeless.

***Experiencing the Opposite so We Can Know Who We Really Are

"In order to fully know freedom, one must fully know darkness."
~Arcturians

The first half of my life I journeyed into the darkness, coming up for air every now and then, only to be sucked back down into the abyss, to experience abandonment over and over again, throughout every chapter of my life. There is only so much one can take before they break, break down, or break through. In my case I broke down, not once, not twice, but many times, before I finally broke through.

I learned about who I am by learning about who I am not.

I learned about what love is by learning about what love is not.

I learned that the healing/balancing/awakening process is a slow journey and not to be discouraged by my progress or lack of progress; *To keep on keeping on, because that in itself is a noble and worthy cause.*

> "Truly, it is in darkness that one finds the light, so when we are in sorrow, then this light is nearest of all to us." ~Meister Eckhart (German Philosopher 1260-1328)

When you are in it, and those of you who have been there know what I mean, in the darkness, lost and scared, lonely and confused, know that this is a good sign. It is a sign of growth, a sign that change for the positive is on the way. You are choosing to awaken to your divinity. Without the darkness here in duality, we would not know the light.

Nobody said it was going to be easy, but it is sure worth it. You are worth it. What are your other choices? Lay down and give up? Keep on keeping on. Persevere in spite of obstacles. Push through in spite of the pain. You can do it. Like Joseph Campbell wrote, "Suddenly you're ripped into being alive. And life is pain, and life is suffering, and life is horror, but my god you're alive and it's spectacular."

When things got really bad and I went into that place of "I'm not worthy and don't want to be here," I thought *if I can't help myself there must be someone else out there that is suffering more than I am that could use my help*. This thought process, the selfless service for others, could be just the thing that saves us and saves the world.

While ignoring our own needs is not the best way to heal, sometimes by offering ourself as a selfless servant to God and the Universe, we actually do heal. **There is always someone you can help.**

***We are ONE

> "The strength of the pack is the wolf and the strength of the wolf is the pack." ~The Jungle Book

What do we hold on to when all falls away? How do we survive the pain and sometimes total devastation? What do we fall back on? I say we hold on to each other and to God.

During my estrangement from Soulmate #4, I needed my soul tribe. However reaching out to others and asking for help was not one of my strengths. I have always been self sufficient and independent, sourcing my help from God and the Universe first. Asking *humans* for help was not as easy for me to do, usually my last resort.

Be that as it may, one early morning when I awoke with the realization that he was really gone, an awful dread spread throughout my being like death had just took occupancy in my body, I had no other choice. I needed help. I hesitantly sent a text message to about ten friends asking them to pray for me. The response I received was overwhelming and immediately I started to feel better.

One particular soul friend said to me that when I was struggling and having a hard time to please reach out to him and ask for help. I agreed but thought to myself *I don't want to keep bothering you with my pain and sadness, what a drag to keep asking for help.*

It was like he read my mind. He added on, "When you reach out and ask for help, you are not just helping yourself, you are helping me as well, and others."

How? I wondered. He continued, reading my mind again, "It forces us to stop whatever we are doing and connect to our hearts, to Spirit and send positive energy out to you, which in turn is sent to the world. It helps us to pause in the craziness of our lives and tune in to the divinity within our hearts."

I have the best friends! Wow, that was a paradigm shift. I don't feel so self conscious about asking for help anymore, like someone is judging me or thinking, "Oh God, you again." It is our inherent nature to want to help others. In helping others we are in essence helping ourselves because the highest truth is that WE ARE ONE.

> "It has been said that when Buddha comes again, he will arrive not as a person but as a community. We will know that God is here on earth when we can see Him/Her in one another." ~*Everyday Grace*, Marianne Williamson

*** New Metaphors

...Mary Catherine Bateson, Margaret Meade's daughter, another brilliant visionary, followed in her mother's foot steps. She declared that, "The family is changing, not disappearing. We have to broaden our understanding of it, look for the new metaphors."

The world is my family. I had to re-define the word family, otherwise I would have continued to feel lost and alone. Although some people might feel sad for me, I look at my life as an opportunity to open my heart even wider and love everyone. Not that that's an easy task, but it's one I strive toward.

New metaphors means we need to expand our thinking and our compassionate hearts. We are a global family, united under the same sun on this beautiful blue and white planet whirling through space; one sky, one heaven, one moon and one family- it just so happens we are different. Our human vessels are different, our personalities are different, our unique contributions are different; but at our core, we are the same. I love Margaret Meade's quote, "Always remember that you are absolutely unique. Just like everyone else."

That means we come from the same underlying essence of love and light and spirit, yet every soul has a unique contribution and imprint to leave on the planet. When our false identities fall away we will realize once again who we really are and embrace a shared identity. Becoming conscious is the greatest gift we can give to the world and our uniqueness is how we might serve the greater whole.

"A human being is a part of the whole called by us universe, a part limited in time and space. He experiences himself, his thoughts and feeling as something separated from the rest, a kind of optical delusion of his consciousness. This delusion is a kind of prison for us, restricting us to our personal desires and to affection for a few persons nearest to us. Our task must be to free ourselves from this prison by widening our circle of compassion to embrace all living creatures and the whole of nature in its beauty." ~Albert Einstein

***For the Greatest Good of All

The mantra: I will become a Buddha, **for the benefit of all** has two parts to it. The first is becoming, the second is *for all.* I know many spiritual seekers that get stuck on the, "I will become," and it stays all about them. The second part of this statement is key...*for the benefit of all.*

Once we reach this understanding and our life transforms, we are not to sit idle, according to Swami Satchidananda, "Once we realize our freedom we should work for the sake of others who are still bound. When a strong person crosses a turbulent river, he or she will not walk away after the crossing but will stand on the bank and help pull out everyone else." This is Humanity's greatest trait: bravery and kindness. Working for the sake of others is our inherent nature, and when we come to the full realization that our happiness is directly linked to every beings happiness our life changes for the better. Side note: when someone doesn't want to be helped, that is a different story. You cannot make someone cross the turbulent river. They have to be a willing participant.

***Life is an Invitation

"Life doesn't happen *to* you, life happens *for* you**."** ~ Me

The universe is inviting you to show up, to participate, to be your own star of your life, not to live vicariously through other peoples lives, through other celebrities, models, sports figures, reality shows. We don't need more of them in the world. We need more of you, everyday wonderful people waking up and becoming empowered co-creators of this world through love and kindness, charity and service. We need more healers, musicians, artists, more conscious parents, conscious couples, conscious uncouples, more conscious men, empowered women, more happy people living on purpose with passion and joy.

There was a time when I thought about becoming an official minister. It's easy now, you can do it right online! But is a piece of paper with a stamp on it going to make you a minister? I believe there is no more important ministry than that of being a parent. Even if you are not a parent in the *traditional* sense, we are all really parents and every day, if we look for it, we will find a chance to bring our ministry of healing and love to someone or something new. You do not have to be 'ordained' to be an official minister in the world. We are all ordained by being here now.

God's gift to us is our life and our gift to God is to become the very best we can for the greatest good of all.

The term "God needs a body," means we are the channels. The call for assistance must come from us since free will choice is our gift here on planet Earth. Just as we can be the cage, we are also the key to experiencing the new heaven and the new earth, here, now. This time it's about us.

I Sent You a Rowboat

> A very religious man was once caught in rising floodwaters. He climbed onto the roof of his house and trusted God to rescue him. A neighbor came by in a canoe and said, "The waters will soon be above your house. Hop in and we'll paddle to safety."
> "No thanks" replied the religious man. "I've prayed to God and I'm sure he will save me"
> A short time later the police came by in a boat. "The waters will soon be above your house. Hop in and we'll take you to safety."
> "No thanks" replied the religious man. "I've prayed to God and I'm sure he will save me"
> A little time later a rescue services helicopter hovered overhead, let down a rope ladder and said. "The waters will soon be above your house. Climb the ladder and we'll fly you to safety."
> "No thanks" replied the religious man. "I've prayed to God and I'm sure he will save me"
> All this time the floodwaters continued to rise, until soon they reached above the roof and the religious man drowned. When he arrived at heaven he demanded an audience with God. Ushered into God's throne room he said, "Lord, why am I here in heaven? I prayed for you to save me, I trusted you to save me from that flood."
> "Yes you did my child" replied the Lord. "And I sent you a canoe, a boat and a helicopter. But you never got in." ~Unknown

PETAL 11

SoulFire/Sunflower

***Holy Love

> "Some people see scars, and it is wounding they remember. To me they are proof of the fact that there is healing." ~Linda Hogan

SHARING MY PERSONAL story has not been an easy process. I resisted it every step of the way. There were times I was sobbing so hard I couldn't write. I had to walk away from my book numerous times.

During this process however, after I rewrote my story for the tenth or so time, I had a shift about Eugene, my daughter's father. When I first starting writing about my experience with him I cried with such deep heartache for me and what I went through. This was the toughest part of my life to re-visit. I actually felt throbbing pain in my throat and then felt it close up. I was back in that space of paralyzing fear again.

> This last time I wrote about my experience, I broke down and cried; but not for me- this time I was crying for him. Eugene was a sensitive, kind man with a beautiful heart. His smile, energy and passion were undeniable. I couldn't imagine what he must have been feeling, plagued with complete hopelessness and utter despair to have committed such drastic violent acts and leave the love of his life, his precious daughter. I feel so much compassion and empathy in my heart for Eugene like I have never felt before. Now this quote is not just a concept in my intellect, I have become

it: "The holiest spot on earth is where an ancient hatred has become a present love." ~*A Course In Miracles*

<u>I am the holiest spot on earth... in this now moment.</u>

<u>If we can turn our corner of the world into the holiest spot on earth and each person turns their corner of the world into the holiest spot then we can holy spot the earth and humanity back to love again. Amen.</u>

This is my first time sharing this part of my life with anyone, including my daughter, and now with the world. After I gave the final manuscript to the publisher, the next day I was in complete panic mode thinking I should call them and ask for it back. It's exhilarating and petrifying all at the same time to be so vulnerable. But to be open and vulnerable is the greatest strength because there is nothing more to defend and protect.

The abandonment issue is in a way a part of me, like a black thread running through the colorful tapestry of my life. I am still sensitive to the feeling of not "being wanted." It still comes up and I get that feeling, but it's not as strong and it doesn't take a hold of me like it did before. I don't know if that will ever go away while I'm in this human body; only now that I am aware of it, I can choose not to let it run my life.

<u>With loss comes growth and with wounds comes wisdom.</u>

"Walking. I am listening to a deeper way. Suddenly all my ancestors are behind me. Be still, they say. Watch and listen. You are the result of the love of thousands." ~Linda Hogan

***Grateful

Although I didn't have a close relationship with my father when he was alive, I do now. I realized as I was writing my book that he made a bigger impression on me than I thought. The two words that my Dad drilled into us as he believed they were the two most important words you could ever say were, **"Thank you."**

If you made it to here, *thank you.* Thank you for sharing my journey with me. I believe each time someone reads about my life story, energetically I am lifted up higher and healed even deeper, since we are ONE. I am humbled, honored and eternally grateful. Blessed be you.

"If the only prayer you ever say in your entire life is 'Thank you," that will be enough." ~ Meister Eckhart

***Meaning of my Logo: The New Yin/Yang for the New Earth

My logo represents a unique artistic version of a sunflower. I was told by Spirit I am the sunflower. I am not entirely sure what that means exactly but in the process of discovering. I use flower essences from Green Hope Farm in New Hampshire and when I found their sunflower essence I felt an immediate connection. Here is the meaning: The Sunflower represents "Owning our divinity, becoming our God-selves, a chalice of wisdom, power and love in perfect and balanced action."

The center, which I describe as the "new yin/yang for the New Earth," was shown to me by Spirit in a dream. It's a beautiful circle of shimmering iridescent white. White is, by the way, the color of all colors. Notice there is no more duality. The white symbolizes our unity consciousness – our true spiritual essence – and the little black dot in the corner represents humanity. The circle represents the sacred circle of giving and receiving, in-breathing and out-breathing, in which all living things come to life through the power of the Almighty Creator Mother/Father God. Sacred Geometry with the Fibonacci Sequence is seen in the center. It is the spiral of life which demonstrates the interconnectedness and Oneness of all living things. The twelve artistic flames or petals of the sunflower stand for the twelve new chakra colors we will be embracing as we ascend into our energetic light bodies back to unity consciousness. **Coalesce, Unite, Soar, Fly, Be Free, One Love.**

My New Trinity

In honor of All That Is
In honor of All That I Am
In honor of bringing my Divine Light here on Earth.

<u>The poem I wrote for my name changing ceremony:</u>

Beautiful Creator, God/Goddess, Mother/Father, Universe, All That Is,

We thank you.
In these new times that we are traversing on this planet earth, help us to be brave.

Soul Fire

Help us to remember that each day is a gift and tomorrow is not guaranteed.

Help us to live from our heart, in harmony with our inner truth and our divine calling, in service to humanity and the world.

Help us to remember that we are creative sparks of Spirit and with every thought and feeling we emit, we are creating our world. Help us to see life's challenges as opportunities to stay focused on creating heaven on earth.

Help us to forgive everyone for everything, including and especially ourselves.

Help us to eradicate fear and doubt from our minds and hearts, so that we can live fully without hesitation, in our light and in our glory, bathing the world with our greatest joy,

Help us to remember that if we want peace and harmony in the world that we must have in it our own hearts. Please help us heal ourselves, our ancestors and our relationships. Heal our families and our communities, and fill them with peace now and forever.

Help us to love each other better, because in the end, love is truly all that matters. Help us to see the best in everyone and honor each person's individual path.

Help us to remember that each moment is a chance to start again, that we are free, free to create the life we imagine, free to be ourselves, free to just be.

Help us to surrender each day to your guidance, knowing that we are never alone and you are just a thought away.

Help us to remember that where there is light, darkness cannot exist and the light is who we are. Help us to see ourselves as the miracle we are.

Help us to remember that at our deepest level of being, we are love, we are light, we are One.

Help us to live in the Oneness as many moments as we can, so our light will ignite the fire in other souls.

Help us to see beauty everyday all around us, in us and in others, even when it's hard.

Thank you for blessing us with true divine abundance in all ways, thank you for this beautiful planet earth, for our health, our friends, our families, for this opportunity to be alive in this unique and momentous new time here on earth. Amen.

Lokah Samastah Sukhino Bhavantu:
May all beings everywhere be happy and free.

PETAL 12

Reflections...What's in your Cage?

*** Effort is Required

LIFE IS SHORT, but life is eternal- another paradox. Buddha says one lifetime is but a blink of an eye, yet for some it can be never ending torture. We have forever to be tortured if we choose it. We also have forever to live beautiful happy peaceful fulfilled lives. It's up to us, *always*- free will choice. In every moment we are either adding to the Light of the world and creating life or adding to the darkness and perpetuating the suffering. What are you dialed in to? The noise in your mind or the divine guidance in your heart? We are not here to suffer- don't listen to Murphy, whoever he was. You can't walk ahead looking backward. Release the past, it's only suffocating you, forgive and let go and embrace the new. Past-future orientation will only bring you suffering and anxiety. Stay in the present moment. You are the Creator. When I start to go down that road of negativity I stop myself and say, "Creator, what are you creating?" Vitality, vigilance and self-reinforcement is needed to stay awake and pull ourselves out of the quagmire of the fear-based collective consciousness of sleeping humanity.

In the deepest core of our being we know there is no separation, that we are all One. Yet in another sense, we are all alone- another paradox. Nobody can change you, nobody can wake you up, nobody can discover who you are for you. As long as we're relying on somebody else, on an external authority for the answers we will continue to be confused, lost and asleep. The hero's journey, the way of the peaceful warrior must be taken alone. Of course we will have help along the way from others and from above; but at the end of the day before you close your eyes at night, the only person you are accountable to and the only person who can change you, is yourself. Inner work and diligence is required. This path is not for the faint of heart. Since you are the one person you are guaranteed to be with forever and through eternity... loving yourself, liking yourself, accepting yourself and being your best friend is a good place to start.

REFLECTIONS:

***Where you are not loving yourself? Accepting yourself 100 percent? Can you practice kindness and compassion toward yourself? "Self-rejection is the greatest enemy of the spiritual life because it contradicts the sacred voice that calls us the 'Beloved.' Being the Beloved expresses the core truth of our existence." – Henri Nouwen

***Are there any areas in your life that you are not being honest with yourself- not in integrity with your thoughts, feelings, words and actions?

***Can you write down your strengths and all the positive traits about yourself?

***What's covering you up? What is in the way of you truly shining? In other words, what old patterns do you want to release that's not in alignment with your authentic self, the angel in physical form. All things that you think are wrong with you are, in truth, the doorway to the discovery of your greatest strengths. Guilt, judgment, criticism, unworthiness are all guises of FEAR. Fear is paralyzing, fear keeps you in a cage and doesn't allow you to be the free heart you are. Fear can be an acronym for **F**alse **E**vidence **A**ppearing **R**eal or **F**ace **E**verything **A**nd **R**ise.

***Is there something in your life that you are not forgiving yourself for? Can you practice acceptance and let it go? There are no mistakes, just experiences.

***Are there people or situations that really bother you, rub you the wrong way, where there is constant conflict? If you reframe it and think, *I chose this*, how does that feel?

Every negative situation or challenge that appears before you is an opportunity to balance and harmonize your thought forms and energetic field in a loving, empowered way and become who you truly are.

***What are the secrets in your heart? If time and money wasn't an issue, what would you do that makes your heart sing? If you don't know think about what were you drawn to when you were a little child or a teenager. For example, when I was in middle school my best friend suffered from bad headaches. I massaged her hands on the school bus on the way to our sports game or before she went to sleep. I was only thirteen and didn't know what I was doing, but it was something natural in me that came out.

Will you (notice I did not say *can you,* we all can, the question is ***will you***) make time in your life for you-to heal yourself, water your spiritual garden and be in your sattwa alpha joy!

Give yourself permission to be fucking happy already!!!
And feel your perfection.
BE FREE!

NOTES:

Thank You Flower

My life is a living example of walking in faith connected to the collective Oneness. I realized finally, I am not alone. In this life time I received the opportunity to witness Humanity at its greatest. Thank you to all the blessed beings who have touched my life with their words, kindnesses, support and love. There are just too many to list here.

I would like to thank my Heavenly Mother and Father for giving me life, my human mother and father for being the vessel to birth me through and my guardian parents for adopting me and giving me a home.

I am forever grateful to Dana Livoti- meeting her changed my life. She is the talented and loving channel who brought through the messages from my angels and multiple Beings of the Light who have guided and assisted me on my earthly sojourn. It's not easy down here! I love being in communication with you!

Lisa Gayle is the Jewish Mom I never had. She has been my biggest cheerleader and Lord knows we could all use some cheering on this path. She is one the most loving giving souls I have ever met. She feeds me and makes sure I am never hungry. I never leave her home empty- full of food in my belly and love in my heart. You can't ask for more than that! I love you Lisa!

I am grateful to Charlie Russo, a tireless servant of God, who has been a rock in my life and the first person to show me unconditional love. I am also grateful to Jim Bishop who stayed in our lives at our darkest hour, supporting my daughter when he had no obligation.

Jack Licitra helped heal my most recent broken heart and was the catalyst in my re-birthing of the year of my confident heart 2016. He was the key to unlocking my fear and insecurity on stage and inspired me to be free in my expression of yoga and dance. I am grateful for his powerful presence in my life.

Cathy Fizz-who told me once she only answers the phone in the middle of the night for her two daughters and myself- is the angel who first planted the seed many moons ago about writing a book. She'd say, "Just write a page or even a paragraph- you gotta start somewhere." I honestly never thought I would accomplish it. Thank you for your continued encouragement and for loving me like family, my dear friend.

Of course, I am forever grateful to my beautiful daughter, Aiyana Natalia Smith, who is a beacon of light. She is also choosing to blaze her own trail like her Mom and I am so proud of her. What I'm the most proud of though, above and beyond all her talents, is that she is a kind person with a loving generous heart. She truly cares about others and the earth and making a difference in the world-that couldn't make me happier.

I believe Humanities greatest trait is kindness and protecting those less fortunate. All of these beautiful souls have been there for me when I was struggling and had no means to pay. They took care of me for free or we bartered services. Many became my dear friends:

Dr. John Gangemi, Dr. Michael Diamond, Dr Richard Mabanta, Dr. John Balsamo, and Dr. Matthew Lewis- all special and unique chiropractors, not just of the spine but of the spirit. Dr. Mabanta continues to take care of me. I couldn't live without your adjustments! Thank you my dear friend.

Valerie Dunne, the angel who guided me during the St.Ignatius Retreat who asked me, "Where was God in your life this week?" refused to take payment from me when I was struggling and is always there for me. Elizabeth Kieffer and Clare Hollywood-powerful healers who became my dear soul sisters; Tom Chambers, the angel who got me to surf, is another healer and huge supporter of my transformation; Anne Oliveri and Grace Grella are also my cheerleaders and soul sisters that I could not have done this part of my journey without.

It takes a village. Word. This book was a cooperative joint effort by many:

Kathy Patterson was the first person to read my original manuscript and ignite my confidence that I had a story worth telling. She encouraged me to tell more of my personal story and gain clarity as to how the book would be best structured.

Joseph Chambers helped with editing and the hardest part- naming the book! Fearless Freedom came from Dana Livoti and Becoming SoulFire came from Joseph. Lisa Gayle also helped me with editing and writing, making me aware that all writing is re-writing. You could not have been more right!

Lisa Mintz- first student, then client, then dear friend is the talented artist who designed my new logo; Wendy Jarva- first student, then dear friend and inspiration designed the cover of my book and helped bring my vision alive with her photography; Hira Akmal- also an amazing photographer, captured my "soul fire," and was responsible for the cover photo, along with other photos throughout the book; Laura Peragallo- the best web designer around, brought my SoulFire vision to the internet and continues to. Being self-employed, doing what I do and starting with nothing was not an easy task. I could not have come this far without all the help from these wonderful supportive loving angels.

Mokshapriya Shakti, my yoga teacher, a wise and beautiful light was the start of my education into true yoga and the shifting into the New Earth. She holds a space for me at her ashram and I am forever grateful to sit beside her.

There are many students and clients who have shared their personal journeys with me over the years. I hold your stories dear in my heart. Thank you for trusting me.Blessed is the influence of one true, loving human soul on another. We are ONE.

***Additional Seeds and Further Study

Marianne Williamson, all books www.marianne.com

Who Am I? Why Am I Here?, Patrica Cota-Robles www.eraofpeace.com

Scripting Your Destiny, Ronna Herman www.ronnastar.com

James Tyberonn www.earth-keeper.com

Lee Carroll, www.kryon.com

<u>Ken Carey's books- all of them</u>

Bruce Lipton, all books www.brucelipton.com

Neale Donald Walsh, all Books www.nealedonaldwalsch.com
(*The Little Soul and the Sun,* one of my favorites)

Proof of Heaven, Dr. Eben Alexander www.ebenalexander.com

You Can Heal Your Life, Louise Hay www.louisehay.com

Power vs. Force, David R. Hawkins, M.D., Ph.D

Gregg Braden www.greggbraden.com

Swami Beyondananda www.wakeuplaughing.com

Eckhart Tolle www.eckharttolle.com

www.chopracentermeditation.com for meditation online

The Autobiography of a Yogi by Paramahansa Yogananda www.yogananda-srf.org

The Second Coming of Christ, The Resurrection of the Christ Within You, (A revelatory commentary on the original teachings of Jesus) by Paramahansa Yogananda

Bhagavad Gita

Doreen Virtue www.angeltherapy.com

The Untethered Soul by Michael A. Singer www.untetheredsoul.com

Chants of a Lifetime by Krishna Das www.krishnadas.com

The Key to Mastery by Robert Peng www.robertpeng.com

The Sermon on the Mount, Emmet Fox

The New Human, Richard Gordon

How Yoga Works by Geshe Michael Roach www.geshemichealroach.com (This is a must for yoga teachers)

The Science of Getting Rich, Wallace D. Wattles

Leadership and Self-Deception and *The Anatomy of Peace* www.arbinger.com
(I feel this is a must for business owners or entrepreneurs)

Dying To Be Me, My Journey from Cancer, to Near Death, to True Healing www.anitamoorjani.com

Quan Yin Speaks, Shih Yin www.quanyinlotuspath.com

The Book of Chakras, Discover the Hidden Forces Within You, Ambika Wauters

Love Thyself, Masaru Emoto www.masaru-emoto.net

The Four Agreements, Don Miguel Ruiz www.toltecspirit.com

Broken Open, Elizabeth Lesser

The Yoga of Relationships, Yogi Amrit Desai

The Greatest Miracle in the World, Og Mandino

Many Lives, Many Masters, Dr. Brian L. Weiss, M.D. www.brainweiss.com

Sivananda Buried Yoga, Yogi Manmoyanand

The Dream Giver, Bruce Wilkinson

The Way of the Superior Man, David Deida and all his work- www.deida.info

Dana Livoti, www.intuitionny.com Channeled messages and healing jewelry

Jack Licitra, artspharmacy.com Music and healing

Laura Peragallo, lpdesignhelp.com Internet presence and web design

www.greeenhopeessences.com Connect to nature

Author Bio

Owning her spiritual name, SoulFire is known to be the spark that ignites the fire in one's soul. Spiritual teacher, yogini, mother, author, pirate, energy healer and awakened being of the new heaven and the new earth, SoulFire lovingly guides and teaches from her own life experience and the myriad of modalities she acquired during her 20 year health and wellness coaching career including: yoga, reiki, Qigong, Thai yoga massage, swimming, personal training as well as the Universal Laws of Science and Spirit. She spent the first half of her life lost in the perceived darkness and is now looking forward to the next part of her journey living in the light as an evolving multi-dimensional human sharing her experience with those open and willing to dream awake. For more information on SoulFire and her services you can visit her at www.igniteyoursoulfire.com

CPSIA information can be obtained
at www.ICGtesting.com
Printed in the USA
BVHW01s0903201217
503308BV00004B/1460/P

9 781542 871051